Hitler's Last Days

Hitler's Last Days

The Führerbunker and Beyond

Mel Kavanagh

Pen & Sword
MILITARY

First published in Great Britain in 2023 by
Pen & Sword Military
An imprint of Pen & Sword Books Limited
Yorkshire – Philadelphia

Copyright © Mel Kavanagh 2023

ISBN 978 1 39904 805 7

The right of Mel Kavanagh to be identified as
Author of this Work has been asserted by him in accordance
with the Copyright, Designs and Patents Act 1988.

A CIP catalogue record for this book is
available from the British Library

All rights reserved. No part of this book may be reproduced or
transmitted in any form or by any means, electronic or mechanical
including photocopying, recording or by any information storage
and
retrieval system, without permission from the Publisher in writing.

Typeset by Mac Style
Printed in the UK by CPI Group (UK) Ltd, Croydon, CR0 4YY.

Pen & Sword Books Limited incorporates the imprints of After
the Battle, Atlas, Archaeology, Aviation, Discovery, Family
History, Fiction, History, Maritime, Military, Military Classics,
Politics, Select, Transport, True Crime, Air World, Frontline
Publishing, Leo Cooper, Remember When, Seaforth Publishing,
The Praetorian Press, Wharncliffe Local History, Wharncliffe
Transport, Wharncliffe True Crime and White Owl.

For a complete list of Pen & Sword titles please contact

PEN & SWORD BOOKS LIMITED
47 Church Street, Barnsley, South Yorkshire, S70 2AS, England
E-mail: enquiries@pen-and-sword.co.uk
Website: www.pen-and-sword.co.uk
or
PEN AND SWORD BOOKS
1950 Lawrence Rd, Havertown, PA 19083, USA
E-mail: Uspen-and-sword@casematepublishers.com
Website: www.penandswordbooks.com

Contents

Introduction		vi
Chapter 1	The Beginning of the End	1
Chapter 2	Bunker Residents	46
Chapter 3	Taking Leave of the Bunker	71
Chapter 4	Aftermath of Hitler's Death	88
Chapter 5	Hitler's Background, and his Physical and Psychological State	106
Chapter 6	The New Flensburg Government and the State of Germany	144
Chapter 7	Political Statements and Hitler's Will	168
Chapter 8	Did Hitler Die?	185
Chapter 9	The Indomitable Hanna Reitsch and her Opinion of Hitler	210
Conclusion		213
Bibliography		214

Introduction

There have been many books written and films made about Hitler and his last days in the Führerbunker.

But Hitler wasn't alone in his last days. There were orderlies, secretaries, troops, very senior officers, at least one wife and even children.

What was Hitler's state of mind? How did he react as the Russians moved closer and closer to Berlin?

Two years or so before what would be the end of the war, the Allies were confident of victory. Hitler was not so convinced.

A report was commissioned by the Office of Strategic Services (OSS), which gathered intelligence information regarding the personality of Adolf Hitler; predictions for his future behaviour and suggestions for dealing with him in 1943 and in the future 'after Germany's surrender'.

What happened to Hitler is well documented, but what about the other inhabitants of the Führerbunker? The men, women and children; how did they react, and what finally happened to them?

Many remained loyal to the Führer, others not so.

This book explores what happened not only to Hitler but also to the other incumbents of the Führerbunker. There are many myths to attempt to unravel before a hopefully clearer picture can emerge of those final days deep underground in the doomed capital of a collapsing Third Reich.

Chapter One

The Beginning of the End

1945

Sunday, 15 April

By this stage of the war, Hitler swung between two moods. Part of the time he was delusional, believing that somehow some unforeseen event would still tilt the war in Germany's favour. On other days he was rational and realistic, fully realizing that the war was lost. To prepare for the latter eventuality, Hitler wrote out orders that, in the event the enemy severed communication between him and the rest of his command, Admiral Karl Dönitz would take command of the northern German forces, while Field Marshal Albert Kesselring would take over in the west and south.

It was not the first time Hitler had made a realistic assessment of the situation. Six months earlier, when Operation *Wacht am Rhein* (Operation *Watch on the Rhine*, better known as the Battle of the Bulge) was crumbling, he had told an aide: 'I know the war is lost. The enemy superiority is too great.' He then dictated a proclamation addressed to the 'Soldiers of the German Eastern Front', part of which read:

'For the last time, our deadly Jewish-Bolshevik enemy has lined up his masses for the attack. He is trying to smash Germany and exterminate our people. To a great degree, you soldiers of the East know yourselves what fate is threatening all German women, girls and children. While the old men and children will be murdered, women and girls will be degraded to barrack whores. The rest will be marched off to Siberia …

'He who fails to do his duty at this time commits treason against our people. Any regiment or division that abandons its position acts so disgracefully that it should be ashamed before the women and children who are enduring the terror bombing against our cities …

'Above all, be aware of the few treacherous officers and soldiers who, in order to save their own lives, will fight against us … . Whoever orders you to retreat must be immediately arrested and, if necessary, killed on the spot, no matter what his rank may be.

'If, in the coming days and weeks, every soldier does his duty at the Eastern Front, then the last Asian attack will be broken, just as the invasion of our enemies in the West will be broken in spite of everything. "Berlin will remain German!"'

Monday, 16 April

The Soviets' final attack was unleashed on Berlin along the Oder River front and in Silesia. The Red Army had gathered 2.5 million soldiers, 6,200 tanks and assault guns, 41,000 artillery pieces (250 guns for each kilometre of front) and 7,200 aircraft. Facing them was Army Group Vistula, with a relatively paltry 200,000 men, 750 tanks and assault guns and 1,500 artillery pieces. Hitler took to his underground bunker.

The Führerbunker

The Germans were highly skilled at building underground facilities of all sorts, and the Führerbunker was no exception. It was an air raid shelter located near the Reich Chancellery (Reichskanzlei) in Berlin, part of a subterranean bunker complex which consisted of two levels of rooms. The bunker had been built in two phases, the first in 1936 and the second in 1944. Hitler took up residence on 16 January 1945, joined by his senior staff, including his Deputy Führer and private secretary Martin Bormann.

Sunday, 22 April

Eva Braun (Hitler's long-term mistress) and Joseph Goebbels – along with Goebbels' wife Magda and their six children – entered the already overcrowded upper Vorbunker level from their apartment on Hermann Göring Strasse. Goebbels, the pint-size Nazi propaganda minister, assured his Führer that he and his family would remain faithful to the end.

Hitler continued to use the undamaged wing of the Reich Chancellery, where he held afternoon military conferences in his large study. Afterwards, he would have tea with his secretaries before returning to the bunker complex for the night. After several weeks of this routine, Hitler seldom left the bunker except for short strolls in the Chancellery garden with his beloved dog Blondi. The bunker was crowded, the atmosphere oppressive, with Allied air raids occurring daily. Hitler mostly stayed on the lower level, where it was quieter and he could sleep.

Two or three dozen support, medical and administrative staff were also sheltered there. These included Hitler's secretaries, a nurse named Erna Flegel and Oberscharführer Rochus Misch, who was both bodyguard and telephone switchboard operator. The Führerbunker had become the centre of the Nazi regime and was to be the last of the Führer Headquarters used by Hitler during the Second World War.

The Vorbunker level was beneath 13ft of concrete and comprised a dozen small rooms (four of which were the kitchens), flanked by a central hallway. At the end of the hallway, a spiral staircase wound its way down to Hitler's quarters.

The Vorbunker was located 1.5 metres (almost 5ft) beneath the cellar of a large reception hall behind the old Reich Chancellery at Wilhelmstrasse 77. There were eighteen rooms, all quite small, where Hitler and many of his staff lived and worked – Hitler and Eva Braun occupied six of the rooms – a far cry from the spacious and elegant offices in the Chancellery.

For the first month or two at least, Hitler's daily life had changed little in the bunker. Life looked much the same below as above ground. After meetings with his generals, he strategized until early in the morning, sometimes as late as 5.00 am. Conferences often took place for much of the night.

> '[Hitler] got up about 11.30 am, bathed quickly, took a hurried breakfast, and held his first conference at noon. The rest of the day was entirely taken up with conversations with political and military leaders. He took lunch in the late afternoon. It consisted of vegetable soup, corn on the cob, jellied omelettes, and whatever delicacies Fraulein Constanze Manziarly, his vegetarian cook, could provide for him.' (Robert Payne, *The Life and Death of Hitler*)

By February 1945, Hitler's personal accommodation had been fitted out with high-quality furniture taken from the Chancellery, along with several framed oil paintings. After descending the stairs into the lower section and passing through a steel door, there was a long corridor. On the right side were rooms which included generator/ventilation rooms and the telephone switchboard. On the left side was Eva Braun's bedroom/sitting room (also known as Hitler's private guest room) and an antechamber (also known as Hitler's sitting room), which led into Hitler's study/office. On the wall hung a large portrait by Anton Graff of Frederick the Great, one of Hitler's heroes. A door led into Hitler's modestly furnished bedroom. Next to that was the conference/map room (also known as the briefing/situation room), which had a door that led out into the waiting room/anteroom.

There were several factors that prevented the bunker's residents from feeling that everything was business as usual. There was the constant threat of death and the dissolution of Hitler's dream of empire. Furthermore, there was a palpable sense of claustrophobia as the underground offices filled with officers and support staff, as well as Eva Braun and the wife and children of Goebbels, according to a report from one of the SS guards who were inside the bunker.

The bunker complex was self-contained. However, as the Führerbunker was below the water table, conditions were unpleasantly damp, with pumps running continuously to remove groundwater. A diesel generator provided electricity, and well water was pumped in as the water supply. Communications systems connecting Hitler and his entourage with the outside world included a telex, a telephone switchboard and an army radio set with an outdoor antenna. As conditions deteriorated at the end of the war, Hitler received much of his war news from BBC radio broadcasts and via a courier.

The bunker's passageway doubled as an 18-square-foot conference room and was unadorned with decoration; a large table contained a situation map showing the latest known front lines. A battalion of 600–700 men of the 1st SS-Panzerdivision 'Leibstandarte SS Adolf Hitler' were billeted nearby, serving as guards, orderlies, clerks, servants and cooks.

The Führerbunker was located 2.5 metres (8¼ft) lower than the Vorbunker and to the west-south-west. It was completed in 1944 and was about 8.5 metres (28ft) beneath the garden of the old Reich Chancellery, 120 metres (390ft) north of the new Reich Chancellery building at Voßstraße 6. Besides being deeper underground, the Führerbunker had significantly more reinforcement against the effects of bombing. Its roof was made of concrete almost 3 metres (9¾ft) thick. Some thirty small rooms were protected by approximately 4 metres (13ft) of concrete; exits led into the main buildings of the Chancellery, and there was also an emergency exit up to the garden. Besides Hitler and Braun, other residents of the bunker complex were Deputy Führer Bormann, one of Hitler's closest lieutenants; Dr Ludwig Stumpfegger, one of SS commander Heinrich Himmler's physicians who now also looked after Hitler's health; Goebbels's adjutant, Günther Schwägermann, and his undersecretary of state at the Ministry of Propaganda, Werner Naumann; plus Hitler's adjutant, Julius Schaub, his two secretaries and his vegetarian cook, Fraulein Manziarly.

The Reich Chancellery bunker was initially constructed as a temporary air-raid shelter for Hitler, who actually spent very little time in the capital during most of the war, preferring the Berghof near Berchtesgaden in the Bavarian Alps and the Wolfsschanze (Wolf's Lair) headquarters in East Prussia. Increased bombing of Berlin led to expansion of the complex as an improvised permanent shelter.

Hitlerjugend Units in the Defence of the Führerbunker
All the Hitlerjugend (HJ, Hitler Youth) members employed in the defence of Berlin were organised as the Panzer Vernichtungs Brigade. This was the

only unit of its kind, consisting of 2,700–2,800 boys who had gone through the Reichsarbeitsdienst, the Reich Labour Service. It was subdivided into four 'Staemme' (troops), numbered from one to four. The brigade was headed by Artur Axmann, and for military operations it came under the jurisdiction of the 9th Army.

The brigade had been deployed in the Frankfurt/Oder area for between four and six weeks before the Russians attacked in that area. Part of the brigade retreated with the 9th Army towards the north-west, while the remaining elements of about 1,000 men went back to Berlin and were committed for the defence of the city. The 1st Stamm (about 600 men) was used in the Heerstrasse-Reichssportfeld area between 18 and 30 April to protect the two Pichelsdorfer Brücken (bridges), which were deemed essential for the approach of General Walther Wenck's 12th Army to relieve the city. The other elements were in the Strausberg area about 25km east of Berlin until 18 April. Between the 25th and the 30th, they fell back towards the Reichssportfeld area, which had been designated as the point where stray units were to regroup. Axmann visited the positions at Heerstrasse and Berliner Strasse several times between 5 and 30 April. He had his command post (CP) at 86 Kaiserdamm in the building of the Reichsjugendführer until 26 April, keeping in close contact with the positions established in the immediate vicinity. On 26 April, when the Kaiserdamm positions had to be abandoned, Axmann established his CP in the cellar of the Parteikanzlei building. This was the last CP he held until about 10.00 pm on 30 April.

Wednesday, 18 April
This day marked the beginning of the last big battle of the war: the Battle of Berlin. For more than two years, the Allied air offensive against Berlin had been increasing. Several large-scale raids successfully targeted huge areas of the capital. Without exception, night after night, Berlin experienced attacks by RAF bombers. The raids came day in, day out; week in, week out; for month after month. Even small raids caused more damage than the larger attacks two years previously, bombs striking their targets successfully.

One part of Berlin after another was laid to ruins. There was no time to dig out the corpses of the dead. Neighbours put flowers on the ruins of houses which now offered better protection to the dead than they had to the living.

Eyes burning because of sleeplessness, Berliners looked heavenwards at every attack. The Luftschutzwart critically examined the sky for every new sign. They did not expect wonders, but they had set their hopes on the new fighters which their comrades in the factories had talked about. What they did not know was that some of those fighters had been senselessly sacrificed;

because of the continuous bombing of London, there was no petrol for the rest of the new fighter planes.

A new terror added to the grief that threatened Berlin from the air – the offensive by the Red Army. A major attack had brought the Russians from the shores of the Vistula to the Oder. East Prussia was lost, having been thought to be an impregnable German fortress.

Millions of refugees from the eastern provinces now streamed to the west: women, children and a few men. They came in cars, lorries and on foot. Many made for Berlin. At one time the city had more than 4 million inhabitants. After the first bombings, this fell to 2½ million. During the city's most difficult time, this number rose to 3½ million with the influx of refugees. They huddled together in the ruins, Berliners helping one another and also the desperate refugees.

Berliners looked to the east, where the stream of refugees came from. They also looked to the west, where, with the Americans and British approaching, the people didn't leave their houses, hoisting white flags from their homes in an attempt to save themselves by proving they had given up the struggle. Berliners looked upwards too, where huge armadas of enemy planes clouded the midday sky to rain destruction on another part of the capital. Berlin was thus between three front lines, yet still the populace heeded their government.

When that government called for the defence of the city, Volkssturm battalions were formed overnight. In February, anti-tank barricades were built around the capital. They were erected from old tram cars and other now-useless items. Those barricades, however, were no hindrance for a tank, but they did hinder other traffic. In the daytime, lorries collided with them; at night, cars with their lights cut sped into them. In March, under the leadership of a few pioneers, the barriers were removed and better barriers were established at bridges and other points of importance. Machine-gun nests were built from sand bags, hideouts dug for infantrymen, parts of the woods mined and trees cut to block the roads. Batteries of anti-aircraft guns were installed. But first of all, broad and deep anti-tank trenches were dug around Berlin.

There was no sign of active fighting from the Wehrmacht. The Volkssturm, who did not even know how to fire a rifle, stood guard.

There were anxious looks on the lower right bank of the River Oder, where the spearheads of the Red Army were waiting for reinforcements.

In this waiting time, something like a front-line was formed. The commander of an artillery depot on the Oder 'collected' lost soldiers. Within fourteen days, he commanded two 'regiments'; after four weeks, double that number, after training and equipping the exhausted men. In the meantime, they had to fight off attacks by Russian spearheads and undertake their own operations. They did 'operate' but had to pay a heavy price for it. It was pointed out to the men that the successes of active Wehrmacht units were 'outstanding examples' worthy of imitation.

Despite all their efforts and their high losses, the Russians infiltrated the German lines by crossing the Oder at night-time and occupied the forests on the left bank of the river, and soon after they stormed the hills near Lebus. Part of the road to Küstrin was lost and could only be reached at night-time. Travelling to Frankfurt required skilful driving, the Russian artillery sending over well-aimed 'greetings'. Slowly, reinforcements started to arrive at the front line there. These men carried a perplexing variety of weapons and munitions of all calibres and systems, including many captured by the Germans.

All power in Berlin was now essentially in the hands of Goebbels. As a Gauleiter before the war, he had already played an important role in the city's administration. The town halls around the country listened to him. Not even the Police HQ, where Himmler had a say, could do anything against the wishes of the Gauleiter. Ground and air attacks increased his influence, his decisions affecting all areas, from the attempted relief of Berlin by some 50,000 soldiers to the delivery of vital food supplies to part of the city. Goebbels was by now Defence Kommissar of the Reich. He put his life into it, taking care of everything, even the discipline of the soldiers on the streets and at their stations. Everything he needed he got, even arms and munitions, far easier than had some army commanders.

When Berlin woke up on 18 April, the news slowly spread about the Russian offensive at Küstrin-Kietz. By midday, it was known that the Russians were on the hills opposite Küstrin. By the evening, every Berliner knew the end was near. Although full of sorrow, many citizens breathed a sigh of relief because the situation was about to come to a conclusion.

Thursday, 19 April
Goebbels had declared that Berlin would be defended along the Oder front and not at the suburbs of the city, with all units in Berlin sent to the danger spots on the Oder. However, Marshal Georgy Zhukov, commander of the Soviet 1st Belorussian Front, destroyed these reinforcements on their way to the front. Time was running out for those in Berlin. Although the atmosphere in the city was loaded with tension, there was a certain quietness that hadn't been known for a long time. There were more air attacks by the Western Allies, while those by the Russians weren't taken seriously by the veterans of the city's anti-aircraft defences. Nevertheless, the air raid sirens were kept silent.

Großadmiral Karl Dönitz ordered his OKM (Oberkommando der Marine) staff to evacuate their Berlin HQ in order to avoid being overrun by the

Soviets advancing from the Oder. The HQ was to move some 50 miles north of Hamburg to Plön, but Dönitz stayed behind in order to attend Hitler's 56th birthday.

Friday, 20 April (Hitler's Birthday)
Hitler ordered *Fall Clauswitz* (Operation *Clausewitz*) as part of the defence of Berlin, which included the evacuation of all Wehrmacht and SS offices in the capital and the destruction of official papers and documents of state. Berlin thereafter became a front-line city.

The Chief of the Personnel Office was found dead in his office. He had shot himself. His body was sewn into a white cloth and taken to a nearby cemetery, where he was the last person to receive a formal funeral for the foreseeable future.

Alarming news arrived, with rumours abounding about a Russian breakthrough towards the city. Because of difficulties with the telephone exchange, getting exact information about events was almost impossible.

Goebbels attended a conference at 11.00 am. He didn't say much about the Russian successes, instead concentrating on planned movements by German forces from the south-west and north-west to attack the flanks of the advancing Red Army.

As it was Hitler's birthday, Goebbels recited from memory extracts from Thomsas Carlyle's biography of Frederick the Great. He added that negotiations had almost been concluded regarding the threat to Berlin and his decision to defend the capital of the Reich, although the troops for this had been sent away. Goebbels apologized for the increasing number of inhabitants in Berlin, pointing out that there was no transport to evacuate any more women and children. As a piece of propaganda, he demanded that under no circumstances should any high-ranking officials leave Berlin, even if the possibility arose for them to do so. To prevent anyone fleeing, he would block the streets leading out of Berlin.

Hitler had originally planned to leave for Berchtesgaden but postponed his flight.

As the Soviets closed in, the thud of artillery shells exploding in the rubble above the Führerbunker began beating an incessant, mournful rhythm. They were like drums accompanying a man being marched to the gallows as Hitler made his last trip to the surface, looking much older than his 56 years as he went to the ruined garden of the Reichskanzlei, where he awarded the Iron Cross to twenty Hitler Youth members who had distinguished themselves.

Artur Axmann was present in the garden at noon when a delegation of soldiers and HJ members brought congratulations for Hitler's birthday. Others present included Himmler, Goebbels, Bormann, General Wilhelm Burgdorf (chief of the Army Personnel Office) and possibly Albert Speer (the Minister for Armaments and War Production). Hitler delivered a short address to the soldiers and the HJ youths, thanked them for their efforts and emphasized the decisive character of the Battle for Berlin. Immediately afterwards, Axmann was granted an interview which he had requested with Hitler; also present were Himmler, Goebbels and Bormann. At the meeting, which took place in the front part of the bunker, Axmann voiced the protests of the Hitler Youth against certain members of the Party who exhorted others to fight but did not participate in combat. Hitler agreed with the criticism and mentioned that he had taken disciplinary action against Gauleiter Wächtler. He also stated that HJ leaders should have been placed in responsible positions earlier. Himmler and Goebbels merely agreed with Axmann's remarks.

While 20 April was an established national holiday, there were few celebrations, just a few Nazi flags still fluttering above the ruins of Berlin.

Armin Lehrmann was one of the boy soldiers with whom Hitler chatted that day. He recalled that Hitler 'shook hands with everybody', but the famous commanding voice was gone: 'It was not an orator's voice. It almost sounded like he had a cold, and his eyes looked watery, and his voice didn't come across very strong.'

Hitler was in denial about the dire situation, placing his hopes on the units commanded by Waffen-SS General Felix Steiner, Armeeabteilung Steiner, coming to the rescue.

As the Soviets smashed deeper into Germany, a wave of panic and hysteria overcame many of the civilians in their path, especially women. Rumours and factual accounts of women and girls being gang-raped by drunken Red Army troops drove thousands of Germans to commit suicide, either taking poison, shooting or hanging themselves, or throwing themselves off cliffs or into rivers. In Berlin alone, during April and May, nearly 4,000 people took their own lives.

One 11-year-old girl who survived nearly being killed by her own mother to prevent her from falling into Russian hands recalled: 'We had no hope left for life, and I myself had the feeling that this was the end of the world, this was the end of my life.' However, somehow she survived.

At a meeting with his staff at the Propaganda Ministry, Goebbels voiced Hitler's complaint that he, the Führer, was surrounded by cowards and traitors and that the German people were no longer worth fighting for. When someone dared to challenge that assertion, the Propaganda Minister lashed out:

'The German people? What can you do with a people whose men are no longer willing to fight when their wives are being raped?

'All the plans of National Socialism, all its dreams and goals, were too great and too noble for this [*sic*] people. The German people are just too cowardly to realize these goals. In the East, they are running away. In the West, they set up hindrances for their own soldiers and welcome the enemy with white flags ... The German people deserve the destiny that now awaits them.'

Hitler had said: 'If the war is lost, then it is of no concern to me if the people perish in it. I still would not shed a tear for them because they did not deserve any better.'

However, Goebbels put on a mask for the sake of national morale. In his final broadcast to the German people, in case any of them were still listening, he declared: 'The Führer is in Berlin and will die fighting with his troops in the capital.'

The Führer may have been in Berlin, but he had no intention of dying fighting with his troops on the barricades that now blocked many of the city's streets. He was hunkered down in his bomb-proof bunker below the garden of the Reich Chancellery, worrying about what the Russians would do to him if they captured him alive.

On the front line, after inflicting heavy casualties on the attacking Soviet forces, the Germans abandoned the dominant Seelow Heights and pulled back toward the capital in an orderly fashion. Elsewhere around the city, the Germans gave as good as they got; some 2,800 Soviet tanks were destroyed during the Battle of Berlin and thousands of Red Army soldiers were killed or wounded by a defence that was growing stiffer and more fanatical by the hour.

Saturday, 21 April
A conference was held at Goebbel's home at 11.00 am. It would prove to be the last one. Between twenty and thirty cold, tired and dirty men sat in the badly damaged film room of the minister's villa in Hermann Göring Strasse. The broken windows were boarded with wood, and because there was no electricity three candles were burning on a long table.

Goebbels was late. He was dressed as smartly as ever, but in those surroundings that elegance was striking in its contrast. He was wearing a dark civilian suit. His usual tanned small face was pale, and his dark eyes were glowing. Once he sat down, he started to speak. His words were slow and low at first, but then became loud and passionate.

His speech was one of accusation against the old officers, opposing political or social progress or reform. He accused them of having committed treason over many years: in 1940, for instance, when they dissuaded Hitler from invading England, and later when they lost their nerve in Russia.

Leaving behind his theme about the treason of the officers, Goebbels began to speak with cynicism and fury against the German people. He repeated the accusation of the cowardice of the German people: 'What shall I do with a people whose men do not fight anymore when their wives are raped?' He then defended Hitler's policy in an outburst which disclosed thoughts which had been very carefully hidden, even denied. His pale face turned red, his veins swelling as he claimed that the German people deserved the fate they were experiencing, repeating that the German nation had chosen its own fate. He recalled that in an election in the early 1930s about Germany leaving the League of Nations, the German people had decided against a policy of submission and for a policy of venture. That venture had now failed.

A member of the conference then stood and said that neither Goebbels nor Hitler had explained to the German people that the plebiscite had been a choice between peace and adventure. Both the Nazi leaders had, he said, always agreed to fight the German *existenzkampf* (struggle for existence) by peaceful means.

Meanwhile, Hitler ordered General Steiner to attack the northern flank of the encircling Soviet salient and the German 9th Army (General Theodore Busse), south-east of Berlin, to attack northward in a pincer attack. Nevertheless, Red Army tanks reached the outskirts of Berlin that evening.

Two cars left Goebbels's house at the Brandenburger Tor at 4.00 pm. They were both full. Inside were Frau Goebbels with her children, who headed west in the direction of the Reichskanzlei. A dozen other cars were standing in the courtyard. Around them were about twenty young women from the telephone exchange, typists and men of the SS-guard. The women were all crying, desperate for information and to escape to Hamburg. Inside the building was Hamel (first name unknown), leader of the Minister Office, dressed in a hat and coat. Goebbels, who had sent for him, declared to Hamel: 'The game is lost. I have no orders any more for you. Together with my family I am going to the Führerbunker.' Hamel was going to drive to Hamburg.

Sunday, 22 April

Oberstleutnant Hermann Brudermüller of the OKW (Oberkommando der Wehrmacht, the High Command of the Armed Forces) accompanied Generaloberst Jodl, the OKW's chief of the Operations Staff, to a Lagebesprechung (situation conference). Present were the Führer, OKW chief Field Marshal Wilhelm Keitel, Jodl, OKH (Oberkommando des Heeres, the High Command of the Army) chief General Krebs and his adjutant, Major Freytag von Loringhoven, General Burgdorf, General Christian of the Luftwaffe, otschafter Hewel (Foreign Minister Ribbentrop's representative at Hitler's HQ), Admiral Voss (Hitler's naval adjutant), Bormann, SS-Gruppenführer Hermann Fegelein (Himmler's liaison officer at Hitler's HQ) and Hitler's Deputy Chief Press Secretary, Heinz Lorenz. SS-Obersturmbannführer Peter Hoegel was in charge of the guards. Goebbels and his whole family arrived at the bunker while the conference was in progress.

During the second stage of the conference, only the most important personalities remained in the conference room, the remainder withdrawing to the anteroom. Remaining with the Führer were Keitel, Jodl and Krebs, and, after his arrival, Goebbels. Burgdorf and Bormann were present for part of the time.

One of the main decisions to be taken at this conference was whether Hitler should move to Berchtesgaden or stay in Berlin. Voss and Fegelein were the main supporters of the plan to go south to the Bavarian retreat.

Immediately after the conference, Jodl stated to Brudermüller that the only thing to do now was to turn the 12th Army towards the east, irrespective of the actions of the Western Allies, in order to demonstrate to the world that Germany's main aim was to fight Bolshevism. Brudermüller did not know whether such a move was discussed at the conference or whether it was Jodl's conclusion drawn from the facts he had heard there. When the transfer of the 12th Army was reported to Hitler the following day, he approved the move.

Later that afternoon, there was a Lagebesprechung in the Führerbunker. Present at the meeting – which lasted for two to three hours – were General Krebs, General Burgdorf, General Weidling (General of the Artillery), Axmann, Goebbels, Bormann and Hitler. There was at least one of these meetings each day, following which orders issued by Hitler were either disregarded or could not be carried out, communications failed and armies ordered to the rescue of Berlin did not appear. The shortage of heavy weapons and ammunition became increasingly serious. At this latest meeting it was revealed that the Pichelsdorfer bridge over the Havel River had no adequate protection in the absence of military units. Hitler ordered a battalion of the Panzer Vernichtungs Brigade HJ to move to the sector to defend the vital bridge. Goebbels, Bormann, Krebs, Weidling and Bergdorf were always present for these meetings. Others present in the bunker at that time were Eva Braun, Frau Goebbels, Hewel Naumann, Hitler's military adjutants and secretaries.

The Red Army had by now penetrated the outer ring of defences around Berlin, which led to several personnel departing the bunker. Among those to do so was Dr Hugo Blaschke, Hitler's personal dentist, who also treated Eva

Braun, Goebbels and Himmler. He was flown out of Berlin to Obersalzberg (the 'Eagle's Nest').

Dr Karl Gebhardt, Chief Surgeon of the Staff of the Reich, also left the bunker. On 27 May 1942, Gebhardt had been dispatched to Prague to attend to SS-Obergruppenführer Reinhard Heydrich, acting Reichsprotektor of Bohemia and Moravia, who had been badly wounded in an assassination attempt. Despite Gebhardt's efforts, Heydrich died eight days after the attack. In early 1944, Gebhardt had also treated Albert Speer for fatigue and a swollen knee. His treatment almost killed Speer and he was replaced by another doctor, Friedrich Koch.

Hitler's Chief Secretary, Johanna Wolf, along with one of Hitler's personal secretaries, Emilie Christine Schroeder – also known as Christa Schroeder – were also ordered to leave the bunker.

Luftwaffe officer General Eckhard Christian, meanwhile, left the bunker complex to become Chief of the Liaison Staff of the Luftwaffe to OKW Command Staff North. Christian's wife, Gerda – one of Hitler's private secretaries – was one of two secretaries who volunteered to remain with Hitler in the Führerbunker. Gerda did not reunite with her husband after the war ended, divorcing Christian in 1946 because he had not remained with her in the bunker until the death of Hitler.

Hitler was told at the afternoon situation conference – what turned out to be his last major conference – that Steiner's forces had not moved to aid those still in Berlin. Hitler flew into a tearful rage, spending several hours venting his anger at the world, at the German people, and at his officers and soldiers who had abandoned him and the Fatherland. Those who witnessed and listened to this venomous outpouring were frightened by Hitler's tirade. Many thought the Führer had, at last, gone completely mad. He openly declared for the first time that the war was lost, blaming his generals. His very public display was the talk of the bunker, and even the most optimistic of Hitler's cohorts were now convinced that defeat was inevitable. Hitler never physically or mentally recovered from this conference room collapse.

Hitler eventually announced that he would stay in Berlin until the end and then shoot himself. Goebbels took the same decision. Thereupon, Hitler dismissed many of his court and advisors, while others left of their own accord. Hitler would remain, surrounded only by his 'family circle' and those officers directly concerned with the defence of Berlin.

Monday, 23 April
Reichsmarschall Hermann Göring, head of the Luftwaffe, had the temerity to flee Berlin and then send Hitler a telegram declaring that because he had heard

that the Führer planned to commit suicide, he wanted permission to assume leadership of the Third Reich. Hitler, furious at what he saw as a treasonous act of betrayal, sacked Göring from all his positions in the Nazi regime.

Jodl, accompanied by Brudermüller, reported at the Führer's bunker as usual. Jodl described in detail the measures taken for the defence of Berlin and parted with the assurance that he would try to make the move to relieve Berlin a success. It was, however, obvious to everyone present that the forces available were inadequate for such a task.

During the night of 23/24 April, Jodl and his staff were forced to withdraw northwards because of the approach of Russian armoured columns.

Hitler, having by now recovered some of his composure after his attack of nervous prostration, and having made the decision to stay, was in a reasonable state of mental serenity. A decision over whether Hitler should leave was never reconsidered, and attempts by others to suggest it were forbidden. From 22–30 April, Hitler awaited the outcome of the Battle of Berlin in some peace of mind. The situation for him was simple: if Berlin was saved, Hitler would live; if it fell, he would commit suicide. He later told Speer that he would tell Field Marshal Robert Ritter von Greim – whom he had summoned from Munich to be head of the Luftwaffe after Göring's fall from grace – of his decision to end his life. Both men were told of the plans for the destruction of his body so that it would not fall into enemy hands.

Hitler appointed Helmuth Weidling, commander of the LVI Panzer Corps, in charge of the Berlin Defence Area, replacing Oberstleutnant Ernst Kaether. The Red Army had consolidated its investment of Berlin by 25 April, despite the orders issued from the Führerbunker. There was no prospect that the German defence could do anything but delay the city's capture.

Thursday, 26 April
Berlin's Tempelhof Airport was captured by the Soviets, and most of Berlin's eastern, north-eastern and southern suburbs and districts had also fallen. Some of the major Nazi 'rats' had already abandoned the sinking ship of state.

Heinrich Himmler, head of the SS and Gestapo, had departed. He had been holding secret negotiations with Swedish diplomat Count Folke Bernadotte and, in a self-serving attempt to save his own skin, promised to release more than 30,000 prisoners from Nazi concentration camps.

A furious Hitler condemned both Himmler and Göring for abandoning him. Speer, who was in the bunker when Hitler exploded, recalled: 'An outburst of wild fury followed in which feelings of bitterness, helplessness, self-pity, and despair mingled.' Hitler blamed Göring for being lazy, corrupt and a drug addict who 'let the Air Force go to pot'.

Then, said Speer, Hitler slumped back into lethargy and resignation: '[He said] "Well, all right, let Göring negotiate the surrender. If the war is lost anyhow, it doesn't matter who does it." That sentence expressed contempt for the German people: Göring was still good enough for the purposes of capitulation.'

Himmler was a different matter. Since the 'faithful Heinrich' was out of Berlin and beyond Hitler's reach, the Führer took out his anger towards the SS chief on Hermann Fegelein, Eva Braun's brother-in-law and Himmler's representative attached to Hitler's staff. Fegelein was arrested and executed on 27 April.

Speer took his leave from the bunker and spent a few minutes in the Court of Honour in the darkened Chancellery that he had designed and built. Wistfully, he recalled: 'Now I was leaving the ruins of my building, and of the most significant years of my life.' He then escaped Berlin and flew to Hamburg, from where he joined Dönitz at his headquarters at Plön in Schleswig-Holstein.

Friday, 27 April
After darkness fell, Hitler decorated Hitler Youth leader Artur Axmann with a Knight's Cross. Between then and 30 April, a number of Knight's Crosses were awarded in Hitler's name to the defenders of Berlin.

Friday/Saturday, 27/28 April ('Suicide Council')
The Russian bombardment of the Chancellery reached the highest pitch so far. The accuracy of the shelling, to those in the shelter below ground, was astounding. It seemed as if each shell landed in exactly the same place as the one before, directly on the Chancellery buildings. This indicated to them that Russian ground troops could overrun the area at any moment. Consequently, a 'suicide council' was called by Hitler. Plans were gone over regarding the destruction of the bodies of everyone in the shelter. A decision was made that as soon as the Russians reached the Chancellery grounds, the mass suicide would begin. Last instructions were given as to the use of poison vials.

The group was hypnotized by the suicide rehearsal, and a general discussion was entered into to determine in what manner the most thorough destruction of the human body could be performed. Everybody made little speeches, swearing allegiance again and again to the Führer and to Germany. Yet through it all there still ran for some the faint hope that Wenck, commander of the 12th Army, might still come to their rescue and hold the line long enough to effect an evacuation. Most, however, only paid lip-service to the hope of salvation through Wenck's efforts to follow the lead of the Führer.

Almost everyone had given up all thoughts of being saved, and said as much to each other when Hitler was not present. At the end of the discussions over the destruction of the bodies, it was suggested that SS men would be assigned to see that no trace remained.

Saturday, 28 April
Throughout the day, the intensity of the Russian fire continued, the suicide, talk keeping pace with the shelling.

Stalin's troops were now within a mile of the Chancellery, which was crumbling under artillery, rockets and aerial bombing. The next day, although the LVI Panzer Corps defending the city was almost out of ammunition, Hitler ordered it to fight to the last man.

The fighting in the streets of Berlin was approaching a climax. Soviet troops had reached the Tiergarten, once a royal hunting preserve, and artillery continued to pound the capital, blowing apart what few walls remained standing. Dug into the rubble with panzerfausts and bolt-action rifles, the old men of the Volkssturm and the young boys of the Hitler Youth fought a losing battle against the better-equipped Red Army troops.

General Hans Krebs, chief of staff of the OKH, made his last telephone call from the Führerbunker to Field Marshal Keitel in Fürstenberg. Krebs told him that all would be lost if relief did not arrive within forty-eight hours. Keitel promised to exert the utmost pressure on Generals Wenck and Busse, commanders of the 12th and 9th armies respectively. Meanwhile, Bormann wired to Dönitz: 'Reich Chancellery a heap of rubble.' He said that the foreign press was reporting fresh acts of treason and 'that without exception [Feldmarschall Ferdinand] Schörner [the last chief of the OKH], Wenck and the others must give evidence of their loyalty by the quickest relief of the Führer'.

Sunday, 29 April (Hitler Marries Eva Braun)
Hitler now did something extraordinary. He told one of his secretaries, Gertrude 'Traudl' Junge:

> 'Since I did not feel that I could accept the responsibility of marriage during the years of struggle, I have decided now, before the end of my earthly career, to take, as my wife, the girl who, after many years of loyal friendship, came of her own free will to this city, already almost besieged, in order to share my fate. At her own request she goes to her death with me as my wife. Death will compensate us for what we were both deprived of by my labours in the service to my people.'

Hitler, of course, was referring to his mistress, Eva Braun, who had existed in the shadows for so long that hardly any German even knew about the plain blonde cipher girl who preferred fashion catalogues and film-star magazines to anything more intellectually stimulating. If it seemed to her that it was a cruel joke as the most powerful man in German history was going to make her 'an honest woman' on the brink of their mutual deaths, she said nothing about it. She just smiled her wan smile and enjoyed her brief moment in the rapidly dimming spotlight.

Much later that day, the couple – with Hitler in his usual uniform and Eva in a black silk taffeta dress – recited their wedding vows in front of a small coterie of eight guests, a minor official having been found to officiate. Throughout the bunker, groups of staffers smiled and celebrated. It was the first time in many weeks there had been anything worth smiling about. The smiles did not last, however, as the artillery continued to drum overhead. It seemed as if the fighting was drawing ever closer to the bunker. Soon the war, and perhaps all of their lives, would be over.

With Goebbels as a witness, the registrar began the wedding ceremony by asking Hitler: 'Are you of pure Aryan descent?' Hitler replied: 'Yes'. Goebbels interjected angrily: 'This is the Führer you are talking to!' 'Yes, sir,' was the nervous reply. The registrar then asked Eva Braun the same question. 'Yes,' she replied. The marriage was quickly solemnized.

Accounts from two of the secretaries present recorded that they had been called together to see the newly married couple. Hitler and Eva emerged from the map room where the marriage ceremony had taken place, accompanied by Goebbels, his wife Magda and Hitler's private secretary, Gerda Christian. Turning to Christian, Eva pointed to the wedding ring on her finger and received her congratulations.

A party followed to celebrate the occasion. According to Gerda Christian, Hitler talked mostly of the past and of happier times. However, he admitted to her that he knew the war was lost. He repeated that he would never allow himself to be taken prisoner by the Russians, instead intending to shoot himself. He then confided to Junge that the wedding had been an emotional experience, but that for him death would only mean a personal redemption of his many worries after what had been a very difficult life.

Gerda Christian, who was accustomed to joining Hitler and Eva for certain meals, was invited to the wedding breakfast after the ceremony but left early, telling Junge that she had been unable to stand the atmosphere of gloom and despondency.

The occupants of the bunker were told that they were all to be received by Hitler. It was 10.30 pm when they were instructed to hold themselves in readiness, but it was not until 12.30 am that they got the call. There was Professor Werner Haase (one of Hitler's personal physicians), SS dentist Doctor Helmut Kunz, Dr Ludwig Stumpfegger and two or three Medical Corps enlisted men. About twenty-five or thirty people had already gathered there – the secretaries, the cleaning women and a few strangers who had taken refuge in the shelter. They were all standing in a row. Hitler had the names of the people he didn't know and shook hands with each one as he walked down the line. A 'brown sister', who was a stranger and had perhaps not grasped the seriousness of the moment and their ultimate fate, expressed her thanks to Hitler because she had been admitted into the shelter, concluding: 'Führer, we believe in you and in a good outcome!' Hitler replied: 'Each one must stand in his place and hold out, and if fate requires it, there he must fall!'

The question of whether Berlin would stand or fall, and therefore whether Hitler should live or die, was now no longer in doubt. Hitler presumably married Eva Braun so that she would have a recognized status entitling her to share in his death.

Those in the bunker received news of the execution by Italian partisans of Mussolini and his mistress, Claretta Petacci. One of the survivors from the bunker interrogated later commented that this would have served to reinforce Hitler's determination that neither he nor Eva Braun should face a similar fate. Hitler shuddered at the thought that the same thing could happen to him. 'I will not fall into the hands of the enemy, dead or alive,' he declared. 'After I die, my body shall be burned and remain undiscovered forever!'

While Hitler and Eva were relaxing with the other residents of the bunker, the Führer decided to hand out a strange gift to the assembled: cyanide capsules. Someone wondered if they would be effective; after all, they had been supplied by the 'traitor' Himmler. Dr Stumpfegger suggested one of the capsules be tested on Hitler's beloved German shepherd dog, Blondi. Strangely, Hitler went along with the idea. A doctor in the bunker hospital was summoned and ordered to give the poison to the animal; it died within seconds. The group put their capsules into their pockets to be used 'when the time was right'.

Hitler then ordered his staff to prepare for the end. An eyewitness noted that Hitler's SS bodyguards were destroying his personal papers.

The Himmler Betrayal

A great blow befell Hitler when a telegram arrived informing him that the staunch and trusted Hermann Himmler (one of the most powerful men in Nazi Germany and the main architect of the Holocaust) had joined Göring on the traitor list. It was like a death blow to the entire assembly. Men and

The Beginning of the End 19

women alike cried and screamed; rage, fear and desperation all mixed into one emotional spasm. That Himmler, seen by many as the protector of the Reich, should now be a traitor was considered impossible. The telegram stated that Himmler had contacted the British and American authorities through Sweden to propose a capitulation to the San Francisco conference (fifty nations gathered at San Francisco's Opera House to sign the Charter of the United Nations). Hitler raged again, like a mad man. His colour rose to a heated red hue, and his face was virtually unrecognizable. Additional evidence of Himmler's 'treachery' was that he asked not to be identified with capitulation proposals; American authorities were said to have abided with this request, but the British authorities did not.

After his lengthy outburst, Hitler sank into a stupor, and for a time the whole shelter was silent. A little later came the news that the Russians would make a full-force bid to capture the Chancellery on the following morning, the 30th. Even small-arms fire could now be heard from the area above the shelter. Ground reports indicated that the Russians were nearing Potsdamer Platz. Everyone looked at their poison.

During the evening of 29 April, Krebs contacted Jodl by radio: 'Request immediate report. Firstly, of the whereabouts of Wenck's spearheads. Secondly, of time intended to attack. Thirdly, of the location of the 9th Army. Fourthly, of the precise place in which the 9th Army will break through. Fifthly, of the whereabouts of General Rudolf Holste's spearhead.' In the early morning of 30 April, Jodl sent Krebs a reply: 'Firstly, Wenck's spearhead bogged down south of Schwielow Lake. Secondly, 12th Army therefore unable to continue attack on Berlin. Thirdly, bulk of 9th Army surrounded. Fourthly, Holste's Corps on the defensive.'

Monday, 30 April

At 2.30 am, some of the residents of the bunker were summoned by the Führer, including SS officers and about ten women. They collected in the dining corridor of the bunker, then Hitler entered and shook hands with all of the women and spoke to most of them. He then left and returned to his own room.

During the late morning, SS-Brigadeführer Wilhelm Mohnke, commander of the Centre Government district of Berlin, informed Hitler that he could not hold out for more than two days. Weidling then told Hitler that the defenders would probably exhaust their ammunition that night and again asked him for permission to break out, finally receiving permission to do so at 1.00 pm.

Hitler lunched with his secretaries 'Traudl' Junge and Gerda Christian from 1.00–2.00 pm. Eva Braun did not join them. During the meal, Hitler appeared calm and under control, telling the women this was the last time they would eat together. Little of importance was said, and there was no mention of any impending suicide.

After lunch, Junge found a room where she could sit down and smoke a cigarette. She then went to Braun's private quarters and found her sorting out and preparing to give away most of her belongings as final gifts. She gave Junge her most valuable fur, saying: 'Here's a present for next winter and your life after the war. I wish you all the luck in the world. And when you put it on, always remember me and give my very best to our native *Bavaria*-das schoene Bayern [Bavaria the beautiful].' Junge then visited Magda Goebbels, who was upset about the fate of her children – she planned to poison them rather than let them fall into Russian hands.

Hitler gave Goebbels and his family permission to leave the bunker, but Goebbels and Magda decided to remain loyal to the bitter, ghoulish end. They knew that if they were captured alive, theirs would be a most unpleasant fate.

Back in March, Magda Goebbels had confessed to her former sister-in-law:

We have demanded monstrous things from the German people and treated other nations with pitiless cruelty. For this the victors will exact their full revenge … we can't let them think we are cowards. Everybody else has the right to live. We haven't got this right – we have forfeited it. I make myself responsible. I belonged. I believed in Hitler and for long enough in Joseph.

Hitler, meanwhile, met with Martin Bormann, who emerged into the antechamber from Hitler's study and went straight up to Otto Günsche (a mid-ranking officer in the Waffen-SS and Hitler's adjutant) and told him that Hitler and Braun wanted to bring their lives to an end that day. Their bodies were to be drenched in petrol and burned in the garden of the Chancellery. That was Hitler's categorical order. Under no circumstances should his body fall into Russian hands. Bormann asked Günsche to make sure that everything was made ready for the burning of the bodies. Günsche said he would take care of things. Shortly after receiving his instructions from Bormann, Hitler came out of his room and told Günsche that he would now shoot himself and that his wife would also depart this life. Their bodies were then to be burnt. He wished that nothing should remain of himself, so the Russians could not desecrate his body or display it in any way. Hitler also charged Günsche with the necessary preparations. The way he expressed it, Günsche would be personally responsible for this; he assured Hitler that he would carry out his orders.

A little later, SS-General Johann (Hans) Rattenhuber and Hitler's personal pilots, Hans Baur and George Betz, made their way, distraught, into the antechamber. They had just run into Bormann and learned from him that Hitler wanted to take his own life. They assailed Günsche with questions. He was just about to answer them when the door opened and Hitler came out. Rattenhuber, Baur, Günsche and Betz gave the Nazi salute to their Führer. Hitler did not react, merely asking them in a tired voice to come closer. Hitler then told them: 'I have ordered that I am to be burned after my death. Make sure that my order is carried out to the letter. I will not have it that they take my body back to Moscow to exhibit in a cabinet of curiosities.' Hitler gave a lethargic gesture of farewell with his right arm, turned round and disappeared behind his study door.

Hitler then suddenly summoned both Baur and Betz to his quarters. As they entered the small study, Hitler clasped one of Baur's hands with both of his and said in an emotional voice: 'Baur, I'd like to bid you farewell! My generals have betrayed me and sold me out, my soldiers don't want to go on, and I cannot go on!' Baur tried to convince Hitler that he could still fly him to safety in Argentina, Japan, Japanese-held Manchukuo in Asia or to some friendly Arabs. Hitler shook his head and explained that if he went to Berchtesgaden or to join Dönitz in Flensburg, he would be in the same situation again within two weeks. According to Baur, Hitler added: 'I will stand or fall with Berlin. A person must have the courage to suffer the consequences of his actions. I will take my own life, today!' Hitler thanked Baur for his long years of service and then presented him, as a gift, with his favourite portrait of Frederick the Great by Anton Graff. It was the painting that Baur had carried from one headquarters to another during the war.

At 2.30 pm, Hitler walked around the bunker with Eva Braun and said goodbye to his immediate entourage.

The final goodbyes came at approximately 3.15 pm, when Hitler and Braun made their last appearance in the main corridor of the lower bunker to say farewell to what was left of the Reich Chancellery group. Present were Joseph Goebbels, Bormann, Hans Krebs, Wilhelm Burgdorf, Walther Hewel, Hans-Erich Voss, Werner Haase, Rattenhuber, Peter Hoegel, Heinz Linge (Hitler's SS valet), Günsche, Frau Christian, Fraulein Else Krueger, Fraulein Manziarly and Werner Naumann. He shook hands with each person, and in a weak voice mumbled something to some of them. While Hitler was saying his goodbyes, Günsche found Junge and told her that Hitler wanted to bid farewell to her. She met him in the central corridor. He shook her hand. Junge later said: 'It seemed as if he were not looking at me … I had the feeling he was not really seeing me.' He said a few words which she did not understand, but thought it was 'all the best' or some such thing. Then Braun, appearing very much composed, took leave of the gathering. She embraced Junge and said: 'See to it that you manage to get through to Munich and give my love to Bavaria.'

Before Hitler entered his room, Linge asked him if he might say goodbye and if he had any last orders for him. Hitler replied: 'Linge, I am going to shoot myself now. You know what you have to do.' He added: 'I have given orders to break out. Try to fight your way through to the west in small groups.' Either at this point or perhaps earlier that afternoon, Hitler had told Linge to take charge of things immediately after his death and that it was Linge who was to give the word when to enter the room where he was to take his life. Linge gave the Nazi salute, they shook hands and as Hitler entered his room, he told Linge to wait at least ten minutes, then to enter if he had heard no sound.

Braun looked sad as she then gave Heinz Linge her hand and said: 'Goodbye, Linge. I hope that you get away from Berlin. If you run into my sister Gretel, don't tell her how her husband died.' After thanking him for everything he had done for Hitler, she went to Frau Goebbels, who was in her husband's room, where she had remained all day, agonizing over the impending death of her children. A few minutes later, Braun left Goebbels's room and went to the telephone exchange, where she found Günsche. She said to him: 'Please tell the Führer that Frau Goebbels has asked him to come to see her one more time.' Depending upon which sources are believed, either Hitler went to Goebbels's room to see Frau Goebbels or she was able to enter Hitler's study to talk to him. Whatever the case, she begged Hitler not to take his life but to escape to Berchtesgaden. Hitler said he had no other recourse than to commit suicide, refusing to discuss the matter further. He thanked her for her commitment and services. Sobbing and trembling, she left the room, walked past her husband in the corridor without saying a word and went to the upper bunker.

Hitler then turned to Dr Goebbels, who begged Hitler to allow the Hitler Youth to take him (Hitler) out of Berlin. Hitler responded brusquely: 'Doctor, you know my decision. There is no change! You can of course leave Berlin with your family.' Goebbels replied that he would not do so. He intended to stay in Berlin and die there. Hitler then said: 'I entrust you with the responsibility to see that our corpses are burned immediately.' Hitler shook his hand and returned to his room, where he was soon joined by Braun, who said goodbye to Günsche. Linge then lost his composure completely and raced up all the steep steps of the emergency-exit staircase, out into the courtyard, where he ran into sharp artillery fire. Just as promptly, he ran back down the steps, speechless and wild-eyed, taking up a position near Günsche, who was till guarding Hitler's door.

Meanwhile, Axmann went to the Führerbunker to see Dr and Frau Goebbels. Dr Goebbels told him that Hitler had already retired to his room to commit suicide with Braun. Axmann wished to bid Hitler a personal farewell, but Günsche told him the Führer would admit nobody, refusing to open the door.

Axmann then went to the conference room, where he joined by Krebs, Burgdorf, Bormann, Naumann, Rattenhuber, Stumpfegger, Hewel and Goebbels. They talked about Hitler saying goodbye, and in a very agitated state waited for the suicides to take place.

Axmann had wanted to take Hitler away from Berlin, but upon receiving no support for his plan he had to give it up. He also sought to organize a kind of emergency messenger service using members of the HJ for dangerous contact missions.

Between 3.45 and 4.00 pm, there were, at different times, at least six people almost as near as Günsche to the door to Hitler's quarters. Goebbels thought he may have heard a shot, but the others did not. Günsche believed none of them could have heard a shot because of the sealed double doors. He later stated: 'Both these doors were fireproof, gas proof and soundproof.' Other witnesses argued that it was impossible to distinguish specific sounds over the constant pounding of the diesel generators and humming of the ventilator fans in the bunker.

After ten minutes or so, in keeping with Hitler's instructions to wait that long before entering his room, Linge remarked to Günsche 'I think it's over' before going into the outer room. Strong fumes made his eyes smart. Choking, Linge left the room, closed and locked the door and went to the conference room. He told Bormann that he had entered the room and smelled gas from a discharged firearm. 'Frankly, I was trembling,' Linge recalled. 'And I simply did not have the gumption to go in there by myself. It was too eerie.' Bormann immediately followed Linge to the door, opened it, and they entered the room together, gasping from toxic fumes. According to Linge, Bormann 'turned white as chalk and stared at me helplessly'.

Hitler had spent 105 days in the bunker before taking his life.

Günsche then began carrying out Hitler's and Bormann's orders. He called SS-Obersturmbannführer Erich Kempka (Hitler's long-time chauffeur and head of the motor pool), who was living in the bunker next to the Chancellery garage, and asked him to bring ten jerricans of petrol to the Führerbunker immediately, leaving it at the emergency exit to the garden behind the Chancellery, and then to report to him. Kempka asked why the petrol was needed, but Günsche said that he could not tell him over the phone. Kempka protested that it would be difficult to find so large a quantity at such short notice, but was told that it must be found. Ultimately, he found most of what had been requested, and it was quickly delivered to the designated spot.

Soon afterwards, Günsche, not wanting any casual observer to witness the final 'tragic' scene, ordered the SS men of the bodyguard and the Security Service who occupied the little room by the emergency exit to vacate the room and move elsewhere. He even told the sentries who stood by the armour-plated door which led from the stairway to the emergency exit to go back into the bunker. One man, SS-Untersturmführer Hans Hofbeck, left by the emergency exit with orders to let no one pass. Günsche then went into the hall of the bunker and took up his position by the antechamber door.

Hermann Karnau, an SS bodyguard of Hitler's, saw four men – subordinates of Kempka – arrive outside the bunker with gasoline cans, which they said were for the air conditioning system inside the bunker. Kempka had siphoned the fuel from damaged cars in the Reich Chancellery garage. Remembering that the air conditioning system was fuelled by diesel, Karnau denied them entrance into the Führerbunker. When pressed, however, he allowed one of the men to enter. The subordinate found Kempka and told him that he and his men had placed around 180–200 litres of petrol at the exit to the bunker.

At that moment, the door of Hitler's sitting room opened and his valet, Linge, shouted desperately at Kempka: 'The petrol! Where is the petrol?' 'It is in position,' replied Kempka.

In Hitler's study, Linge, Bormann, Axmann, Goebbels and Günsche found that the room smelled of gunpowder, smoke and bitter almonds. They saw the bodies seated on the blue and white sofa against the wall opposite the door from the antechamber. Hitler was slumped at the right hand armrest of the sofa. His head was inclined to the right and slightly forward, and his eyes were open. Hitler's right temple had a bullet wound the size of a small coin. A trail of blood ran down from it to about the middle of his cheek. Hitler's lower right arm was between the armrest of the sofa and his right thigh, and his open hand lay on his right knee, palm upwards. The left arm hung at his side. His feet were on the floor; they were pointing forwards and were about 12–15in apart. Next to Hitler's right foot lay a 7.65mm Walther pistol, and by his left foot a 6.35mm Walther pistol; one of the pistols belonged to Braun. On the carpet next to the sofa, a puddle of blood the size of a plate had formed. The rear wall and sofa were spattered with blood. Next to Hitler was the body of Braun, with her head near, or resting on, his left shoulder. She was wearing a blue dress and showed no signs of injuries or blood. She was in the snug position she had assumed before swallowing the poison. Her upper body rested against the back of the sofa, her head upright. Her legs were drawn up under her on the sofa. Her brightly coloured high-heeled shoes stood side by side on the floor in front of the sofa. Her eyes were open and her bluish lips were firmly pressed together.

Linge immediately left the room and fetched the woollen military blankets he had left in the antechamber to wrap Hitler in. Goebbels, Bormann, Axmann and Günsche remained with the bodies for several minutes in stunned silence. Günsche finally snapped out of the trance and directed Linge, who had returned, to move aside the two chairs and table and to spread the blankets on the floor. While Linge was spreading out the blankets, Günsche went to get Hoegel, Franz Schaedle (the last commander of Hitler's bodyguard), Ewald Lindloff (an SS officer) and a certain Reiser, whom he had put on call to assist with the bodies. Apparently, Bormann also left the room to call other people to lend a hand. Meanwhile, Dr Stumpfegger arrived. He examined the bodies and pronounced both Hitler and Braun dead. Goebbels and Axmann were mute spectators to the activities taking place. Linge spread one of the blankets on the study floor in front of the sofa, and with the help of Bormann or another person, laid Hitler's body on the ground and wrapped him in the blanket. Linge then called out to one of the others present that the blanket for Braun was in Hitler's bedroom. He recalled that the person he addressed was already occupied with her body; he did not remember who it was. Axmann, meanwhile, took Hitler's pistol as a memento, for 'better times'.

The next task was to get the bodies out of the bunker and then cremate them in the garden. The bodies, after being carried outside, were laid on the sandy ground in the garden a few yards from the emergency exit of the bunker and soaked in petrol. Those present then retired to the porch of the exit as there was heavy Russian shelling at the time, and from that relatively safe spot Günsche threw a lighted petrol-soaked rag on to the bodies. They then all stood to attention, gave the Nazi salute and retired below ground. The bodies were re-soaked with petrol at intervals to keep them alight and were burnt until little or nothing was left.

Two-and-a-half hours later, with the bodies reduced to ashes and scorched bones, the remains were swept into a piece of canvas, laid in the bottom of a shell hole and covered with dirt. There they would remain until Soviet troops, rummaging through the debris of the Chancellery a couple of days later, came across them and took them to Moscow for identification. Before that, Axmann allegedly collected some of Hitler's ashes and put them in a box, an act that was reportedly witnessed by Junge.

SS-Oberscharführer Rochus Misch

Rochus Misch, who was Hitler's 'last bodyguard', later revealed what happened in the Nazi leader's final minutes in the Berlin bunker.

Misch was a Oberscharführer in the 1st SS-Panzerdivision 'Leibstandarte SS Adolf Hitler' (LSSAH). He served in the Führerbegleitkommando (FBK, Führer Escort Command) as a bodyguard, courier and telephone operator for the German dictator.

Misch described how he once walked in on Eva Braun when she was wearing a 'flimsy nightie' in the guestroom, which had a private passageway into Hitler's room, and she put a finger to her mouth, telling the bodyguard to keep quiet. Misch thought he would be in trouble over the incident.

He had heard Eva Braun and Magda Goebbels swearing to die with their men. The telephone operator was on the switchboard in Hitler's bunker on 30 April 1945 when General Keitel sent a message to say that the army had failed to break the Soviet encirclement in Berlin and that the end of the war was now inevitable. Shortly afterwards, Misch heard Hitler talking quietly to Martin Bormann and others. He saw Hitler walk into his study, with Eva following him.

Misch saw Otto Günsche, the Führer's adjutant, close the door behind the newly married couple. Günsche told Misch that their boss was not to be disturbed. Hitler shook hands with Günsche and told him that all German soldiers were now released from their oath of loyalty. Hitler had already told his adjutant that he did not want his body to be publicly abused, as had happened to Mussolini, and that he wanted his corpse to be burned.

Misch said everyone in the bunker waited nervously, waiting to hear the shot from Hitler's quarters. Then there was some commotion. Linge took Misch to one side and they went in.

Misch recalled: 'My glance fell first on Eva. She was seated with her legs drawn up, her head inclined towards Hitler. Her shoes were under the sofa. Near her ... the dead Hitler. His eyes were open and staring, his head had fallen forward slightly.'

Misch, who survived the war, spoke fondly of his time with Hitler until his later years, describing him as a 'wonderful boss' and 'no brute'.

At 10.26 pm on 30 April, a communiqué was issued by *Nazis in the News*. It read:

'It is reported from the Führer's headquarters that our Führer, Adolf Hitler, fighting to the last breath against Bolshevism, fell for Germany this afternoon in his operational headquarters in the Reich Chancellery. On the 30th April the Führer appointed Grand Admiral Dönitz his successor.'

Tuesday, 1 May
At 4.00 am, General Krebs, who spoke fluent Russian, spoke to General Vasily Chuikov, commander of the Soviet 8th Guards Army, about bringing an end to the fighting in Berlin. Chuikov demanded unconditional surrender of the remaining German forces, but Krebs did not have the authority to surrender so he returned to the bunker.

Keitel was found early in the morning, and he gave the news that all elements of Wenck's relieving 12th Army had long since been destroyed or captured. Keitel said he had sent word to Hitler to that effect. Von Greim, the new chief of the Luftwaffe, and his partner Hanna Reitsch, the famous German test pilot, now knew that Hitler must surely have given up all hope, and both fully expected that the well-rehearsed suicide plans had already been put into operation.

Murder in the Bunker
Most of Hitler's entourage were still in the bunker, hearing and feeling the Russian shells bursting above them. For them, the time had come for the final act. Magda Goebbels gathered her six children. As well as their only son, Helmut, there was Helga, who had the eyes and dark hair of her father, and Hildegard, who was more of a brunette, many believing that she would blossom into a true beauty. Then there was Holde, Hedda and the youngest of the girls, Heide. All their names begin with the letter 'H' as a tribute to Hitler.

With bits of concrete falling from the ceiling after each explosion above, and knowing that the Russians were closing in on the Chancellery, Reitsch pleaded with Magda to allow her to fly the children to safety. 'My God, Frau Goebbels,' Reitsch said. 'The children cannot stay here, even if I have to fly in twenty times to get them out.' Frau Goebbels refused.

Magda, who was reported to have looked tired, said to her children that she had some very exciting news, that tomorrow they would be going to Berchtesgaden. They had hired a plane with a 'top' pilot to get them out. She then dressed her five daughters in long white nightgowns and lovingly brushed their hair. She told them: 'Don't be afraid. The doctor is going to give you a shot now.' At about 8.40 pm, on the direction of Magda, the children were given an injection of morphine by Helmut Kunz, an SS dentist. After the war, Kunz testified: 'I injected them with morphine – the eldest daughters first, then the son, then the other daughters. It took around ten minutes.'

When the children were asleep, Magda went into the room, cyanide capsules in her hand. She went to the children, one by one, and put a capsule in each one's mouth. She put one hand on top of the child's head, the other hand under their chin, and pushed, breaking the capsule that contained the poison. Death was instantaneous. She then covered each child's face with a blanket.

Once their children were dead, Magda and Joseph Goebbels prepared to commit suicide. Joseph said to Rochus Misch: 'Well, Misch, tell Dönitz that we knew how to live. Now we know how to die.'

Dr Goebbels then made a little joke, telling those around them that they were going to walk up to the garden to save everyone from having to carry their bodies up the steep steps. He put on his gloves and his hat, then he and Frau Goebbels, who was near to collapsing, proceeded arm-in-arm up the stairs to the garden and to their deaths.

Goebbels made his adjutant, Günther Schwägermann, promise to cremate both his and his wife's bodies. By some accounts, Goebbels shot Magda and then himself, a *coup de grace* coming from Schwägermann's pistol. Their bodies were then doused with petrol and set alight. However, they were only partially cremated.

With Hitler and Goebbels now dead, those closest to them at the end chose to make their escape from the doomed city. A few made it – Bormann, Kempka, Schwägermann, Stumpfegger, Günsche, Naumann, Linge, Kunz, Junge and several others.

Wednesday, 2 May
At 1.00 am, Soviet forces picked up a radio message from the LVI Panzer Corps requesting a ceasefire. Down in the Führerbunker, Generals Krebs and Burgdorf committed suicide by a gunshot wound to the head. At 6.00 am, General Weidling surrendered with his LVI Panzer Corps staff.

The last defenders in the area around the bunker complex were French SS volunteers of the 33rd Waffen Grenadier Division of the SS Charlemagne (1st French), who remained until the early morning. Soviet forces then overran the Reich Chancellery. They found Joseph and Magda Goebbels's burned corpses, taking their remains to Magdeburg where they were buried. (In 1970, at the direction of KGB director Yuri Andropov, the remains were exhumed, crushed and dumped into the Biederitz River near Berlin.) The bodies of the six Goebbels children were also discovered, found in their beds in the Vorbunker with the clear mark of cyanide shown on their faces.

Johannes Hentschel, the master electro-mechanic for the bunker complex, stayed after everyone else had either left or committed suicide, as the field hospital in the Reich Chancellery above needed power and water. He surrendered at 9.00 am as Soviet troops entered the bunker complex.

Monday, 7 May

With Hitler gone, Nazi Germany's end came swiftly. General Alfred Jodl, commander of the Wehrmacht, arrived at SHAEF (Supreme Headquarters Allied Expeditionary Force) Headquarters in Rheims, France, to sign the official Instrument of Surrender at around 2.30 am. Eisenhower, supreme commander of the Allied Expdeditionary Force, declined to attend, sending his deputy, Lieutenant General Walter Bedell Smith, to act on his behalf. Jodl accepted the Allies' demands that all resistance cease by 11.01 pm on 8 May. Most of the war-weary Axis soldiers gladly laid down their arms, surprised and grateful to find themselves still alive. A few diehards, however, ignored the order and continued to fight.

Why the Redoubt Fortress was not Utilized

Why was the Austria/southern Germany last stand of resistance – the National Redoubt – never put into operation? As late as 15 April 1945, it still seemed that there was every intention of moving the government and military headquarters to Berchtesgaden. All of the bureaus and headquarters in Berlin at the time were on a constant two-hour movement alert.

However, the reports Hitler received were so shocking that he was convinced that preparations to make the Redoubt resistance a success would never be completed in time. It was believed that the realization that the Redoubt, of which so much was expected, would have to be crossed off as useless was the major cause of Hitler's breakdown. It was also said that Göring and Hitler had a 'strained' conversation regarding this matter, with Göring insisting on an early evacuation to the Redoubt area and Hitler declining in the hope that the Oder would hold the advancing Red Army. Göring allegedly claimed that the Redoubt was ready for occupancy, while Hitler preferred to wait until he could have its readiness confirmed. It was later said at the Dönitz war council and elsewhere that Göring's departure was governed by his realization that the Oder would be crossed and his unfulfilled hope that the partially completed Redoubt area would hold.

Had Göring's coup of 23 April succeeded, with him taking over power from the Führer, it was believed that the Redoubt might have been more actively defended. The reasons that it was not are two-fold: first, the failure of Göring's attempted takeover; and second, Hitler's belief that continued resistance in Berlin might be more successful than the sure collapse he saw in an uncompleted Redoubt.

Frau Erna Flegal

One person who was in the Führerbunker until at least 1 May was a nurse, Erna Flegal. Frau Flegal was interviewed by the Strategic Services Unit of the US War Department Mission for Germany in November 1945.

Flegal was a Red Cross nurse from the Märkische Haus training school and was employed as a surgical nurse at the University Hospital in Berlin on Ziegelstraße.

Since there was a shortage of doctors in Berlin, a nurse always had to be present in the air raid shelter in the Chancellery when there was an air raid alarm, to provide first aid in case it was necessary for injuries or any other emergency. The same was true for the Führer's shelter. That service was assigned to Flegal in January 1943. When there was a raid, Flegal was called from the hospital to the shelter and stayed in the First Aid Room. It was a small room adjoining an operating room. Only SS personnel who had been injured were brought there. When the Soviet ring around Berlin drew closer, the injured who had formerly been taken away to the hospitals after air raids were kept in the shelter. During the course of the fighting, it grew to be quite a large hospital, treating about 500 wounded at one stage.

Flegal would have seen a lot of Hitler, as after November 1944 he stayed in Berlin continuously, with the exception of the Christmas holidays and on one occasion when he visited the Oder front. Besides Hitler and the staff at the Chancellery, the Mohnke combat group were always present. Mohnke himself had his quarters in the Reich Chancellery.

During April 1945, the Goebbels family moved into the shelter from the Propaganda Ministry. Hitler was very fond of the Goebbels children. They gave him a great deal of pleasure; even in the last days he invited them for chocolate, which made the children very happy. In the shelter there was only one bathtub, which naturally was provided for Hitler. However, he allowed the Goebbels children to bathe in it, which they always enjoyed. Also present at this time was Martin Bormann – head of the Nazi Party Chancellery – and his brother, Paul. The brothers did not get along. Paul left Berlin because his wife was expecting a baby.

The following aides were present too: Brigadeführer Albrecht, adjutant to Hitler (during the Battle of Berlin, he was last seen defending Hitler's Chancellery with a machine gun and was believed to have committed suicide on 1 May, aged 41, although his body was never found); Oberst Nicolaus von Below, a Luftwaffe adjutant; and General Wilhelm Burgdorf, another adjutant. On 28 April, when it was discovered that Himmler was attempting to negotiate a surrender, Burgdorf was named by Hitler as a member of the tribunal who was to put Himmler and his associates on trial. On the next day, he was among the four men who witnessed and signed Hitler's last will and testament. Following Hitler's suicide, he also killed himself on 2 May.

All the other leading generals were with Field Marshal Keitel outside the cauldron of Berlin. Those that remained were orderlies, soldiers and SS bodyguards, the cleaning staff and kitchen personnel – up to the end, Hitler regularly received his special diet of fresh vegetables.

With parts of Berlin already occupied and the Russians coming closer to the centre of the city, Erna Flegal could almost physically feel the Third Reich approaching its end. She heard that troops were supposed to land by plane to protect Berlin until the Wenck Army Group arrived to relieve the capital. Wenck and his troops were already at Beelitz-Heilstätten, but Flegal heard that Wenck's Army Group required twenty-four hours of rest as the soldiers were completely exhausted. They would eventually be entirely wiped out. Although Flegal still believed in the Führer, she could sense the approaching defeat, blaming what she saw as treachery and cowardice among Hitler's immediate entourage over the recent days and weeks.

Hitler himself required no care; Flegal was there exclusively for the care of the wounded. During her interrogation by the Office of Military Government for Germany (US), Flegal said Hitler had aged greatly over recent weeks, with a lot of grey hair, and gave the impression of a man at least fifteen or twenty years older. He shook a great deal and walking was difficult for him, his right side was still very much weakened as a result of the 20 July 1944 attempt on his life. In the period immediately after the assassination attempt, Hitler always shook hands with his left hand, but towards the end he was using his right hand again. He took great care to favour his right hand. It was not until November that Flegal saw Hitler again for the first time after the bomb attack, when he was in Berlin for a state funeral. She said he was very animated and made all sorts of jokes. Flegal recounted that when Hitler was in the room, 'he filled it entirely with his personality – you saw only him, aside from him, nothing else existed. The fascinating thing about him was his eyes; up to the end, it was impossible to turn away from his eyes.'

Flegal assumed that Hitler now recognized the hopelessness of his position; he was said to have expressed himself on the subject to Professor Werner Hasse, a professor of medicine and member of the SS who was also one of Hitler's personal physicians.

For that reason, Flegal regarded every subsequent rumour that Hitler was still alive as senseless; she felt he would never have had the spiritual and physical strength to build up a new Germany. She thought Hitler had experienced too much disillusionment at the hands of his closest friends. For instance, he no longer believed in the loyalty of Himmler. She heard that the liaison officer between them, Hermann Fegelein – the brother-in-law of Eva Braun – had betrayed the Führer. Fegelein was caught trying to leave Berlin in civilian clothes and was shot. Flegal said his 'treachery' had affected Eva Braun very deeply.

Flegal said Professor Theodor Morell, Hitler's physician, was not present at this time. He had a serious heart ailment and was at Obersalzberg, where he later died of his condition. Dr Stumpfegger was, however, present as Hitler's personal surgeon, and also the dentist, Dr Helmut Kunz. Both doctors were later taken away by the Russians.

When Flegal learned of Hitler's marriage to Eva Braun, it was immediately clear to her that it signified the end of the Third Reich. She thought that if Hitler had believed a continuation of the war was possible, he would never had taken such a step. Flegal believed that with death facing him, he wished to thank Braun for her self-sacrificing loyalty by giving her his name. She had voluntarily stayed with him in order to share his fate.

Flegal recalled that the marriage was of 'little importance to us'. She said that nothing unusual was seen in it, describing Braun as a 'completely colourless personality. When she was with a crowd of stenographers, she was in no way conspicuous among them.' When Hitler had his German shepherd, Blondi, poisoned, Flegal said it affected many in the bunker more than Braun's death.

Flegal went over to Hitler's shelter several times when she needed something urgently for the First Aid Room and saw Hitler on a few occasions. Up until the end, she said, Hitler always took his meals alone and with great regularity. His food was very well prepared and was easy to manage in view of the tiny portions that were involved. She said that the only luxury he allowed himself throughout the war was that he always had fresh vegetables supplied to him from Holland.

Flegal said that as the ring around the Chancellery was drawn tighter, radio connection was broken off. It was then impossible to get any information of the outside world, except through shock troops who went out and brought back reports as to where the Russians had now established themselves in the city. However, she said that there was water and light until the end, thanks to the technical excellence with which the installations in the shelter functioned. She remembered that a rather large staff of technicians had stayed behind to constantly supervise the equipment.

Flegal recalled that at the end, 'we were like a big family'. They were all experiencing a common fate in an atmosphere of camaraderie. The dynamics of the fate which was unrolling held sway over all of them. 'We were Germany,' said Flegal, 'and we were going through the end of the Third Reich and of the war.'

Tuesday, 23 October 1945
Else Krüger
Denis Sefton Delmer, based at the No. 10 German News Service in the British Zone of occupied Berlin as a journalist and propagandist for the British government, wrote to Brigadier R.H. Hayler asking for help (not for the first time). Delmer understood that Bormann's former secretary and a person who was in the Chancellery at the time of Hitler's suicide, Fraulein Else Krüger, had been released from prison after having been held at Altona and Plön. She had been instructed by the British authorities not to talk about what she knew.

Delmer, who was fluent in German, was anxious to tell the story of the last days of Hitler for publication in Germany. He thought that the story would have a world wide circulation. Delmer believed that what Krüger could tell would go a long way towards killing off the Hitler myths: those of his escape and survival – which had been fuelled by 'guileless' pronouncements – and those that Hitler was a superman surrounded by other supermen.

However, the journalist felt that there may be overriding considerations, possibly of an inter zonal nature, which would outweigh the valuable effect on public opinion he thought Krüger's revelations would have.

He wanted to know if Brigadier Hayler could look into the ban on speaking with Krüger and have it lifted.

Saturday, 3 November 1945
Interrogation of SS-Hauptsturmführer Hermann Bornholdt at No. 1 Civilian Internment Camp, Neumunster
SS-Hauptsturmführer Hermann Bornholdt revealed that he was on duty with the SS-Begleitkommando in Berlin until 24 April 1945, when he left with Gruppenführer Fegelein, whom he accompanied to Fürstenberg, near Mecklenburg. Fegelein was on a visit to SS-Obergruppenführer Max Jüttner of the SS-Führungshauptamt. On the following day, Fegelein returned to Berlin by air from Rechlin airport, leaving Bornholdt behind. Bornholdt said he was doubtful whether Himmler's Begleit-Battalion could have marched to Berlin on 25 April (as stated by Obersturmbannführer Grothmann), since the city was already surrounded and there was only an air connection.

Bornholdt said that when he left Berlin, the following officers of the Begleitkommando were still there:

Schedle*	(from South Germany);
Beermann	(from the Harz area);
Frick	(from western Germany);
Lindloff	(from Danzig);

Hansen   (from Ditthmarschen, Schleswig-Holstein);
Griesenbock   (from western Germany).

There was possibly also:

Reisser   (from south Germany);
Weichelt, Obersturmführer   (from Saxony).

* Schedle was Deputy Führer of the Begleitkommando.

Tuesday, 13 November
(From the Memoirs of General Karl Koller, Chief of the General Staff of the Luftwaffe)

'April 27th.
'Take off from Schleissheim: 0330 hours.
  'Landing at Rechlin: 0545 hours.
  'Some AA fire on the Elbe and south-west of Berlin. Numerous fires in the area south and south-west of Berlin. No night fighters in spite of bright moonlight.
  'Met Oberst [Hans-Ulrich] Rudel [the most decorated Luftwaffe ace of the war] on the airfield; he had just landed and was ordered to the Führer. He was just about to drive to Christian's [Luftwaffe general Eckhard Christian] liaison staff in the North officers' mess. The last JUs taking part in the Berlin night operations landed again with their troops still on board. The air movement controller believed that was the last night on which it would be possible to reach Berlin; the latest planes were no longer able to make a landing.
  'Over the city, very large columns of smoke and haze came from the innumerable fires. Orientation almost impossible. A chain of extremely defensive fires along the approach to the [East–West] Axis [an emergency airstrip in central Berlin]. All airfields closed, even Gatow, furthermore, no longer possible to reach the inside of Berlin from Gatow. Crews of transport JUs to whom I spoke supplemented and confirmed the picture. SS men who were to have been flown there gave me the impression of showing great relief that the transport was impossible.
  'To North Mess; Christian's liaison staff still asleep after working all night. I do not want to disturb them. I was informed of the situation in the northern zone and in Berlin and at the OKW command post. After

the experience of the previous day, it is now believed to be impossible to get into Berlin, at least by day.

'I decide to drive to the OKW, which is in a Forester's house in the woods near Fuerstenberg, and report there for the time being. The situation in the Northern zone and in Berlin as already described was confirmed. I was informed that Greim arrived in Rechlin with Hanna Reitsch. She was supposed to bring him to Berlin in a helicopter, but there was none available. If he had told me that before, I could have told him straight away that there was none there. Hannah Reitsch then took Greim to Gatow airfield in a FW 190 and from there they flew to the Axis in a Fieseler Storch. While flying over the Grunewald, Greim was wounded in the leg by heavy fire of light weapons of the Russian infantry. Greim and Hanna Reitsch are in the Bunker and it had not yet been possible to bring them out. It is doubted now whether it will be possible to do so. It is believed to be no longer possible to get to Berlin via the Axis. Departure for the OKW in Fürstenberg, after which events took shape in the following manner:

'(a) During the trip passed numerous treks from the east and south-east towards north and north-west, but road discipline was good, no blocking.
'(b) At OKW first discussion with Jodl of all events since our last conversation in the night from the 22nd to the 23rd of April. Jodl again confirms the accuracy of everything he had told me that night.

'Jodl considers my speedy release from arrest a result of information he had given. During the night 23–24th April he was called up from the Bunker and asked whether the Reichsmarschall had ordered me to go south. Jodl answered:

'"No, Koller came to see me and I informed him of the situation at the Bunker on the 22nd of April and told him of the Führer's decisions. Koller considered it to be his duty to report these facts to the Reichsmarschall immediately. I also thought that was the proper thing to do."

'Jodl, very busy, continually interrupted by telephone calls and by orderly officers bringing reports. We did not get around to having a quiet talk about the overall situation and about future aims. As everywhere else, I got the impression here that everybody is expecting the coming collapse but tries to avoid discussing it at all costs. They pretend that continuation of the war will lead to disagreement between the Russians and the Western powers and that Germany will then be given better conditions.

'(c) Short greetings and conversation with Keitel, who went into Jodl's room. The short conversation is insignificant and without result, Keitel avoids a discussion of the events leading to the Reichsmarschall's arrest, excuses himself with the pressure of work and leaves the room.

'(d) I was given a list of the persons who are with the Führer in the Bunker:

> General Krebs, Oberstleutnant Weiss, Major Freytag Loringhoven, Hauptman Bolt; General Burgdorf, Admiral Voss.
>
> SS-Gruppenführer and Generalleutnant der Waffen SS Fegelein (was originally outside Berlin but he was brought in).
>
> SS-Brigadeführer and Generalmajor Polizei Rattenhuber.
>
> Botschafter Hebel.
>
> Reichsleiter Bormann with an assistant from the Reichsleitung.
>
> Dr Goebbels, his wife and six children.
>
> Staatssekretär Naumann of the Reichs propaganda ministerium.
>
> The adjutants von Below and Johannmeier.
>
> Frau Christian, Frau Junge, Frau Manziarly.
>
> Feldmarschall von Greim, Hanna Reitsch, the usual people of the Führer's Staff, also Eva Braun.

'All the persons were in the Bunker on 22nd April (except, I believe, Fegelein, who is supposed to have left on the 21st, and naturally Greim and Hanna Reitsch, who did not fly there until the 26th). Major Buechs must have been well informed because he was always in touch with von Below by telephone. Furthermore, Christian also confirmed the persons named above. This does not by any means imply that the list of persons I was given can make any claim to completeness. It is absolutely possible that Buechs forgot to tell me the names of one or more persons who might have been there.'

Saturday, 21 April
Kurt Huwe

Kurt Huwe was employed as a sanitiser at the Voßstraße shelter. Huwe reported to the Reichskanzlei in Berlin. Upon his arrival in Berlin, the Government quarter was under ceaseless long-range artillery fire and was constantly being attacked by dive-bombers. There were casualties constantly. Present in the bunker at the time were the hospital doctors, Professor Haase and Dr Stumpfegger, and in addition the dentist of the Reichs Chancellery, Oberleutnant Dr Mueller, three nursing sisters and Professor Brandt's chauffeur, SS-Untersturmführer Neuzeit, who was used as an assistant as well as a driver.

Before Huwe's arrival, most of the officers, male typists and other civilians of Hitler's entourage had left Berlin by plane, on Hitler's orders.

Obersalzberg was to be the new headquarters. According to reports, Hitler intended to leave Berlin several days later. The column of motor-vehicles stood prepared in the garden of the Reichskanzlei but was soon destroyed by artillery fire and aircraft bombardment.

Huwe was occupied in bandaging a fresh amputation when the staff were ordered to the Führer's shelter. As Huwe did not have his uniform jacket with him, he remained behind. Upon the return of the others, he learned that Hitler had taken his farewells from everyone, and it was said that he would not live through the night.

In the days previously, Huwe was with Hitler three times when he fetched instruments and drugs from the medical room of the Führer's shelter. Huwe was unable to say how many people were present at the time Hitler bade his farewell.

On the same day, Huwe was a chance witness to a telephone conversation in the Herman Göring Strasse shelter between the personal adjutant of Hitler, SS-Sturmbannführer Günsche, and Hitler's chauffeur, SS- Ostubaf Erich Kempka. He heard that Günsche had ordered petrol from the Führer's shelter, which was to be carried over at once. Kempka went straight away to the shelter with several people, who each carried two cans. Huwe then learned that Hitler, his wife, Goebbels and his family were soon after burned with this petrol.

A nursing sister told Huwe that Dr Stumpfegger had poisoned Goebbels and his family. They were then told officially that Hitler was dead. Everyone was told they were released from their oath and obligations and could leave the Reich Chancellery. Whoever wished to remain could do so under the protection of an international committee which was to assemble in the Reich Chancellery shelter.

Tuesday, 1 May
Cancellation of the Order to Remain in the Shelter

The notice to remain in the shelter was cancelled by an order that all who were in the Chancellery were to attempt to break through the Russian lines in the evening. The attempt was to be made through the Kaiserhof U-Bahn tunnel to the Bahnhof Frierichstrasse, and from there to reach a street favourable to retreat further. This order was carried out under the leadership of SS-Brigadeführer Wilhelm Mohnke, in charge of defending the Reich Chancellery, and all able officers, men, SD and many civilians departed.

Those who remained were principally the wounded, part of the technical staff, some civilians, women and children. On the staff of the hospital, everyone remained behind except Dr Stumpfegger, who had left the Chancellery. Haupsturmführer Schneider also remained, as he was wounded in the foot, as did Huwe, also wounded in the foot, the only sanitizer who stayed behind in the hospital.

Wednesday, 2 May

During the morning, the first Russian troops came into the Reich Chancellery. The occupants had to put their names on lists of everyone present. They were also interrogated several times but were always sent back to their work. The Russians constantly demanded food and alcohol. As well as that, the occupants had to surrender their watches and other valuables, which were also taken from the wounded. No one was allowed to leave the shelter.

In the afternoon, Professor Haase and Schneider were taken away by Russian officers. It was promised that Haase would be brought back immediately as he was the only doctor. However, they did not see him again.

The dentist, Mueller, took over the administration. The number of wounded had risen to some 300, who were without any medical attention. Furthermore, a fire broke out in the Hotel Adlon on Unter den Linden. The Adlon was occupied by some 300 wounded, who were transferred to Huwe's overfilled rooms, with just one doctor.

Monday/Tuesday, 7/8 May

Huwe was taken by Russian officers to a wounded Russian outside the Reich Chancellery, where he was ordered to dress a wound with a fresh bandage. After he had done so, Huwe – having said that he was a Berliner – was told that he could go home. He was detained once more by a Russian patrol but released again.

1946

Fegelein and Frl Else Krueger
British intelligence officer Major Hugh Trevor-Roper produced a report to the Intelligence Bureau (IB). He wanted the IB to question Fraulein Else Krueger in Hamburg:

> 'Frl Krueger stated that the arrest of Fegelein was carried out by Standartenführer Beetz. She described the visit which Beetz paid to Fegelein in Fegelein's house in the Kurfürstendamm, when Beetz was sent out of the Bunker to find him; how Fegelein had tried to persuade Beetz to obtain a Fieseler Storch for him to escape from Berlin; how Fegelein had then telephoned Eva Braun for her intercession; and how, failing in all these efforts, Fegelein had ultimately been brought back to the Bunker by Beetz. Frl Krueger said that she heard those details from Beetz himself. The occasion on which she made those statements was when I [Trevor-Roper] interrogated her at Plön on 25 September, 1946.'

All other sources agreed that the arrest of Fegelein was carried out by Hoegel, the officer who commanded Dienststelle 1 of the Reichssicherheitsdienst under Rattenhuber. They pointed out that Beetz was merely Hitler's second pilot and had no police functions; although they admit that as a Bavarian and a friend of Fegelein, he may have been employed to intercede personally with Fegelein.

Trevor-Roper wanted to know whether Fraulein Krueger was sure that Beetz, not Hoegel, was concerned. Was she sure that Beetz was her informant, and if so, that it was of himself, not of Hoegel, that he spoke? If so, how did she account for Beetz, who carried out police functions?

Monday, 4 March
Answers to Queries re von Below by Press Correspondents Chamberlain and Wighton Regarding the time of Hitler's Wedding
The original time (the evening of 29 April 1945) given in the statement to the press on 31 October 1945 was based on deductions from statements by various witnesses and was not directly confirmed. Since then Zander, Lorenz and other witnesses had fixed it between midnight and 4.30 am on 29 April. Von Below stated that it took place at 6.00 pm on 28 April, but he had shown himself unreliable on other dates and times. The marriage certificate was definitely dated 29 April.

Zander, Lorenz and von Below all confirmed that the marriage was performed by a Standesbeamter (registrar) of the City of Berlin. This agreed with the signature on the marriage certificate.

Wednesday, 10 April
Christian Lund Ibsen
The IB noted that a man called Christian Lund Ibsen, a Danish national and an armoured car driver, had been told to drive his car to a shelter near the Reichskanzlei. He received the order from an SS officer in a black uniform to drive to the Chancellery and await instructions. He did so, and after a few minutes Hitler came out dressed in a grey uniform and entered the car. A black-uniformed SS officer stood on each running board.

Hitler asked Ibsen whether he knew who his passenger was, and Ibsen replied: 'Yes, it is my Führer.' Hitler then gave orders to drive around in the neighbourhood of Knaackstraße and Brandenburger Platz. Ibsen did not recall the names of the other streets.

Hitler ordered the car to stop on several occasions so that he could issue orders to the officers on the running boards. The trip lasted about half an hour, then Hitler ordered the car back to the Chancellery and re-entered the building.

Ibsen returned to the shelter and received no further orders until 30 April, when the trip was repeated.

Ibsen stated that Hitler said to the two SS officers, who were Sturmbannführers, that if relieving troops did not come from the west by daylight on 1 May, they should forgive him. Ibsen had not seen Hitler since.

He heard at about 10.50 pm on 1 May that Hitler had shot himself and that the defenders were to stop fighting. Ibsen was captured the next day by the Russians.

He was positive in his identification of the car passenger as Hitler, and it was thought by the Danish police that he was telling the truth. Ibsen gave a full description of Hitler's uniform: riding breeches, black riding boots, grey cape, brown Sam Brown belt with pistol holster and an unusual officer's hat without badges of rank. He said he had received his original order from Hauptsturmführer Meyer of the 12th Company, 3rd Battalion, Regiment Danemark, but did not know the names of the other SS officers. As far as he knew, his was the only armoured car in the vicinity.

Ibsen was prepared to swear an oath regarding his testimony. The IB stated that this was the first reference they had to Hitler leaving the bunker on 30 April, which if true would make his death later than that presumed.

Thursday, 20 June
Interrogation of Günther August Wilhelm Schwägermann, Personal Adjutant to Dr Goebbels

Günther Schwägermann served in Hitler's Nazi Government. From approximately late 1941, he was the adjutant for Joseph Goebbels and reached the rank of SS-Hauptsturmführer. He was in the Führerbunker from 22 or 23 April 1945 until the evening of 1 May. His recollection of that period was not very distinct, and dates given by him had been inaccurate in some cases. Schwägermann was aware of that limitation and had been careful to differentiate between knowledge and assumption. As for any definite statements made by him, the information was considered to be reliable.

The Events of Monday, 30 April 1945 (Günther Schwägermann)

Schwägermann did not see Hitler personally at all on 30 April. Around 8.00 am, he heard from Waffen-SS officer Ewald Lindloff that Hitler had given orders to poison his dog, Blondi. This was the first indication for Schwägermann that the end was approaching. Between midday and 1.00 pm, he had lunch in the room above the Führerbunker (where Bauer, Mueller, Beetz, Rattenhuber, Günsche, Lindloff, Schedle and Kempka also ate). He then went downstairs, waited around in an anteroom outside the Lage Vorzimmer (in the 'Zentrale' or HQ/main office) and heard after a while that Hitler has said farewell to his men. Sometime later (he did not recall the exact time), while he stood in the main hallway, he saw through the open door of the Lage Vorzimmer a man carrying a body on his back. Schwägermann could not see the head of the body (which, according to his observation, was not wrapped in blankets), but he saw the olive-green blouse, black trousers and black shoes, all of which resembled Hitler's attire. Therefore, in his opinion, 'there was no doubt that it was Hitler'.

Schwägermann saw the body being carried towards the garden exit; he did not recall having seen anyone else at the time. He immediately went to Goebbels's apartment, saw Goebbels and his wife, Frau Magda Goebbels, who said: 'He should not have done this to us.' This confirmed Schwägermann's opinion that his conclusion as to Hitler's identity had been correct. Both Goebbels and his wife seemed to be deeply moved, but Schwägermann could not talk to Dr Goebbels about Hitler's death as Goebbels had to attend a conference shortly afterwards. Schwägermann did not see the body burnt or buried, but Günsche told him the following day that he had burnt Hitler's body. Schwägermann did not concern himself with the fate of Eva Braun. He had heard about her marriage to Hitler indirectly through the Goebbels children a few days before, and even welcomed her as Frau Hitler.

He recalled that Goebbels, Bormann, Naumann, Axmann, Krebs and Burgdorf had a conference in the Lage Vorzimmer on the evening of Hitler's death. Probably as a result of it, Krebs tried to contact the Russians during the night or the following morning concerning an armistice. It was thought that he came back later in the afternoon of the following day; Schwägermann heard later that the Russians had asked for an unconditional surrender. Goebbels, Bormann, Naumann, Axmann, Krebs Burgdorf (and possibly Wielding and Mohnke) had another conference on the afternoon of 1 May. Naumann told Schwägermann that a breakout of Mohnke's Kampfgruppe, including the remaining personnel of the Propaganda Ministry, had been ordered for 9.00 pm. Schwägermann recalled that a Kreisleiter Ficke, or Vricke, asked Goebbels personally to verify the order.

The Death of the Goebbels Family
Schwägermann had taken his supper about 7.00 pm and was waiting in the anteroom when he saw Frau Goebbels enter the room where the Goebbels children were staying. Shortly afterwards, Frau Goebbels came out of the room, crying; she threw her arms around Schwägermann, indicating to him that she had just poisoned her children. Schwägermann escorted her to the Lage Vorzimmer where Goebbels was, and withdrew. Shortly afterwards, Goebbels called him into the Lage Vorzimmer, talked to him alone and informed him that he (Goebbels) and his wife were going to end their lives too. Schwägermann recalled the following conversation:

> 'Schwägermann, this is the worse [sic] reason. The Army (or the Generals) have betrayed the Führer. Everything is lost. I shall die together with my wife and with my family. You will burn my body. Can you do that?'
> 'Yes.'

Goebbels bade him farewell, and Schwägermann escorted Goebbels to his private apartment. Goebbels then said, 'I give you this as a present' and handed him a picture of Hitler in a silver frame, taken in 1926, which had always been on Goebbels's desk. Frau Goebbels also shook hands with Schwägermann and said: 'Schwägermann, you see that we are dying in a decent manner. If you see Harald again, give him my love and tell him that we have died decently.' 'Harald' referred to Harald Quandt, son of Frau Goebbels from her first marriage.

Schwägermann then left the room. He saw SS-Oberscharführer Rach and ordered him to get some gasoline. After a short while, Rach and an SS-Scharführer brought the gasoline and a small swastika pennant. After about thirty minutes, around 8.30 pm, Goebbels and his wife left their room and, without talking to anybody, went through the Lage Vorzimmer to the garden exit.

Schwägermann said that he and Rach carried gasoline to the foot of the stairs and waited until they heard a shot outside. They saw the bodies lying on the ground, about four or five steps from the exit.

Schwägermann believed that an SS-Scharführer fired two shots to make sure that the pair were dead, then Rach and the SS-Scharführer poured about four cans of gasoline over the bodies and Rach ignited it. By that time it was about 9.00 pm. Schwägermann and Rach went back through the Führerbunker and met Mohnke there for a moment, who told them to ignite some gasoline in the Lage Vorzimmer and left. Rach and Schwägermann emptied the one remaining can of fuel and set fire to it. They did not see anyone else in the Führerbunker; they went upstairs and proceeded to the Voßstraße (New Chancellery) bunker, where many others had gathered. Schwägermann recalled that they saw that Goebbels and his wife were not completely burnt, and their bodies were still recognizable.

Monday, 24 June 1946
Interrogation of Gerhard Boldt
Gerhard Boldt was a German officer who was present in the Führerbunker during the last days of the war in Europe. Boldt regularly participated in the daily briefings held for Hitler. Originally a cavalry officer, Boldt was transferred to Military Intelligence and posted to the bunker. He held the rank of Rittmeister (the cavalry equivalent to Hauptmann/Hauptsturmführer, or captain). Boldt was the only captain in the bunker, and certainly in the briefings.

Boldt stated that he dealt with messages concerning the battle situation only in Berlin. Most of the messages originated from General Helmuth Weidling, the last commander of Berlin, commanding the LVI Panzer Corps. Boldt's job was also to prepare the general situation map. Outgoing messages hardly ever passed through his hands.

He claimed that all telephone connections with the German Army, other than the defenders of Berlin, ceased on 26 April.

Boldt stated that all messages not concerned with the defence of Berlin did not reach him, but went instead to Major Loringhoven.

Boldt left Hitler's bunker on 29 April at 1.30 pm, together with Major Loringhoven and Oberstleutnant Weiss. Except for a few casual words, Boldt said he had no conversation with von Below, and Loringhoven certainly did not tell him anything about von Below's mission.

Boldt, Loringhoven and Weiss had passes signed by General Burgdorf, which stated that that were allowed to pass through the German lines and proceed to General Wenck. Boldt claimed not to know anything about any documents of importance being carried either by his own or any other party.

He stated that they lost Weiss during the night of 1 May, when Weiss made a local recce. They waited for half an hour before proceeding without him. On 4 May, about lunchtime, Boldt and Loringhoven were standing on a road-bridge crossing the autobahn (Südring), when a Russian officer in charge of a lorry stopped and made some enquiries about the road. Apparently, he mistook them for DPs (Displaced Persons), as they were masquerading as French slave workers. Whilst they were talking to him, they noticed about ten German PoWs on the back of the lorry, and Boldt claimed to have recognized Weiss among them.

Boldt stated that he had no contact with any of the bunker personalities after his escape. He admitted, however, having written two postcards to Loringhoven's estate near Leipzig. He claimed he never received a reply

1947

Tuesday, 23 December
Hitler's Last Visit to the Eastern Front: Interrogation of Friedrich Eickenberg
Eickenberg stated that Hitler went for a day's visit to the Oder front at the end of March or very early April 1945. Hitler's party consisted of five or six men and left Berlin in the early morning. Hitler's chauffeur, Kempka, drove the first car, in which were all the members of the group apart from Eickenberg, who drove the spare car. He recalled that about 50km east of Berlin on the main road to Frankfurt (Oder), the party stopped to visit the headquarters of a general. There, they were supposed to change cars, using instead their Mercedes 'Geländewagen'. As there was only one car available, Eickenberg was ordered to return to Berlin with his own car, whilst Kempka took Hitler and his entourage further up the line.

Eickenberg did not know where they then went. He couldn't remember who was present and what the name of the place was where they were to change cars. He only remembered that the whole party returned to the Reichskanzlei about three hours after Eickenberg had got back. He said the whole journey was made by car.

1948

Tuesday, 30 November
Hitler's Cook
It was reported by the Brigade de Surveillance du Territoire, Berlin, that one of Hitler's former cooks was now living at Elmshorn, where he ran a restaurant under the name of Brix.

It was thought that he was one of the last people to see Hitler in Berlin before he disappeared. The French were not in a position to reveal his actual name.

The Director of Security, HQ Intelligence Division, BAOR (British Army of the Rhine), wanted the Intelligence Office (Schleswig-Holstein, British Zone) to see if the restaurant actually existed, if the owner proved to be the former cook of Hitler's and to inform them of his name. Their interest arose from rumours that Martin Bormann was still alive and continued to circulate.

Chapter Two

Bunker Residents

1945

Tuesday, 24 April
Hanna Reitsch and Robert Ritter von Greim
Hitler had sent a telegram from Munich instructing Field Marshal Ritter von Greim to report to the Reich Chancellery on a highly urgent matter. For Greim, the problem of getting into Berlin was a precarious one, as the Russians had practically encircled the city. Greim decided that by availing himself of his mistress, Hanna Reitsch, as pilot, he could enter by means of an autogiro, which could land on the streets or in the garden of the Chancellery.

Hanna Reitsch was no ordinary pilot; she was the first German woman to win a captain's license, the first helicopter pilot and the first female test pilot in her country. During the Second World War, she served as a test pilot for all types of German aircraft, including the jet-powered Messerschmitt Me 262 fighter and the prototype for the V1 rocket. Reitsch had been a test pilot on the Junkers Ju 87 Stuka dive-bomber and Dornier Do 17 light/fast bomber projects, for which she had received the Iron Cross, Second Class, from Hitler on 28 March 1941. Reitsch was asked to fly many of Germany's latest designs, among them the rocket-propelled Messerschmitt Me 163 Komet in 1942. A crash landing on her fifth Me 163 flight left her badly injured; she spent five months in hospital recovering, but received the Iron Cross First Class following the accident, one of only three women to do so. She did everything but fly combat missions during the war. Assigned to a voluntary suicide squad of aviators near the end of the war, Reitsch was one of the last to see Adolf Hitler alive in the underground bunker in Berlin and flew the last German warplane out of Berlin in late April 1945.

Tuesday/Wednesday, Night of 24/25 April
Greim and Reitsch arrived at Rechlin airport and prepared immediately to fly to Berlin, but the only available autogiro that Reitsch could have flown had been damaged. It was therefore decided that a Feldwebel pilot, who had previously taken Albert Speer to the Führer, should fly Greim in because of

the experience the previous flight had given him. Reitsch begged to be taken along. A Focke-Wulf 190 was to be used, which had only a small space behind the pilot's seat, so Reitsch was stuffed into the tail through a small emergency opening.

Some forty fighters would be flown as cover. Almost immediately upon take-off, they were engaged by Russian aircraft. A running, hedge-hopping flight got them to Gatow airfield, the only Berlin field still in German hands. Their own aircraft got through with nothing more than a few wing shots, but the cost was heavy on the supporting fighters.

The landing at Gatow was made through heavy attacks by Russian fighters which were strafing the field when they arrived. Once they landed, immediate attempts were made to phone the Chancellery, but as all the lines were out it was decided to fly an available Fieseler Storch for the remaining distance and land within walking distance of Hitler's shelter. With Greim at the controls and Reitsch as passenger, the plane took off under a whirling cover of German and Russian dogfights. At a height of just a few metres, Greim managed to get away from the field and continue at treetop level toward the Brandenburger Tor.

Street fighting was going on below them and countless Russian aircraft were in the air. After just a few minutes of flight, heavy fire tore into the bottom of the Storch, which severely injured Greim's right leg. Reitsch took control of the aircraft by reaching over her companion's shoulders, and by squirming and dodging close to the ground she brought the plane down on the East–West Axis emergency airstrip. Heavy Russian artillery and small-arms fire sheeted the area with shrapnel as they landed in central Berlin. 'She was my good angel, she piloted me marvellously,' Greim said of Reitsch's efforts. A passing vehicle was then commandeered to take them to Hitler's shelter, and on the way Greim received first aid for his wounded foot.

Thursday, 26 April, 6.00–7.00 pm
Greim and Reitsch arrived at Hitler's bunker. First to meet them was Frau Goebbels, who fell upon Reitsch with tears and kisses, expressing her astonishment that anyone still possessed the courage and loyalty to come to the Führer in his hour of need, in stark contrast to those who had deserted him. Greim was immediately taken to the operating room, where Hitler's physicians tended to his injured foot.

Hitler entered the operating room, his face deep with gratitude at Greim's arrival. He remarked something to the effect that even a soldier had the right to disobey an order when everything indicated that to carry it out would be futile and hopeless.

Addressing Greim, Hitler denounced Göring: 'Do you know why I have called you?'

'No, mein Führer', Greim replied.

Hitler continued:

'Because Herman Göring has betrayed and deserted both me and his Fatherland. Behind my back he has established connections with the enemy. His action was a mark of cowardice. Against my orders he has gone to save himself at Berchtesgaden. From there he sent me a disrespectful telegram. He said that I had once named him as my successor and that now, as I was no longer able to rule from Berlin, he was to rule from Berchtesgaden in my place. He closes the wire by stating that if he had no answer from me by nine-thirty on the date of the wire he would assume my answer to be in the affirmative.'

As Hitler handed Greim the telegram, his shaking hands made the message flutter wildly. It read as follows:

'12.56 am:

'My Führer: General Koller today gave me a briefing on the basis of communications given to him by Colonel General Jodl and General Christian, according to which you had referred certain decisions to me and emphasized that I, in case negotiations would become necessary, would be in an easier position than you in Berlin. These views were so surprising and serious to me that I felt obligated to assume, in case by 2200 hours no answer is forthcoming, that you have lost your freedom of action. I shall then view the conditions of your decree as fulfilled and take action for the wellbeing of Nation and Fatherland. You know what I feel for you in these most difficult hours of my life and I cannot express this in words. God protect you and allow you despite everything to come here as soon as possible. Your faithful Hermann Göring.'

As Greim read the message, Hitler's face remained deathly earnest before every muscle in it began to twitch and his breath came in explosive puffs; only with effort did he gain sufficient control to shout:

'An ultimatum! A crass ultimatum! Now nothing remains. Nothing is spared me. No allegiances are kept, no honour lived up to, no disappointments that I have not had, no betrayals that I have not experienced, and now this above all else. Nothing remains. Every wrong has already been done me [*sic*].'

It was a scene in the manner of Caesar's 'et tu, Brute', full of remorse and self-pity. It was some time before he could gather sufficient control to continue.

With eyes hard and half closed, and in a voice unusually low, the Führer continued:

> 'I immediately had Göring arrested as a traitor to the Reich removed him from all his offices and removed him from all organizations. That is why I have called you to me. I hereby declare you Göring's successor as Oberbefehlshaber der Luftwaffe. In the name of the German people I give you my hand.'

Göring's telegram had implied that Hitler was no longer free to make decisions due to the situation in Berlin, so Göring was going to assume the conduct of government affairs unless he received an answer by his deadline.

To Die for the Honour of the Luftwaffe
Greim and Reitsch were stunned to learn of Göring's betrayal. With one mind, they both grabbed Hitler's hands and begged to be allowed to remain in the bunker, and with their own lives to atone for the great wrong that Göring had perpetrated against Hitler, against the German people and against the Luftwaffe itself. To save the honour of the flyers who had died, to re-establish the honour of the Luftwaffe that Göring had destroyed and to guarantee the honour of their lives in the land, in the eyes of the world, they begged to remain. Hitler agreed and told them that they might stay, stating that their decision would long be remembered in the history of the Luftwaffe. However, it had previously been provisionally arranged with operations staff at Rechlin that an aircraft was to come the next day to take Greim and Reitsch out of Berlin. Despite having now decided to stay, it was impossible to get this information out to Rechlin, which in the meantime was sending plane after plane, each being shot down by the Russians. Finally on 27 April, a Ju 52 – loaded with SS guards and ammunition – managed to land on the East–West Axis, but because of Reitsch and Greim's last-minute decision it was sent back empty.

Hitler Sees the Cause as Lost
Later that evening, Hitler called Reitsch into his room. She remembered that his face was deeply lined, with a constant film of moisture in his eyes. In a very small voice, he said: 'Hanna, you belong to those who will die with me. Each of us has a vial of poison such as this,' with which he handed her one for herself and one for Greim. 'I do not wish that one of us falls to the Russians alive, nor do I wish our bodies to be found by them. Each person is responsible

for destroying his body so that nothing recognizable remains. Eva and I will have our bodies burned. You will devise your own method. Will you please so inform von Greim?'

Reitsch, in tears, sank into a chair, despondent not over the certainty of her own end but that for the first time she realized the Führer saw the cause as lost. She sobbed, but through the tears said:

'Mein Führer, why do you stay? Why do you deprive Germany of your life? When the news was released that you would remain in Berlin to the last, the people were amazed with horror. 'The Führer must live so that Germany can live', the people said. Save yourself, Mein Führer, that is the will of every German.'

Hitler replied:

'No Hanna, if I die it is for the honour of our country, it is because as a soldier I must obey my own command that I would defend Berlin to the last. My dear girl, I did not intend it so. I believed firmly that Berlin would be saved at the banks of the Oder. Everything we had was moved to hold that position. You may believe that when our best efforts failed, I was the most horror-struck of all. Then, when the encirclement of the city began, the knowledge that there were three million of my countrymen still in Berlin made it necessary that I stay and defend them. By staying I believed that all the troops of the land would take example through my act and come to the rescue of the city. I hoped that they would rise to super-human efforts to save me and thereby save my three million countrymen. But, my Hanna, I still have hope. The army of General Walther Wenck is moving up from the south. He must and will drive the Russians back long enough to save our people. Then we will fall back to hold again.'

As far as Reitsch was concerned, Hitler's face showed that he understood the war was over.

At the conclusion of their conversation, Reitsch hurried to Greim's bedside, handed him his poison and they decided, should the end really come, that they would quickly drink the contents of the vial and then each pull the pin from a heavy grenade and hold it tightly to their bodies.

Thursday/Friday, 26/27 April, Late Night and Early Morning
The first heavy barrage bracketed the Chancellery. The splattering of heavy shells and the crashing of falling buildings directly above the shelter tightened everyone's nervous strain, with here and there deep sobbing being heard from behind closed doors. Reitsch spent the night tending to Greim, who was in great pain.

Friday, 27 April, Morning: Hitler's 'Guests' in the Shelter
Reitsch was introduced to some of the other occupants of the bunker, learning for the first time the identity of those who were facing the end with the Führer. She remembered that present in the elaborate shelter were Joseph Goebbels, his wife Magda and their six children; State Secretary Werner Naumann; Reichsleiter Martin Bormann; Walther Hewel from Ribbentrop's office; Admiral Voss (a representative from Dönitz); General Hans Krebs and his adjutant, Burgdorf; Hitler's personal pilot Hans Baur; Eva Braun; SS-Gruppenführer Hermann Fegelein, a general acting as liaison between Himmler and Hitler, and husband of Eva Braun's sister; Dr Ludwig Stumpfegger, Hitler's personal physician; Hitler's Luftwaffe adjutant; Dr Lorenz, representing Reichspresse Chief Dr Otto Dietrich for the German press; two of Hitler's secretaries, Fräulein Christian and Fraulein Krüger; and various SS orderlies and messengers. Reitsch claimed that this composed the entire assembly.

A regular visitor during the last days was Reichsjugendführer Artur Axmann, who was commanding a HJ division committed to the defence of the city. From Axmann came the latest information as to the situation on the ground against the Russians, which was mirrored by the increasingly despondent manner of each visit.

Observations on the Bunker Occupants
Reitsch had little contact with most of the occupants of the bunker, as she was mostly preoccupied with nursing von Greim, but she did have the opportunity to speak to some of them and observe their reactions under the unbearably trying conditions. Of the people she was able to observe closely, the Goebbels family stood out.

Doctor Goebbels
Reitsch recalled that Goebbels was insanely incensed over Göring's treachery. He strode about his luxurious quarters like a caged animal, muttering vile accusations about the Luftwaffe leader and what he had done. The precarious military situation was placed squarely at Göring's door; he said their present

plight was all his fault. Should the war be lost, as certainly now seemed to be the case, Goebbels said, that too would be Göring's fault. Reitsch remembered him adding:

> 'That swine, who has always set himself up as the Führer's greatest support, now does not have the courage to stand beside him. As if that were not enough, he wants to replace the Führer as head of state. He is an incessant incompetent, who has destroyed the Fatherland with his mishandling and stupidity, and now wants to lead the entire nation. By this alone he proves that he was never truly one of us, that at heart he was always weak and a traitor.'

Goebbels gave a very theatrical performance, with much hand waving and fine gestures made even more grotesque by the jerky hobbling as he strode about the room. When he wasn't railing about Göring, Reitsch recalled he spoke about the example those in the bunker were setting for history. Speaking as though he was on a platform, and gripping a chair-back like a rostrum, he continued:

> 'We are teaching the world how men die for their honour. Our deaths shall be an eternal example to all Germans, to all friends and enemies alike. One day the whole world will acknowledge that we did right, that we sought to protect the world against Bolshevism with our lives. One day it will be set down in the history of all time.'

The rooms of Goebbels and Reitsch adjoined each other, and the doors were usually open, so she could hear his oratory sounding out at any hour of the day or night. The talk was always of 'honour', 'how to die', standing 'true to the Führer to the last' and 'setting an example that would long blaze as a holy thing from the pages of history'.

One of the last things Reitsch remembered hearing from the lips of the propaganda master was: 'We shall go down for the glory of the Reich so that the name of Germany will live forever.' Reitsch was moved to conclude that Goebbels's display, even in the tenseness of the situation, was overdrawn and theatrical. In her opinion, Goebbels, as he always had, was performing as if he was speaking to a legion of historians avidly recording his every word.

Frau Goebbels

Frau Goebbels was described by Reitsch as a very brave woman, but whose usual iron control did break down occasionally as the end neared in the bunker, emitting pitiful spasms of weeping. Her main concern was her children, and Reitsch said in their presence her manner was always delightful and cheery. Much of her day was occupied in keeping the children's clothes clean and tidy, and as they had only the clothes they wore, this kept Frau Goebbels occupied. Often she would quickly retire to her room to hide the tears.

She represented the epitome of Nazi indoctrination. If the Third Reich could not live, she preferred to die with it, and nor would she allow her children to outlive it. In recognition of the example she embodied of true German womanhood, Hitler, in the presence of all the occupants of the bunker, presented her with his personal golden party insignia. 'A staunch pillar of the honour upon which National Socialism was built and the German Fatherland founded,' was his (approximate) remark as he pinned it to her dress.

Frau Goebbels often thanked God that she was alive so that she could kill her children to save them from whatever 'evil' would follow the collapse of the Reich. She said to Reitsch:

> 'My dear Hanna, when the end comes you must help me if I become weak about the children. You must help me to help them out of this life. They belong to the Third Reich and to the Führer, and if these two things cease to exist there can be no further place for them. But you must help me. My greatest fear is that at the last moment I will be too weak.'

The Goebbels Children
The Goebbels children comprised five girls and a boy: Helga (12), Hidegard (11), Helmut (9), Holdine (8), Hedwig (6) and Heidrun (4).

They were the one bright spot of relief in the stark, death-shadowed life of the bunker. Reitsch taught them songs which they sang for the Führer and the injured von Greim. Their talk was full of being in 'the cave' with their 'Uncle Führer' (or 'Uncle Aldi') and that in spite of the fact there were bombs outside, nothing could really harm them as long as they were with him. And anyway, 'Uncle Führer' had said that the soldiers would come and drive the Russians away and then they could all go back to play in their garden. Everyone in the Bunker entered into the game of making time as pleasant as possible for them. Frau Goebbels repeatedly thanked Reitsch for making their last days enjoyable, as Reitsch often gathered the children about her and told them long stories of her flying, the places she had been and the countries she had seen.

Eva Braun
Eva Braun remained studiously true to her position as the 'showpiece' in the Führer's circle. Reitsch recounted to her interrogators that most of Braun's

time was occupied in fingernail polishing, changing of clothes each hour of the day and all the other little feminine tasks of grooming, combing and polishing. She seemed to take the task of dying with the Führer as quite a matter of fact, with an attitude that seemed to say: 'had not the relationship been of twelve long years' duration and had she not seriously threatened suicide when Hitler once wanted rid of her, this would be a much easier way to die and much more proper.' Her constant remark was: 'Poor Adolf, deserted by everyone, betrayed by all. Better that ten thousand others die than that he be lost to Germany.'

In Hitler's presence, Reitsch said, Braun was always charming and thoughtful of his every comfort. However, only when she was with him was she completely 'in character', for the moment he was out of earshot she would rave about all the ungrateful swine who had deserted their Führer and that each of them should be destroyed. Her remarks had an adolescent tinge, and it appeared that she believed the only 'good' Germans at the time were those who were caught in the bunker; all the others were traitors because they were not there to die with Hitler.

Reitsch believed that the reasons for Braun's willingness to die with the rest were similar to those of Frau Goebbels: she was simply convinced that whatever followed the Third Reich would not be fit to live in for a true German. Often, she expressed sorrow for those people who were unable to destroy themselves, as they would forever be forced to live without honour and reduced instead to living as human beings without souls. Reitsch thought it unlikely that Braun had any influence over Hitler.

Martin Bormann
Reitsch recollected that Martin Bormann moved about very little, keeping very close to his writing desk and 'recording the momentous events in the bunker for posterity'. Every word, every action, went down on his paper. Often, he would visit this person or that to scowlingly demand what the exact remarks had been that passed between the Führer and the person he had just had an audience with. Comments that passed between other occupants of the bunker were also carefully recorded by Bormann for a document that was intended to be spirited out of the bunker at the very last moment so that, according to the modest Bormann, it could 'take its place among the greatest chapters in German history'.

Adolf Hitler
Hitler's manner and physical condition, Reitsch said during her interrogation, sunk to lower and lower depths as time went on in the bunker. At first, he seemed to be playing the proper part of leading the defence of Germany and

Berlin, and this was in some manner possible as communications were quite reliable. Messages were telephoned to a flak tower and from there radioed out by means of a portable, balloon-suspended aerial. But each day this was more and more difficult, until, late on in the afternoon of the 28 April and all day on the 29th, communications were almost impossible.

Hitler held onto the hope of General Wenck's success in breaking through from the south. He talked of little else, and all day on the 28th and 29th he was mentally planning the tactics that Wenck might use in freeing Berlin. Reitsch said Hitler would stride about the shelter, waving a road map that was fast disintegrating from the sweat of his hands while planning Wenck's campaign with anyone who happened to be listening. When he became overly excited, he would snatch the map from where it lay, pace with a quick, nervous stride about the room, and loudly 'direct' the city's defence with armies that no longer existed. Unknown to Hitler, Wenck's forces had already been routed and destroyed.

Reitsch described the scene as pathetic, the picture of a man's complete disintegration, a comic-tragedy of frustration, futility and uselessness. She pictured a man running almost blindly from wall to wall in his last retreat, waving papers that fluttered like leaves in his nervous, twitching hands, or sitting stooped and crumpled before his table while moving buttons representing his non-existent armies back and forth on a sweat-stained map, like a young boy playing at war.

Friday, 27 April: Another Betrayal
SS-Gruppenführer Hermann Fegelein had attempted to secure his position in Hitler's court by marrying Greta Braun, sister of Eva. Reitsch recalled that it was discovered that he was missing from Hitler's bunker. An SS officer was sent to look for him and he was found in his flat, lying naked in bed with his mistress, a suitcase already packed. It appeared he was trying to escape from the mass suicide that was being contemplated by the inhabitants of the bunker.

Saturday, 28 April, Evening
The news of Himmler's negotiations with the Western powers reached Hitler, who Reitsch said believed that Fegelein was involved to some extent. Oberst Nicolaus von Below even stated that Fegelein had been ringing up the bunker from time to time during the last few days, in order to obtain information about events there. He connected this with a story he was told that Himmler had offered to hand over Hitler's dead body in exchange for peace with the Western powers.

According to von Below, a plot on Hitler's life was to be executed by the SS (a claim unconfirmed by any other source). However, Hitler recognized that Fegelein was connected with Himmler's treachery and had him shot, possibly during the night of 28/29 April.

Letters to be Taken Out of the Führerbunker

Reitsch was given letters to take out by various occupants of the bunker who were to remain in the shelter and die with Hitler. There were letters from Goebbels and his wife to her eldest son by her first marriage, Leutnant Harald Quandt, who was in an Allied PoW camp somewhere in Algeria. There was also one from Eva Braun to her sister, Greta, wife of SS-Gruppenführer Fegelein, liaison officer between Himmler and Hitler; one from Walther Hevel, Ribbentrop's representative on Hitler's staff, to the Foreign Office Headquarters in Fuschl, near Saltzburg; and one from Martin Bormann to the Reich Chancellery Offices which had evacuated to Berchtesgaden. That Reitsch had been given these letters was learned during her interrogation, but the fact that only two letters (from Goebbels and his wife) were still in her possession was discovered quite accidentally, whereupon Reitsch admitted that she and von Greim had destroyed the others.

She willingly gave her reasons for destroying them: the pair had become the arbiters of the correspondence. Hevel's and Bormann's letters were simply official communications, and, as the collapse of the Third Reich occurred before they could be delivered, she and von Greim considered them to be of no further value. The Eva Braun letter was destroyed because Reitsch and von Greim felt that the text was glaringly theatrical and in such poor adolescent taste that only odious reactions would result should the letter fall into German hands. Reitsch remarked that she and von Greim were of the opinion that some Germans might eulogize Braun as a Nazi martyr by reading between the lines of what she had actually written. Von Greim's remark after he had read the letter had been: 'It sounds just as childish and obvious as she looks. Tear it up.'

Hevel's Letter

This letter to the Auswärtiges Amt (Foreign Office) was a brief and insistent request as to why none of the radio messages from the shelter were being answered. The text, as Reitsch remembered it, was as follows: 'Why do you not answer our radio messages? Are you receiving them? Information is badly needed here. Answer immediately.' It was not addressed to any particular person and was to be delivered to anyone on von Ribbentrop's staff who might be at the Fuschl office. Reitsch had no idea as to what the 'information' requested referred to.

Martin Bormann's

When Bormann handed Reitsch his letter, he indicated that it contained nothing of great importance and would not involve any danger should it be lost. It was just addressed to the the Reich Chancellery Offices and asked why communications were not being maintained. It closed with instructions to contact the shelter and gave a description of how this could be done.

Eva Braun's Letter

Braun wrote to her sister, Gretl, Fegelein's wife, whom Hitler had shot because of his planned desertion. The following is how Reitsch remembered the letter (she was interrogated months after reading it):

> 'I must write to you these words so that you will not feel sad over our end here in the shelter. It is rather we who are filled with sorrow because it is your fate to live on into the chaos that will follow. For myself I am glad to die here; glad to die at the side of the Führer; but most of all glad that the horror now to come is spared me. What could life give me? It has already been perfect. It has already given me its best and fullest. Why should I go on living? This is the time to die; the right time. With the Führer, I have had everything. To die now, beside him, would complete my happiness. Live on as well and as happily as you can. Shed no tears nor be regretful over our deaths. It is a perfect and proper ending. None of us would change it now. It is the right end for a German woman.'

Braun thus did not reveal to her sister the fate of her husband.

Dr Goebbels's Letter to His Stepson, Harald Quandt, 28 April 1945

> 'My Dear Harald,
> 'We sit locked in the Führer's shelter in the Reich Chancellery, fighting for our lives and our honour. How this battle will end God only knows. But I know that, alive or dead, we will not leave the shelter unless we leave it with honour and glory. I hardly believe we shall ever see each other again; therefore, it is likely these will be the last lines you will ever receive from me. I expect from you, should you outlive this war, that you do only that which will honour your mother and father. It is not necessary that we be alive to influence the future of our people. It is likely that you will be the only one left to carry on the traditions of our family. Do this always in such a manner that we would never be ashamed of your actions.

'Germany will outlive this terrible war, but only if it has examples upon which to guide its reconstruction. Such an example we want to give here! You can be proud to possess a mother such as yours. Yesterday, the Führer gave her the gold party insignia which he wore on his coat for many years, and she justly deserved it. In the future you must know only one duty: to prove yourself worthy of the great sacrifice which we are prepared and determined to make here. I know that you will do that. Don't let yourself be confused by the uproar that will now reign throughout the world. The lies will one day break down under their own weight and the truth will again triumph. The hour will come when we will stand pure and undefiled above the world, as pure and undefiled as our beliefs and aims have always been.

'Farewell, my dear Harald. Whether we shall ever see each other again lies in the hands of God. If it is not to be, then always be proud to have belonged to a family that even in the face of disaster remained true to the Führer to the very last and true to his pure and holy cause.

'All the best and my heartfelt greetings,

'Your Papa.'

What did Hanna Reitsch think of Dr Goebbels letter? She claimed that it made such a poor impression on herself and von Greim that they decided to make no immediate effort to deliver it. First of all, she claimed that the letter was filled with various figures of speech that had no resemblance to the truth as she and Greim saw it in the shelter. Contrary to what Goebbels writes, they were not 'locked' in the shelter and nor were they 'fighting' for their lives. But more than that, she and Greim objected to the overall tone of the letter. Both felt that Goebbels was not writing to his son, but rather to the German people in an effort to solidify such remnants of the Nazi ideology that might outlive the German collapse. Both Reitsch and Greim held Goebbels in rather low regard and felt justified in deciding that this, 'Goebbels's last propagandistic effort', should not fall into the hands of possible German readers. This obvious bid for martyrdom that the letter reflected, Reitsch and Greim both felt, might work an unhealthy influence should it be publicized in German channels. They would both have preferred to find in the letter some inkling of regret or some faint suspicion that a system which had caused such suffering and useless destruction, both of the German people and the rest of the world, might not be 'pure' and 'holy', as Goebbels claimed.

Frau Goebbels's Letter to Her Son, Harald Quandt, 28 April, 1945

'My beloved son,

'We have already been here in the Führer's shelter for 6 days; Papa, your six brothers and sisters, and I. We are here to give our National Socialistic way of life its only possible and honourable ending.

'Whether you will ever receive this letter I do not know, but perhaps some considerate soul will make it possible for you to receive my last greetings. You must know that it was against Papa's wishes that I remained here with him, and that last Sunday the Führer himself wanted me to get out. You know your mother, for we are of the same blood. For me there was no other alternative. Our beautiful idea is being destroyed, and with it goes everything I knew in this life as fine, worthy of admiration, noble and good.

'Life will not be worth living in the world that will come after Hitler and National Socialism. Therefore, I have also brought the children here with me. They are too precious for the life that will come after us; a merciful God will understand me when I myself help them to a merciful deliverance. You will live on and for you I have but one request: never forget that you are a German. Do nothing against your honour, and take care that you do nothing with your life that will have made our death purposeless.

'The children are wonderful. Without assistance they help themselves in these more than primitive surroundings. Whether they have to sleep on the floor, whether they are unable to wash, or whether they have nothing to eat, there is neither a word of complaint nor tears. Even for me the shells crashing are nerve-racking. The small children comfort the even smaller and the fact of their being here is a blessing if only because every now and then they coax a smile from the Führer.

'Yesterday evening the Führer removed his golden insignia and pinned it to my dress. I am proud and overjoyed. God grant that I will have the strength to accomplish the last and most difficult task of all.

'We have only one aim left to us: To be true unto death to the Führer; that we be allowed to end our lives together with him is a merciful fate upon which we could hardly have counted.

'Harald, beloved boy, I give you the best life taught me, to take on your way with you: Be true! Be true to yourself, true to your people, and most of all be true to your Fatherland – in each and every respect.

'To begin a new page is difficult Who knows whether I shall have time to fill it, but I want to give you so much of my love, so much strength, and to take from you all the sorrow of our deaths. Be proud of us and try to keep us in a proud and joyous remembrance. Everyone must one day die. Is it not better, more honourable and braver to have lived a short and happy life rather than a long one under disgraceful conditions?

'This letter is to go out. Hanna Reitsch will take it along. She is to fly back out again.

'I put my arms about you with the deepest, most heartfelt mother's love.

'My beloved son, live for Germany.

'Your Mother.'

Reitsch's criticisms of Frau Goebbels's letter were almost identical to those she made of her husband's correspondence. Reitsch pointed out that Frau Goebbels found it just as difficult to adhere to the truth as her husband did. While Frau Goebbels remarked that the children had to sleep on the floor, were unable to wash and had little to eat – all the result of 'primitive surroundings' – Reitsch found the living conditions in the shelter the most luxurious she had experienced throughout the war. Reitsch and Greim decided that this letter should not be delivered either, because it too might have help crystallize the martyr-minded leftovers of the Nazi idea. Reitsch was not surprised at the tone of the letter, having described Frau Goebbels as the epitome of her husband's teachings.

Recalling her final days in the bunker, Reitsch said that, still convinced as to the absurdity of attempting an escape, she went alone to Hitler while Greim was making his preparations. Through her sobbing, she begged: 'Mein Führer, why, why don't you let us stay?' He looked at her for a moment and said only: 'God protect you.'

Frau Goebbels gave Reitsch a diamond ring from her finger to wear in her memory. Some thirty minutes or so after Hitler had given their orders, they would leave the shelter with the letters.

Monday, 30 April, 1.30 am
Orders to Leave the Shelter

Hitler, with a chalk-white face, entered Greim's room and slumped down on the edge of the bed. 'Our only hope is Wenck,' he said, 'and to make his entry possible we must call upon every available aircraft to cover his approach.' Hitler then claimed that he had just been informed that Wenck's guns were already shelling the Russians in Potsdamer Platz in the heart of Berlin.

'Every available plane must be called up by daylight, therefore it is my order to you to return to Rechlin and muster your planes from there,' he continued.

'It is the task of your aircraft to destroy the positions from which the Russians will launch their attack on the Chancellery. With Luftwaffe help, Wenck may get through. That is the first reason why you must leave the shelter. The second is that Himmler must be stopped.'

Hitler's voice then became unsteady, both his lips and hands trembling. He told Greim that if Himmler had actually reported making contact with the Allies and could be found, he should immediately be arrested. 'A traitor must never succeed me as Führer! You must get out to ensure that he will not.'

Both Greim and Reitsch protested vehemently that their mission could not succeed and would be futile, as it would be impossible to reach Rechlin. They also said they deserved the honour of dying in the bunker.

Hitler would have none of it: 'As soldiers of the Reich, it is our Holy duty to exhaust every possibility. This is the only chance of success that remains. It is your duty and mine to take it.'

Reitsch was not convinced. 'No, no!' she screamed. 'What can be accomplished now, even if we should get through? Everything is lost; to try to change it now is insane.' Greim thought differently. 'Hanna,' he said, 'we are the only hope for those who remain here. If the chance is just the smallest, we owe it to them to take it. Not to go would rob them of the only light that remains. Maybe Wenck is there. Maybe we can help, but whether we can or cannot, we will go.'

Preparations for them to leave were then quickly made. Von Below, Göring's former liaison officer but now a staunch Greim man, said: 'You must get out. It depends on you to tell the truth to our people, to save the honour of the Luftwaffe, to save the meaning of Germany for the world.' Everyone gave the departing duo some token, something to take into the outside world.

Wednesday, 2 May
Also present in the shelter with Erna Flegal and the wounded were Dr Kunz, Professor Haase, several nurses, civilian personnel of Hitler's residence and the Reich Chancellery, working girls who had taken refuge there, and members of the League of German Girls (BDM) and their leaders. The latter came from Berlin's Reichsportfeld, having fled further into the centre of the city instead of leaving the capital. Flegal admired the work of the BDM. For example, she said that on 2 May, when the Hotel Adlon burned down, with 'their feeble strength' they carried the wounded from the hotel's shelter to the shelter where Flegal was and cared for the badly wounded soldiers. The BDM girls struggled because they were not accustomed to dealing with the wounded and to the oppressive air in the shelter. The fire had allegedly been started in the hotel's wine cellar by drunken Red Army soldiers.

Flegal was also impressed with the German youths who were there towards the end: 'They showed model behaviour; with their slight strength they shifted ammunition. Indeed, up to the end Hitler had an unbreakable faith in German youth.'

Later that day, some people were taken to the Reich's Institute for the Blind, where the Russians had set up one of their GPU (State Political Directorate) offices.

Monday, 8 October 1945
The Last Days in Hitler's Bunker as Experienced by Hanna Reitsch

Reitsch was interrogated by Captain Robert Work, the Air Corps Chief Interrogator. She gave an eyewitness account of what happened in the highest places during the last days of the war.

Her account of the flight into Berlin to report to Hitler and her stay in the Führer's bunker was considered 'as accurate a one as will be obtained of those last days', although the 'is he dead or is he not dead?' fate of Hitler could not be fully answered, only to the extent of describing his mental state and the hopelessness of the last-gasp situation, from which individual opinion may be drawn. Reitsch's own opinion was that the tactical situation and Hitler's physical condition made any thoughts of his escape inconceivable.

Her story was remarkable only in that she played a small part in the events of the war's end and had personal contact with the 'top-rank' Nazis. It was also of interest that Reitsch was one of the last people, if not the very last person, who got out of the bunker alive.

Throughout Reitsch's stay in the bunker, she said Hitler's manner and physical condition sunk to ever lower depths. Bad news followed bad news, until Hitler was so overcome by the persistently hopeless reports that he completely broke down in the presence of everyone who was in the conference room. According to Reitsch, Hitler never recovered physically or mentally from that collapse.

She felt Hitler had enormous faith in General Wenck and talked of nothing but Wenck's breakthrough from the south.

Saturday, 10 November
Major Hugh Trevor-Roper's Report of His Interview With Frau Gerda Christian, One of Hitler's Private Secretaries Before and During the War, and Frau Krau (Gerda's Mother-in-Law)

'Gerda Christian married General der Luftwaffe Eckhard Christian … in 1942. After 20 April 1945, when two of Hitler's four secretaries flew to Berchtesgaden, Frau Christian and Frau Junge remained, as did Frl Krueger, Martin Bormann's secretary.

'On the night 1–2 May, when the occupants of the Chancellery sought to break out through the Russian lines, these three women, together with Fraulein Manziarly, Hitler's personal cook, were in the party which succeeded in crossing the Weindammer Bridge. This party were forced to seek shelter in a cellar, where they were captured by the Russians. The four women, who had civilian papers in order, were allowed to go free by the Russians who were presumably unaware of their positions. Frau Junge became separated from the others, and was seen some days later near Havelberg, alone. Frau Christian and Fraulein Krueger escaped together as far as Hamburg, where they were parted. Frau Christian told Fraulein Krueger that she was going to her mother-in-law, Frau Krau. (Frau Krau was the mother of General Christian. Her maiden name was Krau and, being a professional singer, [she] did not change her surname when she married.)

'I visited Frau Krau on 9 October 1945. She said Frau Christian had left about eight days ago, to seek work in the British Zone. Frau Krau did not know where she was going, but thought it might be Hamburg or Hannover; if she went to Hamburg she would presumably get in touch with Fraulein Krueger (who was now free). Frau Christian would probably seek work as a typist or as a secretary in a commercial law firm. Frau Krau had not heard from her daughter-in-law, but when she was able to communicate with her, she undertook to instruct her to report to the nearest British HQ; she also undertook to inform me of her address if a channel of information could be provided. I therefore asked Major Saxe (UFSET, U-2, CI sub-division) if he would arrange for Frau Krau to be visited at intervals. The necessary instructions have been sent to British Corps Districts, and an order to Frau Christian to report to the nearest British HQ has been broadcast over Hamburg Radio.

'Shortly before 5 November 1945, Fraulein Krueger reported that she had a postcard from Frau Christian giving no address, but posted in the British Zone, stating that she hoped to come to Hamburg or Flensburg, and would write again. Fraulein Krueger has undertaken to report any further developments.

'On 7 November 1945, I re-visited Frau Krau. She said that she was still without news of Frau Christian, but with the introduction of an inter-zonal postal system (announced as imminent on the wireless), she hoped to hear from her. She could add nothing to what she had said on 9 October, beyond saying that Frau Christian had mentioned (without further definition) a Bauernhof [farm yard] in Hanover as a possible *pied-a-terre* in the British Zone.

'I told Frau Krau that a message to Frau Christian had been broadcast over the Hamburg Radio, and that this must be regarded as a final warning; that if Frau Christian reported as instructed, she would not be imprisoned (orders to this effect have in fact been given); but that if she failed to report, and was then traced, she would be arrested and probably imprisoned for failing to comply with the orders. Frau Krau (who gives the impression of being a querulous and perhaps shifty character, expecting more consideration of her convenience than the situation warrants), expressed dislike of the French, in whose Zone she lives, and reacted very unfavourably to a proposal that the matter be placed in the hands of the French, who hitherto merely authorised my visits without asking for details. Frau Krau said that visits from the French would be "*sehr unangenehm*" [very uncomfortable] to her.

'Frau Krau knows that her daughter-in-law is friendly with Fraulein Krueger, and that a message for her, instructing her to report, will be delivered by Fraulein Krueger if contact between the two is made; she probably suspects (what is true) that Fraulein Krueger will also report on Frau Christian to the British authorities. I told her that Fraulein Krueger had been set free immediately after interrogation by me.

'Frau Krau possibly does not know her daughter-in-law very intimately, since she was in Berlin during the war and was only recently married to General Christian. It is possible, therefore, that she will protect her only in her son's interest, i.e., she will conceal her against imprisonment, but not against interrogation, especially if such gratuitous concealment is likely to cause inconvenience to herself. For this reason, and since the only value of Frau Christian consists in her information, I have emphasised:

(1) That a voluntary submission, in reasonable time, will not lead to imprisonment.
(2) That Frau Krau is likely to be pestered, perhaps even by the French, until Frau Christian is found.'

Sunday, 9 December
Interrogation of Major Berndt Freytag von Loringhoven
Major Loringhoven was neither a Party man nor did he prove or support the assassination attempt of 20 July against Hitler.

He strongly despised the SS and its leaders, but had a great admiration for the Führer, to whom he referred in the present tense.

On 25 July 1944, Freytag was informed that his cousin, Oberst Freytag Loringhoven (of the Abwehr), was missing. He traced his moves to his estate in East Prussia, where he found his cousin's body shortly after he had committed suicide. A note was found on his body, addressed to his wife, which proved that it was suicide. The deceased had been arrested by the SD (Sicherheitsdienst, the intelligence arm of the SS) and was thoroughly interrogated by the SD of the Führer's HQ. Only the intervention of General Heinz Guderian, chief of staff of the OKH, had prevented his detention. He was, however, rearrested several times by the SD until the end of August.

On 29 April 1945, Freytag went with General Krebs to the Reichskanzlei in Berlin. Freytag's main duty in Berlin consisted of keeping contact with various commands outside the capital. He also gathered information about the military situation in the city and made daily situation reports, keeping Krebs informed of the military situation around Berlin.

When messages came in, he marked them on the maps and immediately informed Krebs. Consequently, he visited Hitler's bunker fairly frequently to deliver messages to Krebs. The greater part of his time was spent in the other bunker in his office, where he also slept, as did Krebs and Gerhard Boldt.

Until 26 April, there were fairly good telephone connections, but after that date the telephone system started to break down and only sporadic calls went through.

The last telephone call between the Reichskanzlei and the OKW took place at about midday on 29 April, after which a communications balloon near Rheinsberg was shot down. Krebs used the phone in the second anteroom of the Führer's bunker and spoke to Jodl, who informed him of the failure of Wenck's offensive.

Friday, 27 April
General Krebs was called to a conference at the Reichs Chancellery. Although General Burgdorf had indicated that there was a plan for Krebs to stay in Berlin, the final decision was made at the conference. Except for Loringhoven and the driver, nobody else of the staff of the OKH had accompanied Krebs to Berlin.

Freytag believed that there was a broadcasting station in the bunker underneath the Parteikanzlei and that it was from there that Bormann maintained contact with the outside world. It was said that the telegram to Göring relieving him from his post was sent on 26 April by those means.

Fate of Fegelein

Freytag Loringhoven showed utter contempt for Fegelein, stating that he, Fegelein, used his position to interfere and intrigue in all affairs, even if he had no knowledge of the matter concerned. Freytag believed that Fegelein put his loyalty to Himmler before that to the Führer.

Fegelein was a good-looking, dashing, arrogant womanizer, a philanderer par excellence. He was close to Eva Braun, who had admitted to a friend that she had fallen in love with him. Although he flirted with both Braun sisters, he maintained a good relationship with Hitler. Albert Speer, however, called him one of the most disgusting people in Hitler's circle.

Fegelein left the Führer's HQ by plane on 23 April, flying from Gatow airfield. The purpose of the journey was a conference with Himmler. Freytag believed that he had no contact with anyone else before returning on 26 April, landing again at Gatow.

Bormann, who had his own monitoring system, overheard foreign news broadcasts about Himmler's activities. The Führer was thus informed about the negotiations between Himmler and the Swedish Count Bernadotte. Freytag labelled the actions of Himmler *'den* Verrat am *Führer'* (the betrayal of the Führer) and believed that Fegelein was involved in the affair. On 28 April, he said, a Standgericht (court martial) was formed to try Fegelein. Freytag didn't know the composition of the court but stated that General Burgdorf and Krebs were not members.

Freytag's Recollection of Personalities in the Bunker

There were two bunkers at the Reichskanzlei. One was underneath the garden, and was where the Führer lived. With him were Eva Braun, Goebbels and his family and Bormann. There were also a number of SS orderlies and batmen, but Freytag only remembered the name of Linge, Hitler's personal servant.

The second bunker, connected through an underground tunnel approximately 250 yards south-east of the Führerbunker, was underneath the new Reichskanzlei and housed General Burgdorf with his adjutant, Oberstleutnant Weiss, General Krebs, Freytag, three clerks and five batmen. There was a signal office staffed by Army personnel and a monitoring station manned by Bormann's people. The chief clerk was Oberfeldwebel Werner Pardau. Loringhoven maintained that he could not remember any further names.

Herr Müller, Bormann's right-hand man, and Frl Krueger, Bormann's secretary, frequently came over from the Parteikanzle and stayed at the Führerbunker. There were also some journalists connected with Bormann.

Werner Naumann of the Propagandaministerium was seen with Goebbels in the private rooms of the Führerbunker. Freytag also saw Botschafter (ambassador) Hevel of the Auswärtiges Amt.

SS-Begleitkommando
The SS-Begleitkommando (SS Escort Command, charged with protecting the Führer) was commanded by SS-Gruppenführer Hans Rattenhuber, a Bavarian. Freytag estimated the strength of the Kommando at between twenty-five and thirty men, the majority of whom were officers.

Lagebesprechung, 22 April
The situation conference started at 2.00 pm and lasted until 6.30 pm. Present were Hitler, Keitel, Jodl, Burgdorf, Krebs, Bormann, Fegelein and one Luftwaffe officer, either General Christian or General Koller. Loringhoven was not sure whether Goebbels was there. Two stenographers were also in attendance. The meeting took place in the Lage Vorzimmer of the Führerbunker. In the anteroom were Oberstleutnant Ernst John von Freynd (Keitel's adjutant), Oberstleutnant Weiss (adjutant to Burgdorf), Freytag adjutant to Krebs, SS-Sturmbannführer Günsche (adjutant to the Führer) and SS doctor Stumpfegger. Various members of the SS-Begleitkommando were also present.

Freytag was not informed about the problems discussed at the conference, but as a result of the talks the Wehrmachtführungsstab (Operations Staff) and the OKH were contracted into a single body. Freytag believed that the switching of Wenck from the Western to the Eastern Front and the counter-attack to relieve Berlin were decided upon at the conference.

During the night after the conference, the following people left the Führer's HQ: SS-Gruppenführer Schaupp, Professor Morell, some members of the Auswärtiges Amt, the stenographers and several secretaries. During the same night, members of the Heeres-Funkstelle (an Army radio station) were recalled and left.

Thursday, 25 April 1946
Interrogation Report on Frau Gerda Christian.
Frau Gerda Christian, personal secretary to Hitler from September 1939 to April 1945, was interrogated at the HQ of the US European Theatre Military Intelligence Service Centre.

Whereabouts of Frau Christian After 28 February 1945

Frau Christian stated that after 28 February 1945, she stayed at all times within the compound of the Chancellery. Her private quarters were located in the bunker underneath the New Chancellery; during the day she was in the Führerbunker. Around 21 or 22 April, most of the men of the Begleitkommando, Gruppenführer Albert Bormann of the NSKK (National Socialist Motor Corps, a paramilitary training organization), Schaub, Dr Morell, Dr Blaschke and his assistant left for Berchtesgaden. Joining that group were Frl Wolff and Frl Schroeder, the two 'chief secretaries'. Christian said she and Frau Junge stayed in Berlin, where by about 22 April the opinion still prevailed that Hitler might decide to go south and establish his HQ at Obersalzberg. In that case, Christian and Junge would have followed him.

Himmler's Presence at the Führerbunker After 20 April

Christian said Himmler was present in the Führerbunker on about 20 April. She was not sure of the exact date, but remembered that his presence coincided with Göring's visit. Christian did not hear what was discussed, but assumed that it was primarily relating to military topics. As for Dr Gebhardt, Christian stated that she knew him from Berchtesgaden but that she never saw him at the Führerbunker.

The Göring Case

Although Christian was not sure of details, she said that Göring supposedly made an attempt to get Hitler to the south during his visit to the Führerbunker around 20 April. She added that later (at an unknown date), Göring sent a letter renewing his request that Hitler leave Berlin for the south, but Hitler declined with the remark that 'continuation of the fight from the south was impossible'. Of this remark, Christian claimed first-hand knowledge.

Hitler did not say anything to Christian about why he dismissed Göring, and she heard no explanation from anyone else. She said there was no general discussion about Göring in the bunker, and neither she nor, as far as she knew, the other secretaries were present at any meeting where Hitler mentioned the subject. Christian knew that a report of some kind had been received; she assumed that this was from Gauleitung Muenchen to Bormann, who reported to Hitler alone in accordance with routine procedure. She knew that Bormann ordered a telegram that was addressed to some SS Führer at the Obersalzberg. She did not know whether von Greim forwarded Koller's explanation of Göring's actions to Hitler.

Greim's Visit

Christian saw Greim only upon his arrival. She knew that he was initially treated for his injuries, after which he was received by Hitler. She did not see him leave and only heard later that he had been appointed chief of the Luftwaffe. She did not know of any operational orders. Nor did she know of any planes which landed or took off in Berlin after Greim's departure. She believed that any further flights were impossible and that this was partly responsible for Hitler's decision to stay in Berlin.

The Fegelein Case

Fegelein left Berlin by car before 20 April in order to visit Himmler, came back around 21/22 April, then suddenly disappeared on 23 or 24 April. Christian heard that he had tried to leave Berlin by plane and that a search was made for him. He was discovered in his apartment and brought back to the Chancellery, but she did not see him in the Führerbunker. Christian did not know who brought him back, but assumed that Rattenhuber's SS-Begleitkommando men were given the assignment. She believed, but was not convinced, that Fegelein was interrogated by Rattenhuber, who then reported to Hitler. Christian was told that a day or so after his arrest, Fegelein was shot by either the SS or a policeman in the garden of the adjoining building – possibly the garden of the Foreign Office. An official reason for his execution was not given, but the unofficial reason was that Fegelein had tried to flee from Berlin. Christian did not hear any rumours about a plot involving Himmler or General Steiner. She did not know which part Peter Hoegel, Beetz or Gruppenführer Mueller played in the Fegelein incident.

Christian never heard anything from Hitler personally concerning Himmler's treachery. Bur she did hear in general conversation that Himmler had started peace negotiations with the Allies on his own without Hitler's orders. Since this topic was mentioned about the time of the Fegelein incident, she was under the impression that Fegelein was somehow connected with it. Christian was not sure whether Hitler believed that the failure of Steiner's attack was due to treachery. However, at the time that Hitler decided to stay in Berlin, he said to Christian that the fight was now lost and that his only plan was to hold the Russian troops in front of Berlin, but that this would not change the general strategic picture. He contemplated withdrawing units from the Western Front but decided mainly on using Army Group Wenck near Nowawes and 'Himmler's units' under Steiner near Oranienburg. Around 28 or 29 April, he heard that Steiner had withdrawn to the north without having contacted Wenck. Hitler believed that this had been ordered by Himmler, contrary to Hitler's instructions.

Hitler and Braun's Marriage

The reasons which motivated Hitler to get married were not clear to Christian. She believed that Braun proposed marriage, basing this assumption on two observations: Hitler did not think of personal things at the time and under the circumstances; and Eva Braun seemed to be very happy about the marriage in spite of the circumstances.

Christian gave an account as to the sequence of events surrounding the marriage. Late on the afternoon of 28 April, between 5.00 pm and 6.00 pm, she and Frau Junge were called to see Hitler; they had to wait a little while until Hitler and Eva Braun appeared, together with Bormann and Goebbels. Eva Braun pointed to a wedding ring which she wore, whereupon the secretaries congratulated Hitler and Braun before everybody sat down, including Frau Goebbels, who had joined the group. Christian knew that Goebbels and Bormann were witnesses to the marriage ceremony, but she did not see the Standesbeamter who performed the ceremony. The party lasted all evening and through the night. Christian recalled that later on Generals Krebs and Burgdorf came separately for a while, as well as Günsche and Frl Manziarly.

It appeared to Christian that the marriage had come as a surprise for everybody and that no previous discussion about it had taken place. The purpose of the marriage was not clear to Christian, since Hitler and Eva Braun had already made clear their intention to die together. The general conversation that evening concerned primarily old times. Hitler recalled the common work of former days and the successes he had achieved together with Goebbels and other old comrades. No mention was made of any failures or mistakes. Hitler also recalled that he had been a witness at Goebbels's marriage and mentioned the contrast that for him, Hitler, marriage and death were closely linked together, while in the days of Goebbels's marriage things had been happier. Christian recalled that Hitler mentioned at the time that he would never become a prisoner of the Russians, but would shoot himself. He knew that the war was lost and said that there would be no respect and no future for Germany.

Chapter Three

Taking Leave of the Bunker

1945

Friday, 20 April
On this day, Hermann Göring, the head of the Luftwaffe and one of the primary architects of the Nazi police state in Germany, and Heinrich Himmler – leader of the SS, one of the most powerful men in Nazi Germany and a main architect of the Holocaust – left the bunker.

Saturday, 21 April
With time running out for the Nazis, personnel of the Reich Chancellery were taken out of Berlin by air for the last time.

Among those leaving the bunker was Robert Ley, head of the German Labour Front. It was Ley who had invited Edward, Duke of Windsor, and Wallis, Duchess of Windsor, to conduct a tour of Germany in 1937, months after Edward had abdicated from the British throne. Ley served as their host and personal chaperone. When he left Berlin, he headed for southern Germany, the location of the planned National Redoubt.

Admiral Karl-Jesko von Puttkamer, Naval adjutant to Hitler, also flew out of Berlin, with orders to go to the Berghof to destroy Hitler's papers and his personal belongings.

It is thought that on 25 or 26 April, the typing and shorthand secretaries were evacuated by air. Their destination was Obersalzberg.

Friday, 27 April, Evening
The Luftwaffe dispatched six Storch aircraft and some thirty fighters to Berlin to save Feldmarschall Ritter von Greim and other important figures. Two Storch aircraft were reportedly shot down and the mission was aborted due to an extremely heavy Soviet air presence and anti-aircraft fire over the city centre.

However, a single Ju 52 aircraft, one of five sent from Gatow, managed to get through to rescue high-ranking Nazi personnel. Three other Ju 52s turned back as landing was deemed too difficult at night due to smoke that raged from fires across the city. One Ju 52 was shot down, killing all on board, as it came into land. The plan was now for von Greim, Hanna Reitsch and a select few to fly out of Berlin on the single Ju 52 that was able to land. Reitsch resisted the idea; she wanted to fly von Greim out herself in a smaller aircraft. Instead, all spaces on the Ju 52 were given to wounded German soldiers.

Saturday, 28 April
The Flight out of Berlin

At 11.00 pm, Reitsch and von Greim were ready to go, the whole of Berlin aflame and heavy small-arms fire being plainly audible. SS troops, committed to guarding Hitler to the end, brought a small armoured vehicle which was to take Reitsch and Greim from the bunker to where an Arado AR 96 trainer aircraft was hidden near the Brandenburg Gate. Reitsch was certain that this was the last aircraft available. She dismissed as unlikely the possibility of another plane having later gotten in and out again with Hitler as a passenger, as she felt Greim would surely have been informed. She knew that such a message was never delivered. She also knew that Greim had ordered other planes but that each was shot down in the attempt. Therefore, as Russian troops had already solidly ringed the city, Reitsch was certain that Hitler never left Berlin.

The broad street leading from the Brandenburg Gate was to be used for their Arado to take off; about 400 metres of uncratered pavement was available as a runway. There was poor visibility due to smoke. The take-off was made under strong Russian fire, and as the plane rose to rooftop level it was picked up by countless searchlights and immediately bracketed by a barrage of shelling. Explosions tossed the aircraft like a feather but only a few splinters hit the plane. Reitsch (although some reports attribute a Luftwaffe sergeant as the pilot of the Arado, not Reitsch herself) circled to about 20,000ft, from where she could see that Berlin was a sea of flames beneath her. She later described the magnitude of the destruction of Berlin as stark and fantastic. Heading north, 50 minutes later they reached Rechlin, some 100km north-west of Berlin, where the landing was made through a screen of Russian fighter craft at 3.00 am on 29 April.

Meanwhile, General of Artillery Helmuth Weidling had given the order for the survivors in the bunker to break out to the north-west. As the plan got underway, the first group from the Reich Chancellery was led by SS-Brigadeführer Wilhelm Mohnke.

Tuesday, 1 May

The advance of British forces necessitated a retreat from Rechlin to Schleswig late in the day for Greim and Reitsch, who learned of the announcement of Hitler's death and that he was succeeded by Admiral Dönitz.

For those left in the bunker, the plan was to escape from Berlin to the Allies on the western side of the Elbe or to the German forces to the north. Prior to the breakout, General Mohnke briefed all commanders (who could be reached) about the events surrounding Hitler's death and the planned breakout.

Mohnke's group included Hitler's private secretary Traudl Junge, secretaries Gerda Christian and Else Krüger, Hitler's dietician and vegetarian cook, Constanze Manziarly, Dr Ernst-Günther Schenck and Walther Hewel, along with various others. SS-Gruppenführer Hans Baur, Hitler's pilot, also joined them.

Mohnke organized a combat group to help them make the escape out of the shelter. All the able-bodied men who were still there joined them. They tried at first to exit to Potsdamer Platz, which proved impossible, and then turned north and in individual cases got as far as the Stettiner Bahnhof (railway station). Nothing more was heard from them.

A plan to break through the Russian lines was organized by SS-Sturmbannführer Otto Günsche for those who remained in the Führer's shelter in the Reichskanzlei, the Foreign Ministry and Parteikanzlei (Party Chancellery). This breakthrough was to have started in the early hours of 2 May, but it never took place because there was no real command, everyone running around like headless chickens. By then there were scarcely more than forty men left in the Führerbunker, among them Bormann, Rattenhuber, Baur, Kriminalrat Högl of the police and Günsche.

The personal adjutants of the Wehrmacht, Navy and Luftwaffe, as well as SS-Obergruppenführer Schaub, the Press Head of the Reich, Dr Dietrich, Professor Brand, the personal secretary to the Führer and house manager Kannenberg and all left the Führerhauptquartiere between 20 and 28 April, by plane, heading for Berchtesgaden. At the same time, the General Staff with Keitel and Jodl were *Abkommandiert* (relieved of their command). Willi Otto Mueller, a tailor in the Führer Headquarters, added that propaganda Minister Goebbels stayed with his entire family in the Führer Headquarters up until the end of April.

On the night of Tuesday/Wednesday, 1/2 May, Frau Christian, among several others, managed to escape from the Chancellery and was probably not a personal eyewitness to the burning and disposal of the bodies of Hitler and Eva Braun.

Wednesday, 2 May
Willi Otto Mueller succeeded in leaving the Führer Headquarters during the morning, accompanied by his colleagues Wohlfart and Theo Kotch. They managed to sneak into a bakery on Albrechtstraße. They passed themselves

off to the Russians as French civilian workers. Mueller left Berlin on 4 May, intending to go to Strasbourg, but he was picked up in Wiesenburg by the Allied military police and consequently interned.

At 7.00 pm on 2 May, Robert Hintze, the District Forester of Grunewald-Saubucht, was closing his front door when a military car drove up to his house. In it was a high-ranking German general sporting many decorations. The officer declared that he was the last Kommandant of Berlin, General Helmuth Reymann, and that all was lost; he had personally seen the Führer dead and had taken part in a breakout from the Reichskanzlei. He asked Hintze for civilian clothes and a night's lodging. He was alone. Reymann was described as tall, about 6ft, slim and aged about 50, with a vivacious temperament. Hintze gave him a pair of his trousers and some overalls and arranged for him to sleep in the hayloft. Reymann said he had broken out from the Zoo Bunker in Berlin, crossed the Russian lines into Grunewald and was making his way home to Schmargendorf.

With Hintze was Frau Dora Hecker, an employee who lived at Hintze's house, along with a number of people who had evacuated from Berlin. The forester's house was isolated in the middle of some woods and could only be reached along a wooded track. This area was within what became the British Sector once the war ended.

Reymann dressed himself in the civilian clothes and buried his uniform in a foxhole in the forest that had originally been dug by German soldiers. He was not given any food as he had some with him. He showed Hintze his identity papers and told him his address in Schmargendorf so that Hintze could retrieve his clothes from Reymann's home should he wish to do so.

Hintze saw Reymann again at 8.00 am the next morning. Reymann said goodbye and thanked Hintze for letting him stay the night. He went away dressed as a civilian, intending to make his way home. Meanwhile, however, the Russians had penetrated into Grunewald and occupied the forester's house. After several hours, a Russian military car drew up in which sat the former Kommandant of Berlin in his new civilian clothes; he was now a prisoner. Reymann was compelled to point out the place where his uniform was buried. The Russians then took him away in the same car; Hintze did not see him again. Curiously, a little while later, another Russian military car came by, the occupants of which were also looking for Kommandant Reymann, oblivious of what had just transpired.

Monday, 7 May, Night
Greim and Reitsch's Flight to Kesselring; the End at Zell am See
Greim and Reitsch took off in a Dornier 217 to fly to Gratz, where Kesselring was reported to be, but their aircraft was severely damaged by German flak and crash landed on the edge of a field. Reitsch and Greim were of the understanding that the capitulation would come on the night of 9 May, and when they learned that Kesselring had left Gratz for Zell am See in Austria, they took off again in an effort to instruct him to combine some of his troops with those holding back the Russians.

Greim and Reitsch arrived at Zell am See in a Fieseler Storch and immediately reported to General Koller, Chief of the General Staff of the Luftwaffe, asking the whereabouts of Feldmarschall Kesselring, now in charge of all German forces fighting the Western Allies. They now learned that the German capitulation was to be on 8 May, but said they still wanted to locate Kesselring. However, Koller either chose not to tell them where Kesselring was – because it was already too late – or else he did not know that he was in the village of Almdorf, a few miles north of Zell am See. Hearing this news, Reitsch and Greim decided any further efforts on their part were useless. Just before the capitulation, they left Zell am See for Kitzbühel to place themselves under the care of a well-known doctor who had just opened up his hospital there.

Tuesday, 8 May
Both von Greim and Reitsch were captured by the American Army. Reitsch would spend eighteen months in various internment camps. She later learned that her father, fearful of what the Soviets might do to his family, had killed his wife, Emy, Hanna's sister Heidi, her three children and himself on 3 May.

Wednesday, 19 December
Interrogation Report on Major Freytag von Loringhoven's Escape
Thirty-one-year-old Loringhoven was considered to be an intelligent and shrewd young General Staff Officer. His army career was strongly influenced by the fact that General Guderian took a special liking to the young man, whom he first met on the staff of the 1st Panzer Division in 1939. It was Guderian who called him to the OKH and later selected him as adjutant when he became Chief of the General Staff.

Loringhoven had said he agreed with his counterpart, Oberstleutnant Weiss, to ask their respective superiors to grant them permission to join a fighting unit as there was no further scope for any employment on the staff.

Loringhoven approached General Krebs early that afternoon and was granted permission to leave Berlin. He was given a pass to help him reach Spandau.

He left at 4.30 pm with Weiss. Both were in uniform and carrying a pistol, and the only documents they had was the pass. They made their way on foot through the Tiergarten, where they encountered Russian fire. They reached the Zoo Bunker, where HQ Berlin was still working in spite of the number of women and children who had taken refuge there. Loringhoven recalled that the flak gun on top of the bunker was firing against ground targets.

After some time, Loringhoven and Weiss continued and went to Pichelsdorf, which they reached in the early hours of 30 April. There they met an HJ unit, whose members gave them food and shelter.

The pair then found a canoe and later that evening started down the River Havel to the Wannsee. They passed a little peninsula and crossed the mouth of the Wannsee, never entering the lake proper, landing on the opposite side, where they were challenged by a German sentry.

Loringhoven said he and Weiss were taken to the HQ of the staff of Luftflotte Reich, which was housed in the former bunker of the 20th Panzer Division. The unit had about 3,000 men who were completely isolated. Loringhoven identified himself with his pass, and they spent the remainder of the day in a nearby house.

The following evening, 1 May, the unit tried to break out in the general direction of Potsdam. Loringhoven lost contact with Weiss and never heard from him again. He believed that Weiss had been taken prisoner. Loringhoven spent the remainder of the night and the following day hiding in a ditch in the woods.

During the night of 3 May, he said he made his way to Zehlendorf, where he entered an empty house, found civilian clothing and discarded his uniform. He prepared himself a meal and stayed in the house until the following day.

On 4 May, he set out towards Wittenberg, marching openly on the road. He was stopped several times by Russian troops, but each time told them that he had documents and was permitted to proceed. He walked via Wittenberg to Leipzig, where he was captured by American military police (MPs) on 12 May.

Wednesday/Thursday, 9/10 May
Kurt Huwe, sanitizer at the Voßstraße shelter, left Berlin to search for his relatives.

Thursday, 24 May
Greim committed suicide by taking poison, having discovered that he was to be given over to the Soviet Union and possibly tortured by the NKVD (secret police).

Thursday, 29 November
Interrogation of Hans Arthur Farson
Hans Farson served as a radio operator on a reserve plane Ju 52 of Fliegerstaffel des Führer's (Hitler's Squadron). The plane and crew were in the part of the squadron known as the Flugbereitschaft Reichsmarschall and made transport flights connected directly with Göring.

Tuesday, 17 April to Monday, 23 April 1945
On 17 April, Farson was stationed at Pocking airfield near Berlin, awaiting further orders. To his knowledge, none of the squadron's other planes were at Pocking during his stay there of several days. On the afternoon of the 17th, Farson and his colleagues were ordered to Berlin's Tempelhof Airfield by Oberstleutnant Henke, the local representative of General Baur, CO of Hitler's Squadron. Farson's Ju 52 flew otherwise empty. They stayed at Tempelhof until 21 April without knowing why they had been moved. An FW 200 of Hitler's Squadron was on the field when they arrived, and during the evening of 21 April two Ju 290s arrived from Fernaufklärungsgruppe 5 which were to fly with the squadron. Those three planes were still on the field when Farson left late that night.

Farson said they had taken off for Salzburg airfield with a load of eighteen SS men who appeared to be on some priority mission. Farson later learned that one of the Ju 290s took off a short time later with thirty more SS men who were part of the same mission.

Upon arrival at Salzburg, they were immediately ordered to return to Tempelhof airfield, getting back to Berlin before morning. The field there was under terrific fire in the early morning of 22 April, and upon reporting in they discovered that no one had the slightest idea why they were there. They were later able to contact Standartenführer Beetz in the Reich Chancellery and were told to wait until a group of women and children arrived who were to be taken to Salzburg. Farson recalled that everything at Tempelhof was completely disorganized, the result of Russian fire blanketing the surrounding area. During the morning of the 22nd, the passengers arrived (twelve women and five children) and were put on the plane by an SS-Obergruppenführer Schaub. Farson and his crew were not aware of the identity of any of the passengers. Upon returning to Salzburg, they were told that the SS men they had brought there had been taken back to Berlin; they were supposed to have had something to do with the arrest or shooting of Göring.

Monday, 23 April to Tuesday, 1 May 1945

Farson remained in Salzburg until the 23 or 24 April, when an order from the Berchtesgaden Berghof instructed him and his crew to fly to Berlin in their unarmed Ju 52. Farson considered it utter insanity making any flight at that time without proper armament, and the crew simply refused to take off. On the 28th, they received orders to fly a spare undercarriage to Rechlin for a FW 200 which had been damaged. As they knew that a properly equipped Ju 290 was stationed at Prague, they flew there and transferred their load to the 290, which then went to Rechlin.

It became evident that the entire German flight structure had quickly broken down. It had been certain for several days that there was no direct communication between Berlin and Berchtesgaden, as the orders emanating from those two command centres were consistently conflicting.

On 29 April, Farson and his colleagues returned to Salzburg with the Ju 52 empty. Upon their return, they received an order to fly the diplomat and politician, Baron von Steengracht, to Lübeck, where he was to enter into armistice discussions with the British. However, at the last moment this mission was given to an He 111. On 29 April, Farson and his crew learned that a Ju 52 and a Ju 352 transport aircraft had been shot down, both on flights from Berlin to Salzburg.

During the last week in April, the airfield at Salzburg was initially guarded by a strong detachment of SS troops and later by an Army unit. Their orders were secret and no plane could take off without clearance from them. Farson recalled that it was generally suspected that the purpose of the guard was to foil the possibility of Göring escaping to Spain, but noone believed the story that Göring had been arrested or shot.

During those final days, Obersteutnant Baer arrived with some thirty to forty Me 262 jet fighters from Riem, near Munich. Further evacuation of these jets to Klagenfurt or Hörsching was spoken of, said Farson, but never accomplished.

During the last three days of April, all military units on the airfield were in the process of dissolution. Soldiers were changing to civilian clothes and, either with or without the knowledge of their commanding officers, were leaving for their homes.

On 1 May, Farson was given a piece of paper by a Luftwaffe major which indicated that Farson had been released from his duties and was free to go home.

Wednesday, 5 December

Heinz Lorenz, Hitler's Deputy Chief Press Secretary and Hauptschriftführer of the DNB (German News Service) attached to Hitler's staff, who left Berlin on 29 April, stated under interrogation that he met Major Bernd Freytag von Loringhoven, Oberstleutnant Rudolf Weiß (adjutant to General Wilhelm Burgdorf) and Specht (adjutant to General Krebs) on the Pfaueninsel (an island in the River Havel) on the night of 30 April to 1 May. Lorenz said they told him that they had left Berlin during the late afternoon of 29 April and had spent the night and the following day in Pichelsdorf. They also stated that they had been given permission to leave Berlin and that the Luftwaffe adjutant von Below had accompanied them to Pichelsdorf but stayed there.

Lorenz added that these men had put on civilian clothing while on the Pfaueninsel but he thought that they later changed back into uniform since they intended to join the German troops at the Wannsee bridgehead who were trying to make a last attempt to break out of Berlin.

The CIB (Criminal Investigation Bureau) wanted von Loringhoven to confirm this story, and in particular wished to interrogate him on the question of whether he or either of the others were given any special mission by anyone in the bunker or were carrying documents of importance from there.

Monday, 28 January 1946
Interrogation of Rittmeister Gerhard Boldt

On 23 April 1945, Rittmeister Gerhard Boldt, an officer in the German Army, said he was summoned at very short notice to the Führerbunker under the Chancellery to act as Ordonnanz officer (batman) to General Krebs. Boldt found that a militia HQ had been established next to the Führerbunker. He said he saw little of, and had no conversation with, the party leaders in the next bunker.

By 29 April, with the situation obviously hopeless, Boldt, Loringhoven and an unknown officer who was adjutant to General Burgdorf applied for, and received, permission to leave the bunker to go to fight in the streets of the capital. They received an order, purported to be signed by Hitler, to make their way to Geltow-Ferch, where they should join up with advanced elements of General Wenck's forces who were believed to be trying to break through the Russian ring around Berlin.

Boldt said that the three of them left the bunker at 1.00 pm on 29 April. They made their way via Hermann-Göring-Straße, Heiligensee and Adolf Hitlerplatz to the Spandau Hafenbrücke, where they fell in with a company already fighting a defensive action. Further progress was impossible so they remained there for the rest of the night, the whole of 30 April and part of the following morning. During the night of 30 April/1 May, a breakout was attempted. Boldt believed that all personnel were either captured or killed, with the exception of Loringhoven and himself. The unknown officer who accompanied them was known to have been captured.

Boldt said he and Loringhoven spent the night of 1/2 May in a slit-trench in a wood, having previously obtained civilian clothes from a ruined house, and they destroyed their uniforms and papers. While in the slit-trench, Boldt claimed he attempted suicide by taking an overdose of morphine which he had obtained from a medical officer. However, Loringhoven made him vomit the entire dose, saving his life, but it left him in a very weak condition. Boldt complained that he was sick and as a consequence could not remember clearly the detailed events of the next few days.

He said they finally left on 2 May, pretending to be French slave workers – both could speak French fluently. They spent the night of 2/3 May at Kreilinden, their objective being to cross the Elbe (which they erroneously assumed to be the demarcation line between the Western Allies and the Soviets) and so avoid falling into Russian hands.

Between 3 and 7 May, they had travelled in the direction of Teltow and Jüterbog, avoiding roads and keeping to country paths and the woods. On the afternoon of 7 May, they were stopped by a Russian patrol about 5km north of Wittenberg and put into a displaced persons camp, where they spent the following night. Boldt said they escaped from the camp on 8 May and made their way through Wittenberg to the River Mulde.

Owing to the concentration of patrols on both sides of the river, he said they did not succeed in crossing it until midday on 11 May, swimming across at Raguhn. They immediately pushed on about 5km and spent the night of 11/12 May in a wood.

The pair separated on 12 May, with Loringhoven heading for Leipzig, where his family had an estate, on a lady's bike he acquired. Boldt, meanwhile, left on foot for Lübeck, where he was reported to the police and was admitted to hospital. He was discharged on 19 August.

Boldt was anxious not to mention Loringhoven as he had saved Boldt's life. He volunteered a statement that the political future of Germany had at no time been of interest to the military staff and that in the bunker there had been little personal contact between the staff of Hitler and Krebs. He added that there had been no mention of stay-behind organizations. His interrogators felt that Boldt appeared to be telling the truth.

Thursday, 25 April 1946
Interrogation Report on Frau Gerda Christian, One of Hitler's Personal Secretaries
Escape from the Bunker

Gerda Christian said that when she left the Führerbunker, Goebbels was still alive, but she believed that his family were already dead. Otto Günsche told her that afternoon that an escape would be attempted from the New Chancellery, and 9.00 pm had been mentioned as the time for them to meet. The departure from the Chancellery eventually took place toward 11.00 pm in several sections. Christian said she left in the first of ten breakout groups together with Gertrude Junge, Else Krueger, Constanze Manziarly and Günsche *et al.* They passed through underground corridors, went upstairs at Voßstraße, continued to the Kaiserhof U-Bahn station, followed the U-Bahn tracks to Bahnhof Friedrichstraße and then to an S-Bahn tunnel as far as the Spreekanal. They crossed the Spree River on an iron foot bridge which ran parallel to the Weidendammer Brucke, went into houses on the other side of the Spree and arrived at the Charite buildings.

At that point, the group consisted of Mohnke, Günsche, the four women and about twenty soldiers, and they stayed there for a while. Mohnke and Günsche tried unsuccessfully to establish contact with other groups. Eventually, they continued on their way towards Chausseestraße. There, near the Maikäferkaserne, Christian said a Russian tank opened fire on the group, so they retreated and stayed overnight in the cellar of a house at Chausseestraße. In the vicinity of the house, Christian saw Admiral Voss but said he did not enter the cellar. At about 6.00 am on 2 May, the entire group left the cellar in the direction of Alexanderplatz. At Schönhauser Allee, close to Alexanderplatz, a large number of soldiers, including some generals unknown to Christian, collected in a large bunker. Christian saw Walther Hewel and SS-Gruppenführer Rattenhuber, who had been wounded. At about 2.00 pm, the Russians sent an emissary requesting the surrender of those in the bunker within two hours. Christian recalled that the negotiations were carried out by Mohnke and an unknown general. Mohnke then told the women to leave the bunker, giving no instructions except that they should try to escape Berlin in a northerly direction in order to contact British units. The men stayed in the bunker, with Hewel saying that he was going to shoot himself. Rattenhuber mentioned that SS-Obersturmbannführer Hoegel had been killed at the Weidendammer Brücke and also talked about some tanks which had been destroyed there. The four women left shortly before 4.00 pm, about fifteen minutes before the bunker surrendered, and continued towards Seestraße. In order to avoid being mistaken for soldiers, Christian said she and Krueger changed into skirts, while Manziarly left with a German civilian in order to obtain one. When she did not return by 5.30 pm, Junge went after her, but she did not return either (she was eventually apprehended on 26 June 1946 in Munich). Krueger and Christian stayed with a civilian woman near Seestraß until the morning of 4 May, when they left Berlin and headed towards Kremmen and Alt Ruppin. They eventually reached the Anglo-Russian demarcation line on 14 May. After considerable difficulties with the Russian border guards, Christian said she and Krueger ran off, reached Crivitz in Mecklenburg and then Garwitz, where they stayed for almost a month with a farmer. They finally succeeded in boarding a British convoy at Parchim, reached Lüneburg and walked to Hamburg, which they reached on 10 June, continuing to Elmshorn where Krueger's mother lived. On 25 June, Krueger left for Hamburg, while Christian went to Ebernburg, near Bad Kreuznach.

Interrogation of PoW SS-Obergruppenführer Max Jüttner

Max Jüttner was a German officer and paramilitary activist. He served from 1934–45 as deputy chief of staff of the SA and head of the main leadership office of the Supreme SA Leadership.

Jüttner was in Berlin at Bendlerstraße until 21 April 1945. He said the majority of his department had moved south to Munich; he had practically no work left and was merely receiving situation reports from Wehrkreise and liaising with OKW. Jüttner said he and his staff left for Fürstenberg on 21 April, and about three days later moved to Tommendorfer Strand.

An English captain called on him on 13 May and interrogated him, looking to make an arrest. He was, however, not taken into custody and was told that he was to establish a camp (Auffangslager) for all the SS personnel remaining in the area.

Jüttner said that on 4 May he had gone to Flensburg, where he saw Keitel, and then attended a conference with Himmler at which he was officially thrown out of the SS.

Later he saw Jodl, who gave him his previous orders from the English captain in writing and told him to send his reports to the English C-in-C via Generalfeldmarschall Ernst Busch, commander of Army Group North-West. He was also told to keep in touch with the German Area Commander, General Müller.

On 16 May, after the end of hostilities, Jüttner went to Arensdorf near Schleswig, where Oberst Blume told him that Intelligence Officers of the British Armoured Brigade were expecting him. Jüttner returned that afternoon and was told to start his work the next day and attend an interview with a brigadier. Later that evening, however, an Intelligence Officer returned and took him to Rendsburg, where he was arrested by FSS or MPs.

During his interrogation, Jüttner spoke of SS-Gruppenführer Fegelein's visit to see him at Fürstenberg on 24 April. It appeared that the visit was not intended for Jüttner at all, as he said Fegelein was on his way from the Chancellery to see Reichsführer-SS Himmler, merely stopping at Fürstenberg en route.

Jüttner said Fegelein arrived during the afternoon, worn out after a strenuous journey from Berlin, immediately rang Himmler and then went to see him. He came back later that night and told Jüttner that Hitler had sent him to tell Himmler of the attempted Göring putsch at Berchtesgaden, and of the fact that Martin Bormann has ordered the SS guards to arrest Göring, an order which they had carried out. Jüttner could not supply any reason why Hitler should have been so anxious to inform Himmler of this at that critical stage of affairs. He believed, however, that the trip may have been Fegelein's idea as he was anxious to get out of Berlin. Fegelein's last remark leaving Jüttner had been: 'I certainly don't intend to die in Berlin.'

Fegelein had also received the Führer's orders to fly back with Himmler to Berlin the next day, probably for the latter to answer for his secret negotiations with the Swede Folke Bernadotte, of which Hitler had heard. However, plans changed and Fegelein flew back alone.

Sunday, 2 June
Interview with Oberst Nicolaus von Below
Nicolaus von Below was a young Luftwaffe officer who spent practically every day for eight years in Hitler's presence.

Von Below admitted that he left Hitler's bunker at midnight on 29/30 April 1945 bearing two letters, one from Hitler to Generalfeldmarschall Keitel and another from General Krebs to General Jodl. He said he had burnt those letters on his way through the Russian lines, as he had strict instructions that they should not fall into enemy hands and it appeared likely that he would be stopped and searched by the Russians. He did, however, reproduce the gist of the letters from memory:

(1) The letter from the Führer to Generalfeldmarschall Keitel, dated 29 April 1945.

> 'The fight for Berlin is drawing to a close. On the other fronts as well the end can be expected within a few days. I am going to commit suicide rather than surrender. I have appointed

Großadmiral Dönitz my successor as Reichspräsidenten and Oberbefehlshaber der Wehrmacht. I expect you to remain at your post and to give my successor the same zealous support you have granted me; and to do your upmost to fight gallantly to the end.

'Two of my oldest supporters, Göring and Himmler, have broken faith with me at the last minute. The people and the Wehrmacht have given their all in this long and hard struggle. The sacrifice has been enormous. My trust has been misused by many people. Disloyalty and betrayal have undermined resistance throughout the war. It was therefore not granted to me to lead the people to victory. The Army General Staff cannot be compared with the General Staff in the [First] World War. Its achievements were far behind those of the fighting front. The Luftwaffe fought bravely.

'Its Commander in Chief has been unable to maintain the superiority of the years 1939 and 1940. The Navy has wiped out the disgrace of 1918 by its morale during this war. It cannot be blamed for its defeat. The efforts and sacrifices of the German people in this war have been so great that I cannot believe they have been in vain. The aim must still be to win territory in the east for the German people.'

(2) The letter from General Krebs to General Jodl, dated 29 April 1945.

'The encirclement of Berlin by the Russians is complete. Our own resistance against enemy superiority can only last a few days. Arms and ammunition are lacking. Supplies by air are insufficient. It is no longer possible to land in Berlin. There is no information about the position of Wenk's Army here. Their help in saving Berlin is no longer being reckoned with. The Führer expects that the other fronts will fight on to the last man.'

While there is, of course, no proof that the above were the actual contents of the letters, they are at any rate consistent with evidence obtained from other sources.

Von Below also gave further information on the following points:

(1) Hitler's children
Von Below was certain that Eva Braun bore Hitler no children. He saw her frequently and regularly between 1937 and 1945, and her condition never indicated pregnancy. Owing to his intimacy and friendship with Hitler and Hitler's entourage over a long period, he would certainly have learnt of the existence of children had there been any. Hitler himself told von Below how impossible and wrong it would be for him, Hitler, to have descendants, for both personal and public reasons.

(2) Hitler's wills
Von Below was shown a photostat of Hitler's personal will and identified it as genuine. It was signed in the early morning of 29 April. He did not see the political will in the bunker, but thought it must have been signed shortly before, when Burgdorf and Krebs were with the Führer.

(3) Hitler's suicide
Von Below stated that Hitler announced his intention of committing suicide after his decision to remain in Berlin on 22 April. Eva Braun followed suit. At the time von Below left the bunker, he did not know if any definite date had been fixed for the suicides or any definite arrangements had been made for the disposal of the bodies, apart from Hitler's intention to have his and his wife's bodies burnt, as stated in the personal will. However, he was quite certain that Hitler carried out his intention, for the following reasons:

(a) The suggestion of suicide was made as early as 22 April and, more strongly, on 27 April.
(b) That intention was expressed in the personal will.
(c) A conversation took place between von Below and Oberfeldwebel Werner Pardau on 6 May 1945 in Friesack. Von Below and his batman, Matthiesing, met Pardau by chance and each had a short conversation with him. Von Below said Pardau told him: 'In the afternoon of 30 April Hitler and Eva Braun committed suicide and their bodies were burned. The Goebbels family also committed suicide.' After the Below–Pardau conversation, Matthiesing had a longer conversation with Pardau, being told: 'On the afternoon of 30 April 1945, Eva Braun took poison and died shortly before Hitler shot himself. Bormann and Burgdorf were present when the bodies of Hitler and Eva Braun were wrapped in sacking and carried out into the garden by members

of the Begleitskommando. There the bodies were soaked in petrol and set alight. Goebbels and his family also committed suicide.'

Despite how close von Below had been to Hitler, he had no knowledge of a plot to drug and remove the Führer at the last moment. He knew nothing of orders given to Hitler's adjutant Günsche and the chauffeur Kempka about the disposal of Hitler's body after the suicide, nor what orders were given to Rattenhuber. Nor did he know of orders given to Hitler's pilots to fly out the body, dead or alive. He also neither knew nor had heard anything of the two Storch aircraft landing on the Charlottenburger Chausse on 30 April, nor of an aircraft sent from Dönitz's HQ landing at Wannsee.

20 June
Special Interrogation Report on SS-Haupsturmbannführer Günther August Wilhelm Schwägermann

Günther Schwägermann, personal adjutant to Goebbels, was in the Führerbunker from 22 or 23 April 1945 until the evening of 1 May. His recollection of that period was not very distinct, and dates given by him had been quite inaccurate in some cases. Schwägermann was aware of that limitation and had been careful to differentiate between knowledge and assumption. As far as definite statements that had been made by him were concerned, the information was considered reliable.

Escape from the Reichskanzlei

Schwägermann did not recall specifically who left in which groups from the Voßstraße bunker, but he recalled having seen Günsche there but not Mohnke. He claimed that everybody moved out through the inner courtyard towards Wilhelmsplatz, crossed Wilhelmsplatz and entered the U-Bahn tunnel. He left the U-Bahn tunnel somewhere along Friedrichstraße and reached Bahnhof Friedrichstraße between 10.00 and 11.00 pm. At that time, the group included Schwägermann, Rach, Naumann and Dietrich (who guided Schwägermann but was handicapped in the dark due to the loss of an eye). From Bahnhof Friedrichstraße, they proceeded to the far side of Weidendamer Brücke. Held up at an anti-tank barrier by machine-gun and rifle fire, he said they took shelter in some ruins to the left ahead of the barrier, where they met Bauer, Beetz, Kempka, Bormann and Axmann (together with approximately a company of HJ). Schwägermann said he did not see Rattenhuber in the vicinity of the Weidendamer bridge at any time. Schwägermann, Rach, Naumann and Dietrich tried to get ahead through some houses on the right-hand side of the street, but received fire from the other side of Ziegelstraße and were forced to withdraw.

He said this was about 1.00 am and that at roughly the same time a number of tanks tried to break through together with small groups of people on foot. Schwägermann remembered that one of those tanks was hit and exploded just before reaching Ziegelstraße. He was definite that Naumann was next to him in the house to the right at that time and was not near this or any other exploding tank at Weidendamer Brücke. Since all attempts to get ahead failed, Bormann, Axmann, Naumann, Stumpfegger, Dietrich, Hauptfeldwebel Weizin and Schwägermann withdrew to Bahnhof Friedrichstraße and took shelter in a shell crater. When they discovered that Rach had not come along with them, Naumann sent Schwägermann back to find him. He was not successful. The remainder of the group then went along the canal to the railroad tracks, went up the tracks near the S-Bahn bridge and followed the tracks to Lehrter Bahnhof. After a short while, everybody removed their shoulder straps.

He continued that close to Lehrter Bahnhof they ran into a Russian patrol, then went up on a street bridge, crossed the tracks and split up. Bormann and Stumpfegger went to the right, while Naumann, Axmann, Dietrich, Welzin and Schwägermann went to the left, in the direction of Alt-Moabit. They ran into another Russian patrol, which stopped Axmann and Welzin (Schwägermann was under the impression that they were arrested), while Naumann, Dietrich and Schwägermann ducked into a house on the left of the street and hid between some tiles. They stayed there from 2–3 May and left during the night of 3/4 May in the direction of Moabit, followed the railway tracks of Lehrter Güterbahnhof and hid on 4 May in some freight cars there. On 5 May, Dietrich looked around the rail yard and managed to procure some civilian clothing. During the night, the trio unsuccessfully tried to cross the bridge towards Wedding. However, they got across during the daytime on 6 May and reached Wedding, Hermsdorf, Frohnau and Wittenau. Near Wittenau, they stayed overnight in a garden lodge. The following day, they were stopped near Frohnau by a Russian patrol but were not arrested. They proceeded towards Oranienburg and Friesack. About a kilometre before Friesack, near a railroad, they finally separated. Dietrich mentioned at the time that he intended to go to the Harz Mountains, while Naumann wanted to see his family, then believed to be in Thuringia. Schwägermann said it was possible that Naumann and Dietrich continued together for a while. Schwägermann, meanwhile, went to Ueltzen near Hannover in order to see his family. He said he did not see Naumann or Dietrich again. On Whitsunday 1945, he met Rach by accident at Ueltzen, who told him he intended to go to southern Germany.

Chapter Four

Aftermath of Hitler's Death

1945

Sunday, 29 April
By the end of the day, the question over whether Berlin would stand or fall, and therefore the question of Hitler's fate, was no longer open to doubt. The inhabitants of the other bunkers under the two Chancelleries were told not to go to bed as the Führer wished to say goodbye to the ladies.

Monday, 30 April
Erna Flegal
Nurse Erna Flegal, who worked at the emergency casualty station at the Reich Chancellery, announced during the afternoon: 'He departed this life.' No questions were asked of her as to how; none at all. Each of her colleagues had the feeling that the previous evening had been Hitler's farewell to them. Flegal's first question to the doctor each morning had been: 'Is Hitler still alive?' The answer kept coming: 'Yes.' The same anxious question was raised at each meeting with Dr Haase. When Haase came out of the Führer's shelter at 6.00 pm on 30 April, Flegal asked the same question again. Haase gave no answer; the truth dawned on Flegal. She felt that it was natural that such an event was not discussed, as it affected the occupants of the bunker very deeply; at such a time, unimportant matters were of no interest at all. They all feared that they would not come out of that living hell alive; they knew precisely what may be in store for them. Flegal said everyone had made up their mind on that subject; there were no more questions about it and they were paying attention only to what was essential.

During the evening, Bormann, Goebbels, Burgdorf and Krebs (and possibly Weidling and Wilhelm Mohnke) had a meeting lasting from 7.00 pm until midnight. Immediately afterwards, Krebs left the bunker in order to bring from Bormann and Goebbels a letter to the Russians. Gerda Christian had typed that letter, which advised the Russians of Hitler's death. It indicated that Bormann and Goebbels were sending the letter by virtue of their newly assumed government positions and contained an authorization for Krebs to conduct negotiations for an armistice or truce. No future plans were mentioned. The letter was signed by Bormann and Goebbels, and possibly also by Burgdorf. Krebs returned during the afternoon of 1 May with the answer, not surprisingly, that the Russians requested unconditional surrender and extradition of all those still in the bunker. That ended all attempts of a negotiation. Christian was not aware of any communications sent or received from Dönitz. She claimed that Dönitz had already been notified at the time of the Göring or Himmler affair that he was to succeed Hitler. When confronted with the fact that Dönitz actually had received a telegram, she stated that the message could have been delivered only through Wehrmacht W/T facilities.

Tuesday, 1 May
The day after Hitler's death, the occupants of the bunker were all conscious of a vacuum. However, their fate could not be postponed and Flegal saw that the end was about to come. Upon the news that Hitler was dead, they were told that they were released from their oath, and everyone was permitted to choose their own fate. The able-bodied men prepared a sally, but the others decided not to go out with the combat group, instead remaining at their place beside the wounded. Flegal could not understand why the orders were not given for the breakout on the 30th, but only on the 1st, as in consequence there were a large number of people killed.

Martin Bormann was among the men who took part in the breakout attempt. Flegal assumed that he met his death there, purely because as most of the young battle-experienced SS men fell, a relatively older man could not have come through alive.

How Flegal Viewed Magda Goebbels
Flegal considered Magda Goebbels in a much better light than she did Eva Braun. Flegal perceived Magda as having been her husband's guiding light, but could not judge if she had been wavering. Magda was having dental treatment and Flegal often spoke with her for an hour at a time, considering her 'far superior to the average human being'. Flegal felt that it took a resolute spirit to decide to sacrifice your own children, much more so than for Hitler to take his own life. Magda said: 'Now, we too will give up our lives.' About the children she said: 'Where shall my children go? The shame of being Goebbels children will always rest upon them.'

The two women shook hands. Not a word was said; there was nothing to say. Mrs Goebbels had told the children that they would have to live in the shelter for quite a long time and that with this in view they had to be inoculated. The children were accustomed to inoculations as a result of the war. Flegal said the children died during the afternoon and their parents that evening.

Flegal said that Hans Fritzsche, the Ministerialdirektor at the Propagandaministerium (Reich Ministry of Public Enlightenment and Propaganda), was now the only high-ranking Nazi official left. He took great pains after the death of Goebbels to keep everything more or less in order and to find the best way of making the surrender to the Russians. He went over to the Soviet lines in Berlin to offer the surrender of the city to the Red Army on 1 May and was taken prisoner.

Tuesday, 1 May
Hilco Poppen was a member of the Reich Security Service (the Reichssicherheitsdienst, or RSD) in the bunker. At 6.00 pm on 1 May, Hermann Karnau, an SS bodyguard friend of Poppen, told him: 'Hitler is dead. They [Hitler and Eva Braun] are lying in the garden and burnt.'

Poppen stated that Hitler really did marry Eva Braun on 28 April and that they then 'poisoned themselves'. He said that petrol was poured over their bodies and set alight, and that they were buried in a tomb crater in the garden in front of the *notausgang* (emergency exit).

As to whether he knew that Braun's left foot had not been burned, he simply answered: 'I didn't know.' He claimed not to have seen the bodies himself because he was on duty and could not leave his post.

Poppen had confidentially spoken to Fliegner at Rotenburg Hospital. Poppen claimed that he was on duty and didn't see Braun's foot. Poppen was lying, and why should Fliegner make that up?

Paul Fliegner, an inmate at Milag PoW camp spent time in Rotenberg hospital two weeks previously.

He shared the same room with Hilco Poppen, who made this 'very confidential' confession to him.

Poppen made a sketch which indicated the bomb crater in the garden of the Reichskanzlei. The other side of the sketch gave the names of the nine people who were working with Poppen.

Wednesday, 2 May
The Russians entered the bunker at 10.00 am. Flegal and her colleagues had marked their section of the bunker with Red Cross flags, which the Russians initially respected as they went through the shelter. The wounded were left alone, as were Flegal and her colleagues, and nor was anything taken from them. Furthermore, they were surprised to hear they were permitted to lock themselves in overnight. She said the Russian commandant's behaviour was

exemplary, although he had admitted that he could not vouch for the behaviour of his soldiers. According to Flegal, the Russian officer did not appear to have full authority over his soldiers, something that was anathema to Flegal. The Russian headquarters, meanwhile, were established at Mohnke's battle post.

Sunday, 30 September
Interrogation Report of Hilco Poppen in Rotenberg Hospital by Captain Godreau
Hilco Poppen was a burly SS policeman with considerable experience in partisan fighting. He was a Revier-oberwachtmeister der Schupo (sergeant in the security police) in Wilhelmshaven, attached to Hitler's HQ. From August 1944 until the end of September that year, the HQ was located at Rustenburg in East Prussia. Poppen stated that he saw Hitler every day when he made his daily walk in the Chancellery garden. He said that Hitler's left arm was constantly trembling as a consequence of the 20 July assassination attempt.

In November 1944, the HQ was moved to Berlin. Poppen had previously moved there to organize the guard system of the Reichskanzlei. Hitler reduced his walks in the garden once the Chancellery came under fire from the Russians.

Saturday, 6 October
Report by Captain W.M. Ingham Regarding the Interrogation of Hilco Poppen – Classified 'SECRET'
It was considered that Poppen had given the information in his statements to the best of his ability and that as far as Ingham was concerned, the statements were true.

Regarding Hitler's death, the following information was obtained:

(1) Poppen was employed on guard duties at the Reichskanzlei in Berlin from January to 2 May 1945.
(2) He last saw Hitler around 16–18 April 1945.
(3) On 29 April, Poppen heard from various people in the building that the Führer had married Eva Braun.
(4) At about 9.00 pm the same day, he was told by the soldier in charge of Hitler's dog, Blondi (a Schäferhund, or German Shepherd), that on the Führer's orders he had the dog killed with poison (presumably to see if the poison worked as it was supplied by Himmler).
(5) On 1 May at about 6.00 pm, Revier-Wachtmeister Karnau spoke to Poppen and told him that Hitler and Eva Braun were dead, having 'poisoned themselves' at approximately 5.00 pm. At about 6.30 pm, the Wachtmeister came to Poppen, confirmed the above and added

that the two bodies were burnt in the garden. Poppen gained the impression that Harry Mengershausen, one of Hitler's bodyguards, had actually seen the burning bodies. At about 9.00 pm, Karnau went to Poppen and told him that he had seen the bodies and that they had been buried in a crater immediately to the right of the emergency exit in the garden.

(6) Poppen was under the impression that the burning and burial was done by SS-Sturmbannführer Heinz Linge and SS-Sturmbannführer Schedle. He could not explain how he came to such a belief, except that it was the general impression that they would be the people to do the job.

Poppen said he left the Reichskanzlei on 2 May, moving down a street parallel to Friedrichstraße and various byways to a brewery, where he met a number of the Führer's staff. He subsequently worked his way through the Russian lines and on to Wilhelmshaven, where he reported himself and was consequently made a prisoner of war, interned at Fallingbostel in northern Germany.

Friday, 26 October
Special Investigation Squad Counter Intelligence Corps, Detachment 970, Headquarters United States Forces European Theatre: Interview with Frau Elisabeth Krau, Mother-In-Law of Frau Gerda Christian (One of Hitler's Private Secretaries)
Two special agents from the United States Army Counter Intelligence Corps (Army CIC), Edward J. Majowicz and Otto W. Knauth, produced the above report.

The agents were instructed to interview Frau Krau at her address, Haus Ursula, Ebernburg, near Bad Münster am Stein-Ebernburg, in an effort to learn the whereabouts of Frau Christian, who was wanted for questioning as a possible witness to the death of Hitler.

Frau Christian had left her mother-in-law on 2 October 1945 in order to look for work elsewhere, and had not notified Frau Krau of her new address.

The special agents found that Gerda was a 31-year-old brunette with dark eyes, the wife of Eckhard Christian, a major general of the Luftwaffe. She was employed as a secretary in the office of the Reich Chancellery in Berlin prior to its capture by the Russians. Her husband was interned as a prisoner of war in Strupp, near Berchtesgaden, in August, but may have been evacuated to England. Frau Christian and her husband lived at Niersteiner Straße, Berlin-Grunewald, before the end of the war. The couple had no children of their own, but General Christian had three young children by a previous marriage;

those children lived with Frau Krau. No other relatives of Frau Christian were known.

Arrangements were made with Frau Krau to detain her daughter-in-law in the event of her return, or at least to get her new address. The special agents would return to Frau Krau on 7 November to learn of any new developments.

Friday, 9 November
Erich Kempka
A secret cipher message from HQ United States Forces European Theatre, to the Commanding Officer, Civilian Internment Camp Number 6, Moosburg, Bavaria:

SECRET (.) REQUEST THAT ERICH KEMPKA, FORMER CHAUFFEUR FOR HITLER PRESENTLY HELD IN YOUR CAMP BE ASKED THE FOLLOWING QUESTIONS AND THAT ANSWERS BE CABLED SECRET THIS OFFICE FOR MAYBURY SOON AS POSSIBLE; WHEN HITLERS BODY WAS BURNED, WAS IT BURIED WHILE STILL WRAPPED IN BLANKET OR WAS IT UNWRAPPED? WHAT DID HE ACTUALLY SEE? HOW WAS HE SURE IT WAS HITLERS BODY?

Thursday, 15 November
Death of Hitler: Present Position of Enquiry and Recommendations for Further Action in British and US Zones
The following were considered by the British and the Americans to be a source of further useful evidence:

(1) Frau Christian, Hitler's secretary in the bunker at the end and familiar with all the incidents, although probably not a personal eyewitness of the burning and disposal of the bodies. She was believed to be in the British Zone of occupation.

   Frl Krüger (secretary to Martin Bormann) was in Hamburg and would report if Frau Christian communicated with her.

(2) The SS-Begleitkommando. There was a very significant gap in the Allies' knowledge because the British had not been able to locate any members of this unit who were on duty in the bunker in the last days of the war. The relevant officers were:

> SS-Sturmbannführer Franz Schedle, Stellvertretender Führer (deputy commander), was said to live in the Allgäu area near Memmingen. He gave Erich Kempka (a US prisoner at No. 8 Internment Camp, Moosburg, formerly Stalag VII-A) a message to his wife that he would stay in the bunker and would not fall alive into Russian hands. He had been injured in the foot by a grenade and could only walk with the aid of a stick.
>
> SS-Obersturmführer Helmut Beermann was believed to live in the Harz area of northern Germany. He was reported to be a PoW by the US 9th Army, but had not been located.
>
> SS-Hauptsturmführer Otto Hansen was said to live in Barlt, Dithmarschen, Schleswig-Holstein. He was last seen in Friedrichstraße on the night of 1/2 May.

These men were known to have been on duty on 30 April and were believed to have been direct eyewitnesses of what happened; their evidence was much needed. Apart from them, the following officers were also known to have been on duty during Hitler's last days and may have been witnesses of some of the events of 30 April:

> SS-Obersturmführer Helmut Frick, said to be from western Germany. He was last seen in Friedrichstraße on the night of 1/2 May.
>
> SS-Obersturmführer Pat Lindlof, said to be from Danzig.
>
> SS-Obersturmführer Hans Reisser, said to be from Memmingen.
>
> SS-Hauptsturmführer Grießenböck, said to be from western Germany. He was last seen in Friedrichstraße on the night of 1/2 May.
>
> SS-Obersturmführer Weichelt, said to be from Saxony.

Local investigation by CIC Memmingen (US 3rd Army area) may have produced evidence about Schedle and Reisser. The exact address of Schedle could have possibly been obtained from Kempka. The name of Weichelt had only been recently known, and it was suggested that lists of PoWs and civilian internees be examined in case he had been captured.

> (3) Reichssicherheitsdienst, Dienststelle I. Apart from Rattenhuber, who was reportedly a Russian PoW in the Russian communiqué of 7 May, there were three members of this unit still unaccounted for,

who were believed to have been eyewitnesses of the burning and/or burial of the bodies of Hitler and Eva Braun. They were:

Hans Hofbeck, from Munich.

Harry Mengershausen, the guard who had allegedly buried Hitler's body. He was said to live in Theodor-Körner Straße, Bremen.

Max Koelz, whom it was thought may live in the Augsburg area. It was claimed that he was the only man who knew where Hitler was buried.

Sunday, 14 December
Frau Gerda Christian
Major L.H. Long, CIB, BAOR, visited Hamburg to see Denis Sefton Delmer, of the Allied News Desk, to ask him to arrange a transmission regarding the search for Frau Christian. Long wanted to speak to her in connection with Hitler's death. Text along the following lines was agreed to be put out:

> 'Will Frau. Christian, Christian name Gerda, née Daranowsky, wife of General der Luftwaffe Eckhard Christian, call personally or otherwise communicate with Missing Persons Bureau, Hamburg.'

A transmission prepared and approved by Long was left at Delmer's office. Long wanted it cleared with the Missing Persons Bureau before it was put out. The bureau was closed on Sundays, so Long visited Major Hockliffe's office to ask him if he could clear it the following day (Hockliffe was Area Security Officer, Hamburg). Hockliffe was not present and a message was left with with his sergeant, explaining the full circumstances of the case. Hockliffe eventually gave his clearance and informed Delmer's office to go ahead. Long assumed that this was done and wanted Delmer to arrange for a rebroadcast.

Wednesday, 28 November
Major Gerhard Engel and Major Freytag Lohringhoven
The CIB were interested in Engel and Lohringhoven, who were believed to be members of Hitler's immediate entourage at his personal HQ, and they were therefore included in the list of wanted characters originally circulated. Subsequent information had suggested that they were not present at the end in the bunker, which reduced their value. Nevertheless, it was recommended that they be interrogated on the following matters:

Engel

Engel was reported to have been Wehrmacht Adjutant at Führerhauptquartiere, but had been transferred from that post sometime before the end and sent to Armee Wenck; Wenck's 12th Army operated east of Berlin. He needed to be interrogated on his work, with special attention paid to the following questions:

1. When was he last in Berlin, and in what capacity?
2. Who succeeded him as Wehrmacht Adjutant at the Führer HQ, and when?
3. What were the exact circumstances of his transfer?

If Engel was at the Führer HQ at any time after 20 April, the fullest details of persons present, incidents and dates needed to be sought, along with any other matter which would have made it possible to check his veracity.

Loringhoven

Freytag Loringhoven was thought to have been on the staff of General Krebs. He was said to have been in the bunker up until 27 April and to have left with Hauptmann Bolt (who was also probably on Krebs's staff). He was wanted to be interrogated in general about his work and in detail about his experiences in the bunker between 20 April and his departure. In particular:

1. Did he know about the shooting of Hermann Fegelein? When did it take place? (Before, after or simultaneously with what other events?)
2. Who else was in the bunker, at what times and for what purposes and occasions?
3. Did he see Ritter von Greim and Hannah Reitsch? If so, when, and in connection with what events?
4. Was he present at the Lagebesprechung of 22 April? If so, could he give the fullest details?
5. What did he know about the personalities of the SS-Begleitkommando?
6. When did he leave the bunker, with whom and how? If by plane, from which airstrip and in what plane?
7. Did he know the fate of Krebs?
8. What did he know about the Hitler–Braun marriage? When did this take place? What was the exact time of day? Who solemnized it?
9. Was he in the bunker when news of (a) Himmler's negotiations with Bernadotte or (b) Mussolini's death was announced? If so, when was

this? What details were announced, and by whom? What was the reaction?
10. What did he know about Hitler's will? When was it made, and who typed it? How many copies were made? To whom were they given, and for delivery to whom?
11. What did he know about the functions, last instructions and means of escape, destination and present whereabouts of Weiss, Specht, Zander and von Below?

Wednesday, 5 December
The CIB wanted the following people for interrogation in connection with events surrounding the death of Hitler:

Alwin-Broder Albrecht. Aged about 42. Adjutant (National Socialist Motor Corps). Originally a naval adjutant. Became the subject of controversy for marrying a woman with a bad reputation. On 1 July 1939, he was appointed an NSKK adjutant. Albrecht was believed to have committed suicide when the combat group started out from the Chancellery on 1 May 1945.

Georg Betz. Aged about 45. A pilot on Hitler's staff and former captain for Lufthansa prior to joining the Schutzstaffel (the SS). It was later discovered that he was killed during the Battle of Berlin.

Nikolaus von Below. Aged about 38. Adjutant (Luftwaffe). One of only a few people with an aristocratic background to serve in Hitler's inner circle. He became closely associated with the Führer over the years.

Wilhelm Burgdorf. Aged about 50. Adjutant (Army). He was promoted chief of the Heeres Personnel Office and Chief Adjutant in October 1944.

Otto Günsche. Aged about 28. Originally an SS adjutant. From August 1943 to 5 February 1944, he fought on the Eastern Front, and in France until March 1944, when he was again appointed as a personal adjutant.

Professor Dr Haase. Aged about 42. SS personal physician and surgeon for Hitler.

Frau Traudl Junge (nee Humps). Aged about 25. Hitler's youngest secretary, she was married to Hans Hermann Junge, an aide-de-camp and valet.

Hans Krebs. Aged about 50–55. Chief of Staff of the OKH. Infantry general.

Heinz Linge. Aged 32. Member of the Schutzstaffel and Hitler's longest-serving valet. He would wake up Hitler each morning and keep him stocked with writing materials and spectacles.

Frau Constanze Manziarly. Aged about 32. Cook/dietician. Began working for Hitler from 1943 and was present in the Führerbunker during the dictator's final days.

Franz Schädle. Aged about 38. Schädle was the fifth and last commander of Hitler's personal SS guard at the Führerbunker.

Günther Schwägermann. Aged about 28. Adjutant for Joseph Goebbels.

Dr Ludwig Stumpfegger. Aged about 38. Became Hitler's personal surgeon after a recommendation from Heinrich Himmler.

14 December
Interrogation of Frl Else Krüger (Martin Bormann's Secretary)

'Zander was not one of Bormann's adjutants, but one of his advisors. She saw Zander for the last time approx. 29 April 1945, in the Bunker at Reichskanzlei. Zander disappeared suddenly on 29 April 1945, and she had not seen or heard anything of him since that time. Zander was married and his wife was believed to be living in Munich and was believed to have one child. Frl Krüger did not know Zander's home address. Frl Krüger did not know any more about Zander as he lived on the opposite side of Wilhelmstraße and only came to the Bunker during lulls in the bombardment.

'Frau Junge was believed to have written Hitler's Will, which was typewritten, [but] she did not know who witnessed the Will. Frau. Christian was present in the Bunker and told Frl Krüger that Frau Junge was typing Hitler's Will.

'As far as Frl Krüger knew, no will was made by Göring, who had left previously for Berchtesgaden.'

Thursday, 20 December
Artur Axmann, Leader of the Hitler Youth

Artur Axmann was arrested by the Americans. It was possible that he was in Hitler's bunker in the last days of April 1945. Axmann was later reported as being seen dead in Wilhelmstraße. The General Staff (GS) requested that Frl Krüger should be interrogated about Axmann. It was requested that she should not be told that Axmann had been arrested. The GS wanted to know when she last saw him, what his intentions were when collapse seemed imminent and what his intentions were in Hitler's bunker. He was described by Heinz Lorenz as a frequent visitor to the bunker.

1946

Wednesday, 2 January
Alleged Discovery of Hitler's Body
An article appeared in the evening newspaper, *Nachtexpress*, which stated:

> 'According to an Associated Press report, the correspondent of *France Soir* reported on Tuesday that the body of Adolf Hitler had been found on December 19th by the Russian High Command and had been identified.'

The *Nachtexpress* appeared in the Russian sector and would presumably have been published under Russian control.

A similar article appeared on the same date in the *Der Kurier*, a newspaper that appeared in the French sector.

In Britain, the *Daily Telegraph* of 2 January quoted Reuters as an authority for a similar report which appeared in that paper. In the same column in the *Daily Telegraph* appeared a reference to Krbbs, Hitler's deputy in Bohemia and Moravia and a witness of Hitler's will, who, according to the *Daily Telegraph*, was about to be handed over to the Czechs by 'the Allies'.

Major Hugh Trevor-Roper – known as 'the sleuth of Oxford' – felt that if Krebs could be found he would be a valuable witness regarding investigations into Hitler's death. Trevor-Roper believed Krebs to be either in the US or British Zones.

The Allies agreed to extradite Krebs, according to the *Daily Telegraph* of 2 January 1946:

> 'The Allies have agreed to the Czechoslovak Government's request for the extradition from Germany of Hans Krebs, Hitler's deputy in the "Protectorate" of Bohemia-Moravia stated an Exchange message from Prague. Krebs was one of the four men who witnessed Hitler's Political Testament.'

The Reuters correspondent in Berlin explained that the source was the *France Soir* report. However, the offices of the French Press camp, *et al.*, claimed that no correspondent was in Berlin representing *France Soir* and that all correspondents were away temporarily.

Monday, 7 January
General Hans Krebs, Last Head of the German General Staff (OKH)

The CIB were informed on the telephone by Major Trevor-Roper that if Krebs could be found he would be a valuable witness regarding Hitler's death. However, Trevor-Roper told the CIB that Krebs was believed to be dead and was certainly not in the British or US Zones. The CIB informed Trevor-Roper it would do its best to find out the truth in the report about Krebs or on the general subject of the discovery of Hitler's body.

Monday, 14 January
Interrogation of Ursula Druesedau

Ursula Druesedau was a nurse, aged about 17, who was employed in the large bunker under the Reich Chancellery towards the end of the fighting in Berlin. The following report on her interrogation was prepared:

> 'A party of nurses were asked to be allowed to see the Führer through an SS Lieut who was the boyfriend of one of their number. The Lieutenant who belonged to the Führer's bodyguard arranged for a communal interview on Wednesday afternoon, 26 April, but owing to the arrival of a lorry load of wounded, she was unable to attend. She did, however, see the Führer take a walk in the garden alone with his big dog the following day, Thursday. He looked very worn and ill, on being greeted by Druesedau with the words, "Heil mein Führer", he thanked her for her work in helping the wounded, and asked her to carry on with the good work. Thereafter, he shook her by the hand and carried on with his stroll around the garden. After this interview, she neither saw nor heard of the Führer again. When he spoke to her he seemed depressed, but otherwise quite normal. On the 1st May, Druesedau escaped with some walking wounded, walking via the underground railway tunnels. Later she walked to Rathenau, and there met an old friend of hers who was an SS guard on the Bunker door which belonged to the Führer. This man was named either Linge or Linker and came from Westphalia.
>
> 'He claimed to have been on guard when Hitler shot himself, and to have seen the body wrapped in a blanket. Unfortunately, Druesedau has no real name or whereabouts of this man. The man gave the date when he [Hitler] shot himself as 29th April. Although the Bunker was packed with SS at the time, Druesedau can think of no names or addresses of persons who could give further information.'

Friday, 25 January
Erich Kempka
SS-Obersturmbannführer Kempka's statement of 20 June 1945: HQ Military intelligence Service Centre – labelled 'TOP SECRET'.

SS-Obersturmbannführer Erich Kempka served as Hitler's primary chauffeur from 1934 to April 1945. He was present in the area of the Reich Chancellery on 30 April 1945 when Hitler shot himself in the Führerbunker. Kempka delivered petrol to the garden behind the Reich Chancellery, where the remains of Hitler and Eva Braun were burned.

Kempka's Statement, 20 June 1945
Kempka was questioned over the circumstances of his arrest and his report of 20 June 1945. Kempka was arrested during the night of 19/20 June and was interrogated by Berchtesgaden CIC; the morning interrogation was conducted by a CIC agent in the presence of two newspaper reporters – Mr Fleischer and Mr Hus – and a German photographer, Amtagerichtsrat Hergesell. In the afternoon, he was interrogated by the CIC agent alone. On the basis of those two interrogations, a report was prepared. About two weeks later, the report was presented to Kempka by a CIC captain in five white and one pink copies for his signature at the CIC office at Hotel Jahreszeiten. Kempka signed the white copies. He was not aware of any formality which would have indicated that the report was notarized; he believed that the stenographer signed the report in order to certify the accuracy of the notes taken and the transcript prepared by him.

During his interrogations, Kempka stated that Gerhardt Herrgesell used to work as a stenographer in the Reichskanzlei and he left Berlin on 22 April 1945.

Kempka also said he saw SS-Gruppenführer Heinrich Müller once between 25 and 28 April at the Reichskanzlei in connection with the Fegelein case. He never saw Müller there before or after that time. Kempka stated that he saw two pistols lying on the floor in Hitler's room: one in front of the sofa and another to the right of it. He did not describe them in any detail as regards their make or calibre.

Additional Information Obtained from Artur Axmann
Axmann confirmed that Otto Günsche was the person who brought the news of Hitler's death to the assembled people in the Lage Vorzimmer, apparently having come from Hitler's private room. Questioned whether Hitler had shot himself in the right temple (as Axmann had stated previously) or through the mouth (as other reports claimed), Axmann repeated that Hitler had

shot himself through the right temple. He saw most of the blood on Hitler's right temple and on the right side of the face, although there were also some traces of blood on the left-hand side of the face. The lower jaw was sagging and slightly protruding, which, in Axmann's opinion, possibly created the impression of a shot through the mouth. Axmann stated, however, that there were no signs of a bullet having left the back of the head, which would have been probable in the case of a shot through the mouth. Axmann stated that he did not notice any pistols in the room, although he remembered having later heard some talk about two pistols. When asked again about the exact position of the two bodies, he stated that Hitler was sitting at one end of the sofa (the left end from the viewpoint of the observer), leaning slightly to the outside. Eva Braun's body was to Hitler's left, towards the middle of the sofa, leaning against Hitler's body.

Willi Otto Mueller
Mueller was found to have been employed as a tailor in the Führerhauptquartiere over a period of fourteen months and was in the bunker at the time of Hitler's death.

Mueller stated that he was 'well informed' of Hitler's death. He dismissed all the current stories as groundless rumours. His knowledge came from the fact that up until Hitler's death, Mueller was in direct contact with the Führer. As far as Hitler's death was concerned, Mueller claimed that in the last days of April 1945, when the situation for Berlin and the Führer Headquarters was extremely critical, Fegelein – one of the closest colleagues and a 'relative' of Hitler – was ordered to lead Wenck's Army from the west, and Steiner's Army from the north, for the relief of Berlin. Fegelein, who personally did not report to Hitler and had already aroused distrust because of this, was caught sabotaging his orders and was immediately condemned to death by Hitler and executed. Mueller personally observed this and also learned about events from Eva Braun, when 'she was talking to some high officers'.

Fegelein's treason had caused Hitler to collapse completely. His execution, according to Mueller, took place on 28 or 29 April. Mueller felt that Hitler's belief he could no longer trust anyone and the fact that he did not wish to fall into the hands of the Russians under any circumstances led him to decide to commit suicide.

Mueller said that Hitler – apparently to justify to some extent before the world his commitment to Eva Braun – married her on 29 April at 2.00 am. He said the marriage was performed by the state secretary, Dr Naumann, and on the same night Hitler said goodbye to all those present and went to his private living quarters. Mueller did not see Hitler's farewell as he was on duty at the guard post in the watchtower next to the emergency exit from the Führer's shelter.

Mueller added that because too much noise was being made in the bunker, a command came from the Führer's apartment that people must be more quiet. What particularly struck Mueller when he returned to the shelter was that Gruppenführer Rattenhuber slapped him on the back and said good evening to him as if he was a high-ranking officer, asking about conditions outside. It was the first time that Mueller had ever heard a high-ranking officer say good evening. He noticed that the mood had completely changed. Theo Koch, who was employed in the Führerhauptquartiere, informed Mueller that Hitler intended to shoot himself. Hitler had given this order to the head of the Gestapo, Heinrich Müller. During the following morning, Mueller saw three picks and three shovels leaning against the wall on the first floor by the watchtower. It was clear to him that those tools had been put there to dig a hole for the cremation of Hitler's body. It was already known that Hitler had given the command that his body was to be burned so that not the smallest bit would remain and nothing would fall into the hands of the enemy.

Mueller said that at about 4.30 pm on 30 April, Feldwebel Fritz Tornow, who was Hitler's personal dog handler and was very close to the Führer, told him that Hitler was dead. However, he was told that Hitler had not been shot but poisoned. Mueller noticed the same odour in Hitler's apartment as two days previously, when Hitler's dog, Blondi, had been killed with poison. Mueller thought that the last time he saw Hitler in the shelter was 28 April. His impression was that Hitler was in a state of complete collapse. He did not see Hitler's body, but he thought it must have been in a hole dug between the emergency entrance of the shelter and the watchtower. Mueller's belief that Hitler's body must have been burned was strengthened by the fact that he saw five men with ten petrol cans going towards the indicated spot at about 5.00 pm on 30 April. He thought that Eva Braun must have been disposed of in the same way as her husband.

Mueller said the events that followed caused such panic that no one was interested any longer in the details concerning the disposal of the bodies. It was a case of *sauve qui peut* (run for your life). Mueller believed that the Führer and Eva Braun had been killed with a lethal injection by Hitler's private physician, Dr Stumpfegger, an SS-Standartenführer who was at the time the only doctor present in the Führer's coterie. Mueller had heard Hitler express the opinion that in the event of the worst, he would kill himself and the wounded by injection. The preparations for this had already been made. Present at the killing, according to Mueller, would have been Heinrich Müller and Hitler's personal servant, Linge.

Tuesday, 5 March
Erika Treutler
The Intelligence Bureau (IB) wanted to interrogate Erika Treutler, who in September 1944 had volunteered as a chambermaid at the Berghof in Berchtesgaden on a salary of 45 Reichmarks per month. She had helped to clean the personal rooms of Hitler, Eva Braun and others. In June 1945, she was employed as a waitress at the Holiday Inn, Velden am Wörthersee.

The IB wanted her interrogated regarding who had arrived at the Berghof during the last week of April 1945. It was known that Hitler originally intended to arrive at Berchtesgaden on 20 April but subsequently postponed his decision. However, on the night of 22/23 April, an aeroplane left Berlin for Berchtesgaden containing Dr Morell, Admiral von Puttkammer, two of Hitler's secretaries – Frl Wolf and Frl Schroeder – and his stenographers, Herrgesell and Hagen. However, did these people proceed to the Berghof?

Saturday, 9 March
The events concerning Hitler's death had by now been fairly well substantiated from a number of independent sources, with only a few loose ends remaining.

The chief points outstanding were:

(1) The burning and disposal of the bodies.
(2) The fate of Bormann.

It was felt it was only worth interrogating actual eyewitnesses of the events from 29 April to 2 May.

The following principal witnesses had still not been located:

(i) Frau Junge, Hitler's secretary. She was last seen on 3 May near Havelberg.
(ii) Ambassador Walther Hewel, who had been in the bunker to the end.
(iii) Dr Naumann of the Propaganda Ministry, who left the bunker with Bormann.
(iv) General Krebs, Chief of the General Staff. (It was later learned that he had committed suicide in the Führerbunker during the early hours of 2 May 1945, his body being disposed of by the Russians.)
(v) General Burgdorf, Hitler's Chief Military Adjutant. (It was later learned that he had also committed suicide in the Führerbunker on 2 May 1945.)

(vi)   Admiral Voss, Hitler's Naval adjutant.
(vii)   Hitler's pilots, Hans Baur and George Betz.
(viii) Sturmbannführer Günsche, Hitler's personal adjutant.
(ix)   Sturmbannführer Linge, Hitler's personal servant, who was present in the Führerbunker when Hitler committed suicide.
(x)   Members of the SS-Begleitkommando on duty in the bunker.
(xi)   Members of the RSD Dienstelle (Department).
(xii)   Oberfeldwebel Werner Pardau, chief clerk in the bunker.
(xiii) Professor Stumpfegger, Hitler's personal doctor. It was claimed, by Axmann, that Stumpfegger and Bormann were killed in Berlin on the night of 1/2 May.
(xiv)   Günther Schwägermann, secretary to Goebbels.
(xv)   Professor Dr Brigadeführer Alwin-Broder Albrecht, adjutant to Hitler.
(xvi)   Professor Dr Haase, Medical Officer in Hitler's adjutants office.
(xvii) Frl Manziarly, Hitler's cook.

Saturday, 4 May
American newspapers quoted a British Intelligence officer who stated that Hitler's body had been identified by dental surgeons and that this fact had been known to the Russians for some time.

Chapter Five

Hitler's Background, and his Physical and Psychological State

Hitler's Early Life

Was Hitler born a despot, a brutal tyrant, or did he adopt these characteristics? To try to gain an insight as to the Führer's personality, it is worth investigating one man who knew him closely for five years – Karl Wilhelm Krause.

Krause was a Waffen-SS officer who rose to the rank of SS-Hauptsturmführer. He was a personal orderly and bodyguard to Hitler from 1934 until mid-September 1939, and was thus a close witness during a key period in the Nazi dictator's rise to power, seeing at first-hand the personal preferences and foibles of the man behind the Holocaust. Historian Roger Moorhouse noted that Krause 'was perhaps as close to his master as anyone would get: waking him in the morning, serving him breakfast, managing his wardrobe and travelling with him wherever he went'.

The following excerpts are from Krause's eyewitness account of the time:

'Here is a question many people asked themselves: why didn't Hitler get married? What I can state here is that Hitler certainly did not hate women. Proof of this are the many actresses who were invited during the early years to afternoon and evening performances. Often, during our travels, he would suddenly be totally enchanted, exclaiming, "My God, isn't that a beautiful girl (a beautiful woman)." He then turned around, making me, who was behind him, move to the side so that he had an unrestricted view behind him and could follow the lady with his gaze. If, in any given place, an exceptionally beautiful girl would catch his eye, Brückner [Hitler's chief adjutant] more often than not had to find out her address. After that, the lady was invited for coffee, either to Munich, Berlin or on the Obersalzberg, just so that Hitler could have a chat with her. In the earlier years, he also often joined members of the KDDK [Kameradschaft der Deutschen Künstler, the Fellowship of

German Artists] when they gathered after performances in the theatre and opera houses.'

'Rumours about Leni Riefenstahl [a German dancer, actress and film director, best known for her imposing propaganda films in support of the Nazi Party], and Frau Winifred Wagner [English-born wife of Siegfried Wagner, who served as Hitler's personal translator during treaty negotiations with Britain; Winifred remained personally faithful to Hitler but denied that she had ever supported the Nazi Party] bore no substance. He certainly respected Leni Riefenstahl because she was an ambitious woman who, based on remarkable commitment, had put together the films on the Party convention days, and the Olympic Games. "A woman has more sensitivity for this whole thing than a man," Hitler once said, referring to Riefenstahl. And he revered Frau Wagner as the bearer of the Wagnerian legacy, but marriage was never a likely possibility. They certainly were close, however. I was once present during a private conversation between Frau Wagner and Hitler where he mentioned that he was thinking of dissolving the Party. His reason was that for the sake of the unity of the German people, no difference should be made between Party and non-Party members, and they should all be on equal footing.

'Frau Wagner was very surprised to hear this and asked him to consider what his old Party comrades would say to such a decision. This is just an example of their frank relationship.'

'He was overjoyed when the BDM [Bund Deutscher Mädel, the League of German Girls] came out to openly celebrate him during his trips, and he went out of his way to treat them as being very special. They received gifts of money from him of two to ten Reichsmarks per head with the words: "Why don't you extend your stay for a little bit", or "Coffee and cake are on me", and so forth. All that was simply a reflection of his appreciation of beauty. If an especially attractive actress performed in an opera or play on stage (and provided she was also talented), he asked to be introduced to her at the end of the event. Among the film actresses he especially liked were Olga Tschechova and Brigitte Horney.

'What Hitler didn't care for was women who got involved in politics. While he conceded that women had achieved big things, he stood firm in his opinion that politics was exclusively to be left to men. This is how he explained his status of remaining unmarried; his principle was that every married partner should lead a decent family life. This was, however, not something he himself could ever offer, considering the colossal amount of work he had to cope with. He would only come home late at nights, and a wife and family would have nothing to gain from him. At most – if he were married with children in real life – they could perhaps have a chat about him. That was his reason to remain unmarried.

'Sometimes he made reference to his wartime activities and said that it was a good thing he hadn't been married at the time, as "the wave of enthusiasm [he] received mostly came from women". He didn't believe that, had he been married, he would have garnered so much support. "Just based on instinct alone, females are more inclined to be attracted to (single) men."'

'How Close was it to Not Being 'Heil Hitler' but Being 'Heil Schicklgruber'?
Adolf Hitler was born 20 April 1889 in Braunau, west of Linz in northern Austria. He could easily have been called Adolf Schicklgruber or Adolf Hiedler; his father, Alois, was born the illegitimate son of Maria Anna Schicklgruber and was given her surname. Adolf was Alois's fifth child, the third of his own mother (Alois's third wife) but the first to live more than two years.

When he was aged about 40, Alois decided to adopt the last name of his stepfather, Johann Georg Hiedler, who some speculated was actually his biological father. On the legal documents, Hitler was given as the new last name, though the reason for the spelling change is unknown. Alois Hitler was married twice and had several children before taking Klara Pölzl, a distant cousin, as his third wife. The couple had six children, though only Adolf and a sister reached adulthood. Adolf had a difficult relationship with his father, who died in 1903, but adored his mother and was reportedly grief-stricken when she died from breast cancer in December 1907.

According to an inquiry ordered by the Austrian Chancellor, Engelbert Dollfuss, Maria Anna Schicklgruber became pregnant while in the employ as a servant to a Jewish-Viennese family. As a result, she was sent back to her home in the country. If true, Alois Hitler may well have been half-Jewish. The fact that he selected a Jew, Herr Prinz of Vienna, to be Adolf's godfather would lend support to that hypothesis. What was known was that Alois was illegitimate and made to suffer the contempt of the little community of Spital, where he was raised.

Alois was a cobbler, but by the age of 40 had improved his status when he achieved the position of an Austrian customs official. For a time, he patrolled the German–Austrian border, and he was known as the 'man-hunter'. As part of his job, he wore a uniform, his badge of status and carried a gun. He was very proud of his position, believing that it entitled him to lord it over the class that once scorned him. It was said that he frequented the local pubs; he was a coarse man who would boast and swear, and would recount his accomplishments to anyone who would listen. He was also a womanizer.

Because of Alois's age – twenty-three years older than his wife – his social status and his over-weaning pride, he maintained a master–servant relationship with his wife. At home he was a tyrant.

Not surprisingly, Frau Hitler was mild, submissive, an inordinately lenient woman who was devoted to her family. As far as Adolf was concerned, Alois was stern, harsh and unusually severe; beatings of the young Adolf were frequent. Alois seemed to have looked upon his son as a good-for-nothing, a moonstruck dreamer and a weakling.

Adolf himself was timid and submissive in his father's presence, but away from his father's immense authority he could be unruly, quarrelsome, stubborn and defiant. He smoked cigarettes and cigar stubs from the gutter or obtained from roisterers in the bars.

At the age of 11 or 12, Adolf committed a serious sexual indiscretion with a little girl. For this he was punished but not expelled from his school.

February 1908: Down and Out in Vienna

Hitler dreamt of a career as an artist. His father had rejected the idea, but after he died in 1903 Hitler would try to make his dream a reality.

He applied to the Vienna Academy of Fine Arts but was promptly rejected in October 1907. Shortly afterwards, Hitler's beloved mother died. He then moved to Vienna and scratched a precarious bohemian existence sleeping in hostels and painting postcards. Here he began to develop many of the views which would later characterize his ideology and desire to unite Germany and Austria. The anti-Semitic politics of Vienna's mayor, Karl Lueger, were particularly influential.

Hitler's Development and Personality
August 1914: Fighting for the Fatherland

Hitler hated the multi-ethnic composition of Austria's ruling Habsburg Empire. Determined to avoid military service, he moved to Munich in 1913.

Hitler was keen to prove his loyalty to Germany. In August 1914, the world plunged into a war unlike any seen before. Hitler quickly enlisted. In the German Army, he finally found purpose, a cause with which he could wholly identify. Serving in both France and Belgium as a runner, he was twice decorated for bravery and was promoted to corporal. In 1916, Hitler was wounded at the Somme, one of the bloodiest battles of the war. Convalescing in Germany, he affected his distinctive toothbrush moustache.

November 1918: 'Stabbed in the Back'

Hitler was wounded for a second time following a British gas attack in October 1918. While recovering in Pasewalk, the unthinkable happened – Germany surrendered.

Before the surrender, facing serious discontent at home and the prospect of defeat at the front, Germany's High Command sought to shift the blame. The majority parties in the Reichstag were handed a poisoned chalice: they were given more power but implicated in the impending defeat. Kaiser Wilhelm II abdicated days before the Armistice. Like others, Hitler was enraged by what he saw as the betrayal of an undefeated German Army by Jews and socialists at home. He thus resolved to go into politics.

June 1919: Treaty of Versailles

To the victor came the spoils, and when the Treaty of Versailles was signed in summer 1919, Germany was forced to accept sole responsibility for the war.

Just as damagingly, the peace obliged Germany to pay large amounts in reparations. The huge loss of territory it also dictated came as a further devastating blow. Hitler bitterly resented the loss of German territories. Defeat and then humiliation at Versailles challenged his whole sense of worth. Nevertheless, still in the army, Hitler was sent to report on an emerging far-right group, the German Workers' Party (which was soon renamed the National Socialist German Workers' Party, or NSDAP, becoming better known as the Nazi Party). Finding that he agreed with their nationalist, anti-Semitic beliefs, he joined them.

July 1921: Der Führer

Hitler's oratory skills helped him rise quickly through the ranks of his new party. In February 1921, he spoke before a crowd of nearly 6,000 in Munich. To publicize the meeting, he engaged in propaganda tactics, sending out party supporters in trucks adorned with swastikas to leaflet the area. However, the party executive, including founder Anton Drexler, were uneasy at Hitler's growing popularity. In an effort to weaken his position, they formed an alliance with a socialist group while Hitler was in Berlin visiting other nationalist parties. It backfired spectacularly: Hitler promptly resigned and rejoined only when he was handed sole control, acquiring the title of Der Führer.

November 1923: Beer Hall Putsch

Germany's Weimar Republic government was on the brink of collapse in 1923, with hyperinflation seeing the price of a loaf of bread rise from 250 marks to 200 billion marks by November that year.

Sensing an opportunity, Hitler sought to start a revolution. On 8 November, Bavarian Prime Minister Gustav Kahr addressed a meeting of businessmen at a beer hall in Munich. Hitler burst in with his storm troopers (the SA), a motley crew of far-right paramilitaries. At gunpoint, Kahr was forced to pledge his support for the Nazis. The next day, Hitler led 3,000 supporters onto the streets, but the police were waiting for them. In the ensuing violence, sixteen Nazis and three policemen died. Hitler was arrested and sentenced to five years in prison for treason.

Despite his conviction, he was out of jail before the end of 1924, his political position stronger than ever. He had used his time behind bars to pen *Mein Kampf*, his ideological manifesto which later became a best-seller after Hitler's rise to power.

October 1943
Langer's and Murray's Wartime OSS Reports

During the Second World War, the Allies wanted to understand Hitler's psychological make-up in order to predict his behaviour as they continued their prosecution of the war and to anticipate his response to a German defeat.

The US wartime intelligence agency, the Office of Strategic Studies (OSS, predecessor of the CIA), was quietly confident regarding the eventual outcome of the war and was possibly preparing for an 'exit strategy', as far as Hitler and the German people were concerned. They wanted to know the psyche of Hitler, and consequently that of the German people. On behalf of the OSS, Dr Henry A. Murray, MD, of the Harvard Psychological Clinic, Cambridge, Massachusetts, and W.H.D. Vernon, of Harvard University, issued reports entitled 'Analysis of the personality of Adolf Hitler with predictions of his future behaviour and suggestions for dealing with him now and after Germany's surrender' and 'Hitler the man – notes for a case history'. Obviously, their reports were compiled at a distance and not on a face-to-face basis with the psychologists and their subject.

Vernon and Murray's reports had three main aims:

(1) To present an analysis of Adolf Hitler's personality with a hypothetical formulation of the manner of its development.
(2) On that basis of the above, to make various predictions as to Hitler's conduct when confronted by the mounting successes of the Allies.
(3) To offer some suggestions as to how the US Government might influence Hitler's mental condition and behaviour (assuming it saw fit to do so) and might deal with him, if taken into custody after Germany's surrender.

The document stated:

> 'The proper interpretation of Hitler's personality is important as a step in understanding the psychology of the typical Nazi, and – since the typical Nazi exhibits a trait that has, for a long time, been prevalent among Germans – as a step in understanding the psychology of the German people. Hitler's unprecedented appeal, the elevation of this man to a demi-god can be explained only by the hypothesis that he and his ideology have almost met the needs and longings of the majority of Germans.
>
> 'The attainment of a clear impression of the German people is essential if, after surrender, they are to be converted into a peace-loving nation that is willing to take its proper place in a world society.'

Identification with his Father

According to Vernon, it was evident that, consciously or unconsciously, Adolf Hitler imitated many of his father's traits and none of his mother's. His will for power, aggressiveness, and cult of brutality were all in keeping with what was known of the personality and conduct of Alois. Moreover, Adolf's declaration that he demanded nothing but sacrifices from his adherents was reminiscent of his father's attitude toward his family.

The father's loud, boastful and perhaps drunken talk were said to have provided Adolf with an 'impressive' model for emulation.

Hitler sported a walrus moustache – just as his father had – for a number of years. He eventually trimmed it to the one that he would forever be associated with.

It was said that Alois had a great respect for the class system and was proud of his rise in status; he envied those above him and looked down on those below him. Vernon stated that if this was true, Alois was instrumental in establishing a pattern of sentiments which was of determining importance in his son's political career. Adolf Hitler had always been envious of his superiors and was deferential; he never showed affinity with the proletariat.

A picture of his father hung over Hitler's desk at Berchtesgaden. This was indeed an honour, since only the likenesses of three other men – Frederick the Great, Karl von Moltke and Mussolini – had been selected for inclusion in any of Hitler's rooms. Nowhere was there a picture of his mother.

The figure of power admired by Hitler was marked by courage, military valour, brutality and absence of sympathy of compassion. He regarded humane feelings as a weakness.

Repudiation of Past Self and Family Connections

Vernon noted that knowing Hitler's fanatical resentment against mixed marriages, impure blood, the lower classes and the Jewish race, it was important to record the following:

> 'His forebears came from a region in which the blood of Bavarians, Bohemians, Moravians, Czechs and Slovakians have mixed for generations. Without doubt all of these strains are represented in him.
>
> 'His father was illegitimate; his grandfather may have been a Viennese Jew.
>
> 'His godfather, Herr Prinz, was a Viennese Jew.
>
> 'His father had three wives, one a waitress, one a domestic servant, and a number of women on the side (hearsay).
>
> 'His father begot at least one child out of marriage.
>
> 'Klara Poelzl, his mother, was Alois Hitler's second cousin once removed and also his ward [and she was] twenty three years younger [than Alois]. Special permission from the church had to be obtained before he could marry her.
>
> 'Angela Hitler, Adolf's older half-sister, ran a restaurant for Jewish students in Vienna.
>
> 'Paula Hitler, Adolf's younger sister, was the mistress of a Viennese Jew for a while.
>
> 'A cousin of Hitler's was feeble-minded; most of the other members of his clan are ignorant, illiterate or mentally retarded. He himself had to repeat the first year of Realschule [Technical High School] and failed to graduate.'

Consequently, Vernon argued, Hitler spent time cursing and condemning people who belonged to his layer of society, people who resembled members of his own clan and who had characteristics similar to his own.

The dossier predicted possible finales for the Führer, including going insane, sacrificing himself in battle, contriving to be killed by a German or Jewish assassin or committing suicide: 'Hitler has often vowed that he would commit suicide if his plans miscarried; but if he chooses this course he will do it at the last moment and in the most dramatic possible manner ... For us [the Allies] it would be an undesirable outcome.'

Dr Murray, meanwhile, predicted that because Hitler's chief concern was the immortality of his legend, he would endeavour to plan his own end according to the most heroic, tragic and dramatic pattern.

114 Hitler's Last Days

Murray recommended that up until the cessation of hostilities, the aim should be to accelerate Hitler's mental deterioration or to prevent him from ensuring the perpetuation of his legend by ending his life in sensational fashion.

Vernon further claimed that Hitler's energies would never have been fully involved if it had not been for Germany's defeat and collapse in the Second World War. He believed that the critical point for Hitler, what gave his political convictions sufficient stimulus, came when, in October 1918, he lay in a German military hospital having been temporarily blinded by a British gas shell and made a vow to reinstate his fallen motherland.

Need for Sex
A large number of observers of Hitler have concluded that he was asexual – not involving himself in sexual activity or feelings. It was generally said that Germany was his beloved – his mother, his wife – and that when he addressed the masses, whom he thought of as feminine, he was courting, appealing to, complaining to and arousing the woman of his heart.

It is interesting to note that Hitler – according to one informant – was in the police records in Vienna as a sexual pervert.

Femininity, Passive Homosexuality, Masochism
Vernon wrote that the hypothesis of Hitler's identification on a physical, erotic level called for a strain of feminism, combined with a trend of passive homosexuality.

Regarding feminine traits in the Führer, Vernon recorded:

'His sentimentality, his emotionality, his shrieking at the climax of his speeches, his artistic inclinations, his sudden collapses, his occasional softness, these are all typical not so much of a woman as of a woman in a man.'

On Hitler's identification with his mother, Vernon said:

'Hitler believed that he was going to die young from a major illness like cancer, as did his mother, which suggested an underlying empathetic relationship.'

Vernon had the following to say about Hitler's attraction to homosexuals:

'He was attracted to homosexuals, followed by their murder. It was known that Hitler had a special admiration for Ernst Röhm [German Army officer and chief organiser of Adolf Hitler's Storm Troopers, and feared as a rival by the Führer]. It is unclear whether it was Röhm or Hitler himself responsible for attracting such a large number of homosexuals to the Nazi party, but what was known was that after two or three months of anxiety and delusions that Röhm and his fellow homosexuals were planning to usurp power, Hitler had them all murdered in the purge of 1934 [the 'Night of the Long Knives'].

Homosexual Panic
Some of Hitler's nightmares described by several informants were very suggestive of homosexual panic. Hermann Rauschning, a German Conservative revolutionary, was known for his book *Gespräche mit Hitler* (*Conversations with Hitler*), in which he claimed to have had many meetings and conversations with the Führer. Rauschning wrote:

> 'Hitler wakes at night with convulsive shrieks. He shouts for help. He sits on the edge of his bed, as if unable to stir. He shakes with fear, making the whole bed vibrate. He shouts confused, totally unintelligible phrases. He gasps, as if imagining himself to be suffocating ... Hitler stood swaying in his room, looking wildly about him. "He! Ho! He's been here!" he gasped. His lips were blue. Sweat streamed down his face. Suddenly he began to reel off figures, add odd words and broken phrases, entirely devoid of sense ... then he suddenly broke out, "There, there! In the corner! Who's that?" He stamped and shrieked in a familiar way.'

Hitler also had a fear of being poisoned by some deathly powder sprinkled on his bedclothes. His bed therefore had to be made up in a particular way by a woman, never by a man.

Narcisensitivity
Vernon described Hitler's narcisensitivity (being narcissistically sensitive) as his having the following features: low tolerance, belittlement, deprecation, criticism, mockery, sense of failure, inability to take a joke, tendency to harbour grudges and not forgetting or forgiving.

Reinhold Hanisch, an Austrian migrant worker, first met Hitler before the First World War in a Viennese dosshouse. On his very first day there, sat next to the bed that had been allotted to Hanisch was a man who had nothing on except an old torn pair of trousers; the man was Hitler. His clothes were being cleaned of lice, since for days he had been wandering about Vienna without a roof and in a terribly neglected condition. The two men became friends.

Hanisch recalled: 'Hitler could never stand any criticism of his paintings ... Hitler could not stand to be contradicted. He would get furious. He couldn't restrain himself; he would scream and fidget with his hands.'

These characteristics in Hitler were echoed by Hermann Rauschning: 'He [Hitler] looked round apprehensively and suspiciously, with searching glances at us. I had the impression that he wanted to see if anyone was laughing.'

Recognition (Self-Exhibition)
Vernon wrote:

> 'Hitler's appearance at meetings and rallies are dramatised to the fullest extent. He is careful to have electric lights shining on him in such a way to produce the most striking effect possible, etc etc. However, one gets the impression the exhibitionism is limited to talking before a crowd – at which times it is extreme – but that ordinarily he is self-conscious and ill at ease, and does not particularly enjoy showing himself in public, although he must do this to maintain his power.'

Autonomy
Hitler was unruly as a youth, intolerant of frustration. After his father died, he was given his own way, and after leaving school became increasingly resistant to rules and regulations. Consequently, he was not able to hold down a job. He wanted to be an artist and live like a bohemian. Vernon placed him high on the autonomous variable, although in Hitler it did not take its usual form – defensive individualism – due to his political ambitions; Hitler needed the alliance of the masses.

In *Mein Kampf*, Hitler wrote: 'The thought of being a slave in an office made me ill; not to be a master of my own time, but to force an entire life-time into the filling in of forms.'

In many respects, Hitler was deficient, especially in the practices of orderly administration. However, he was capable of finding sufficient skill among his adherents and making them work for him regardless of their failings in other respects.

Konrad Heiden, a journalist who worked for Frankfurter Zeitung and the Vossischen Zeitung, suggested that the Führer needed to be educated in systematic work. To this purpose, an officer was selected to act as Hitler's secretary, to map out the day's work according to the clock and in general to introduce order and a programme into the Führer's day. When Hitler heard of this, he banged his fist on the table and shouted: 'Who do those fellows think they are? I shall go my own way, as I see fit.' He did, however, accept the secretary.

Rejection
Hitler distrusted anyone who tried to explain political economy to him. He believed that the intention was to dupe him, and he made no secret of this. Hitler wrote: 'My mind was tormented by the question, are these still human beings, worthy of being part of a great nation? A torturing question it was … it brought me internal happiness to realise definitely that the Jew was no German … armed in one's mind with confidence in the dear Lord and the unshakeable stupidity of the bourgeois.'

Defendance (Defending one's Self-Esteem Verbally)
Hitler's prime method of defending his status was by blaming others. For example, he stated:

> 'If we committed high treason, then countless others did the same. I deny all guilt so long added to our little company those gentlemen who helped [sic]. I believe that as a National Socialist I appear in the eyes of many bourgeois democrats as only a wild man. But as a wild man I still believe in myself to be a better European.'

Almost all psychologists who have analyzed Hitler's personality – by referring, among others, to Alfred Adler, an Austrian medical doctor who emphasized the importance of inferiority and the inferiority complex – have found that his craving for superiority came out of unbearable feelings of inferiority.

Rauschning, for example, wrote:

> 'Every conversation, however unimportant, seemed to show that this man was filled with immeasurable hatred. Hatred of what? It was not easy to say. Almost anything might inflame wrath and his hatred. He seemed always the need of something to hate … Hatred – personal hatred – rang out in his words, revenge for early years of poverty, for disappointed hopes, for a life of depravation and humiliation.'

And according to Heiden:

> 'Anyone acquainted with the unhappy life of this lonely man knows why hatred and persecution mania guided his first political footsteps. In his heart he nursed a grudge against the world, and he vented it on innocent

and guilty alike. His cracking voice, his jerking gait, and his sawing gestures expressed a hatred of which all who saw him were conscious.'

Cathexis (Unhealthy Concentration of Mental Energy on One Subject) for the Hitler Youth
Hitler was quoted by Rauschning as having said the following about members of the HJ:

'But my magnificent youngsters! Are there finer ones anywhere in the world? Look at these young men and boys! What material! With them I can make a new world … how did the eyes of my boys shine when I made clear to them the necessity of their mission … vanity in a beautiful, well shaped body (to be encouraged by men wearing less concealing clothes).'

Negative Cathexis of Weakness
Vernon declared that Hitler's sentiments in this category were the natural complement of his high positive cathexis for power. Hitler himself would later state:

'A stronger generation will drive out the weaklings, because in its ultimate form the urge will again and again break the ridiculous fetters of a so-called "humanity" of the individual, so that its place will be taken by the "humanity" of nature, which destroys weakness in order to give its place to strength.

'… these upper layers [of intellectuals] lack the necessary will power. For will power is always weaker in these secluded intellectual circles than in the masses of the primitive people.

'… the Jewish Christ-Creed with its effeminate petty-ethics.

'Anybody who is such a poltroon that he can't bear the thought of someone nearby having to suffer pain had better join a sewing-circle, but not my party comrades.

'Unless you are prepared to be pitiless, you will get nowhere. Our opponents are not prepared for it, not because they are humane … but because they are too weak.'

His father, Alois, was understood to be a smoker, a drinker and a lecher; Adolf was remarkable for his abstemiousness, so in those respects the two were quite different. However, it should not be forgotten that, as a young man, Hitler junior had picked up cigar butts and smoked them. He drank beer and wine in his early Munich days, and later in his life he showed a good deal of interest in women.

There was no doubt that Hitler greatly admired and envied the power and authority of his father. Although he hated his father as the tyrant who opposed and frustrated him, he still looked upon him with awe and admiration, desiring to be like him. Adolf confessed: 'unconsciously he had sown the seeds for a future which neither he nor I would have grasped at that time.'

Vernon proposed that one of the most potent impressions of Hitler's early life was that of a relationship in which a domineering and severe old man (his father) bullied and scornfully maltreated a gentle, compliant woman (his mother). The effects of being reared under these conditions were lasting; the experience made it impossible for him to believe in, hope for or enjoy a relationship marked by peace, love and tenderness.

Schizophrenic Features and Sanity
Hitler was possessed by a complete semi-delusional system of paranoid schizophrenia. It must be acknowledged that conditions in Germany had been such and his success in imposing his delusional system on his fellow countrymen had been so phenomenal that he remained within the bounds of technical sanity.

Dr Henry Murray claimed that Hitler exhibited classical symptoms of a paranoid schizophrenic: hypersensitivity, panics of anxiety, irrational jealousy, delusions of persecution, delusions of omnipotence and having a messiah complex. Murray felt that the possibility of a complete mental breakdown was not a remote one. He predicted that Hitler's neurosis would increase in frequency and duration, and his effectiveness as a leader would diminish. Murray claimed there was some evidence that his mental powers had deteriorated since November 1942.

Hitler May Go Insane
Vernon wrote the following regarding the possibility of Hitler being insane and its effect upon wartime Germany:

> 'He has the make-up of a paranoid schizophrenic, and the load of frustration and failure that is coming to him may crack his will to the turbulent forces of his unconscious. This is not undesirable; because, even if the truth be kept hidden from people, the greatest source of strength in Germany will be removed from the scene of action, and morale will rapidly deteriorate as rumours spread. Furthermore, the legend of the hero will be severely damaged by such an outcome. There is no good

historical evidence of the deification of a military or political leader who was defeated and went insane. Finally, if Hitler became insane, he would presumably fall into the hands of the Allied Nations, and this, as I shall argue, would be the most desirable possible outcome.'

Superego

Hitler was not an amoral brute like Hermann Göring or the majority of his close followers. He did have a superego, but it was repressed.

Vernon attributed a good many of Hitler's later acts of aggression to his superego. He believed that having once started on a career of brutality, the Führer could only stem the pain of a bad conscience by going on with even greater ruthlessness to achieve successes, and to demonstrate to himself and others that God approved of him in his methods.

Hitler not only saw himself as Germany's greatest strategist and war lord, but as the chosen instrument of God, the saviour of the German people and the founder of a new spiritual era which would endure for a thousand years. Indeed, Hitler often identified himself with Christ:

> 'Therefore, I believe today that I am acting in the sense of the Almighty Creator: by warding off the Jews I am fighting for the Lord's work.
>
> 'My feeling as a Christian points me to my Lord and saviour as a fighter. It points me to the man who once in loneliness, surrounded by only a few followers, recognized these Jews for what they were and summoned men to fight against them and who, God's truth! [*sic*] was greatest not as a sufferer but as a fighter.

Hitler's Need for Aggression and Sadism

As far as Hitler was concerned, the will for power was the central principle, fused with it being a vindictiveness which took pleasure in the painful humiliation of his adversaries. Hitler's ideology of power had been expressed in definite acts of aggression, particularly against weaker, helpless individuals and groups. Statements made by Hitler that were reported by Hermann Rauschning and Konrad Heiden (who as well as being a journalist was also a member of the German Social Democrat Party and remained an active opponent of Hitler) illustrate the precursors of Hitler's unprecedented brutality.

Heiden quoted Hitler as having said: 'There will be no peace in the land until a body is hanging from every lamp post.'

Rauschning, meanwhile, quoted the Führer as stating:

'I shall spread terror by the surprise employment of all my measures. But even if we could not conquer them, we should drag half the world into destruction with us, and leave no one to triumph over Germany. There will not be another 1918. We shall not surrender.'

Hitler's Attitude to Old Men
In *Mein Kampf* and his recorded conversations, Hitler spoke of old men in a derogatory and contemptuous manner, possibly suggestive of his sentiments to his elderly father.

Rauschning wrote: 'Everywhere, Hitler complained, there were nothing but sterile old men in their second childhood, who bragged of their technical knowledge and had lost their sound common sense.'

Heiden quoted the following comments by Hitler: 'My great adversary, Reichspräsident von Hindenburg, is today eighty-five years of age. I am forty-three and feel in perfect health. And nothing will happen to me, for I am clearly conscious of the great task which Providence has assigned to me.'

Hitler May Get Killed in Battle
Dr Henry Murray wrote of the Führer:

'At a critical moment Hitler may decide to lead his elite troops against Russians, exposing himself so that he will be killed, and so live in the hearts of his countrymen as a valiant hero.

'He is very likely to choose this course, most undesirable from our Allied point of view. It is undesirable, first, because his death will serve as an example to all his followers to fight with fanatical death-defying energy to the bitter end, and second, it will insure [sic] Hitler's immortality.'

Hitler May be Killed by a German
Hitler was most efficiently protected, and it was not likely that anyone would wilfully attempt to kill him. But he may have contrived to have someone, a half-crazed paranoid like himself, instigated to do the deed at some prearranged moment when he purposely exposed his person in public.

If he could have arranged to have a Jew kill him, then he could have died in the belief that his fellow countrymen would rise in their wrath and massacre every remaining Jew in Germany. Thus, he would get his ultimate revenge. This would be the most dastardly plan of all, and the most undesirable. It would increase the fanaticism of his soldiers and create a legend in conformity with the ancient pattern – Siegfried stabbed in the back by Hagan, Caesar by

Brutus, Christ betrayed by Judas – except that in Hitler's case, the murderer would not be a close follower.

Hitler May Commit Suicide
Hitler often vowed that he would commit suicide if his plans miscarried; but if he chose that course, Vernon noted, he would do it at the last moment and in the most dramatic manner.

Vernon also predicted that he may retreat to the impregnable fortress he had built for himself on the top of the mountain beyond the Berghof at Berchtesgaden. There, alone, he would wait until troops came to take him prisoner. As a climax, Vernon felt he could either blow up the mountain and himself with dynamite, make a funeral pyre of his retreat and throw himself upon it, kill himself with a silver bullet or possibly throw himself off the parapet. While this would not be unlikely, Vernon said it would have been an undesirable outcome for the Allies.

Teetotaller, Vegetarian and Drug User?
In attempting to build a master 'Aryan' race, the Nazis promoted health-conscious policies. So it is perhaps not surprising that Hitler was reportedly a teetotal, non-smoking vegetarian. However, his healthy habits were undermined by his alleged use of opiates. According to research, from 1941 his personal physician, Dr Theodor Gilbert Morell – who was well known in Germany for his unconventional treatments – assisted Hitler on a daily basis in virtually everything he did. Morell was beside the Führer until the last stages of the Battle of Berlin, injecting him with various drugs, which included oxycodone (an opiate painkiller), methamphetamine (a powerful, highly addictive stimulant that affects the central nervous system), morphine (a strong painkiller) and even cocaine (a powerfully addictive stimulant drug). Drug use was reportedly prevalent throughout the Nazi Party, and soldiers were often given methamphetamine before battle. Near the end of his life, Hitler was prone to shaking, and while some have attributed this to Parkinson's disease, others have speculated it was due to withdrawal from drugs which by then were hard to obtain.

In an uninspiring 240-page assessment, Dr Murray and his colleagues concluded that Hitler was insecure, impotent, masochistic and a suicidal neurotic narcissist who saw himself as 'the destroyer of an antiquated Hebraic Christian superego.' They continued:

> 'There is little disagreement among professional, or even among amateur, psychologists that Hitler's personality is an example of the counteractive

type, a type that is marked by intense and stubborn efforts (i) to overcome early disabilities, weaknesses and humiliations (wounds to self-esteem), and sometimes also by efforts (ii) to revenge injuries and insults to pride.'

The report also stated that Hitler had suffered from 'hysterical blindness' while he was a soldier in the First World War:

'This psychosomatic illness was concomitant with the final defeat of Mother Germany, and it was after hearing of her capitulation that he had his vision of his task as saviour. Suddenly his sight was restored.

'There was a dichotomy in Hitler's makeup. He admired brutal strength, had contempt of weakness, and worshipped physical force, military conquest and ruthless domination.'

Furthermore, he had many weaknesses. The report suggested that Hitler had a large feminine component in his constitution:

'As a child he was frail and sickly, emotionally dependent upon his mother. He never did any manual work, never engaged in athletics, and was turned down as forever unfit for conscription in the Austrian Army. Afraid of his father, his behaviour was outwardly submissive, and he was annoyingly subservient to his superior officers. After four years in the [German] army, he never rose above the rank of corporal. At the end he broke down with a war neurosis and hysterical blindness. Later, in all his glory, he suffered frequent emotional outbursts in which he yelled and wept. Sexually he was a fully fledged masochist.

'Hitler was not from noble stock; he came from illiterate peasant stock derived from a mixture of races, not a pure German among them. His father was illegitimate, married three times, and was sexually promiscuous. His mother was a domestic servant. It was considered that his father was a Jew, and it "is certain that his Godfather was a Jew". One of his sisters managed a restaurant for Jewish students in Vienna and another was, for a time, the mistress of a Jew.

'During his outcast days in Vienna, Hitler, sporting a long beard along with a long overcoat, given to him by a Jewish friend, made him look like a certain type of Oriental Jew, uncommon in Vienna at that time. His friend, Reinhold Hanisch, joked with Hitler that he must have Jewish blood, "since such a large beard rarely grows on a Christian's chin".'

According to Murray, Hitler was impotent. At the time the report was written, Hitler was unmarried, and his old acquaintances had testified that he could not consummate a sexual act 'in the normal fashion'. This infirmity was recognized as an instigation to exorbitant cravings for superiority. Unable to demonstrate male power through a woman, he was impelled to compensate by exhibiting unsurpassed power before men in the world at large.

Hitler could not change his origins or his potency, neither change himself physically nor change his origins, but for a while he became the most powerful individual in the world.

Murray felt that Hitler started his career as a nonentity with nothing to lose; he selected a fanatical path for himself which required as an ending either complete success (omnipotence) or utter failure (death). No compromise was possible. Since it was not him personally who was doing the fighting, his collapses could occur in private at Berchtesgaden, where he could recuperate, and then once again come back with some new and always more desperate plan to destroy the enemy. Hitler had a powerful compulsion to sacrifice himself and all of Germany to the revengeful annihilation of Western culture, to die while dragging all of Europe into the abyss.

Hitler and Anti-Semitism
Hitler's personal frustrations required a scapegoat as a focus for his repressed aggression. The Jew has often been seen as the classic scapegoat because they do not fight back with fists and weapons. Furthermore, there was a long history of widespread anti-Semitic sentiments in Europe.

That Hitler's hatred of Jews was of a more than usual pathological nature is suggested by the morbid connection he made between the Jew and disease: blood disease, syphilis and 'filthy excrescences of all sorts'. As far as Hitler was concerned, the Jew was not even a beast but a 'creature outside nature'. The Jew was at the root of all things evil, not only in Germany but elsewhere, and the Führer believed that only through their destruction could the world be saved.

As far as Vernon was concerned, Hitler possessed an inner emotional connection between sex, syphilis, blood impurity, Jewishness and the degeneration of pure, healthy and virile racial strains. Like his need for aggression, Hitler's fear of the tainting of blood was a major element in his personality structure.

The Jew was an object upon whom Hitler could suitability project his own inferior self-sensitiveness, weakness, timidity and masochistic sexuality. After the Versailles Treaty of June 1919, the German people also needed a scapegoat; Hitler offered them the Jewish race as an act of political strategy.

Having assembled a veritable army of gangsters – his Nazi stormtroopers – and aroused their fighting spirit, it was necessary for Hitler to find some object upon which these men could vent their brutish passions to divert their anger away from himself.

Hitler felt that Jews, being non-militaristic, could only impede his programme of conquest. In revealing that he wished to eliminate them, he lost no sizeable support in Germany.

Jews were associated with several of Hitler's pet antipathies: business, materialism, democracy, capitalism and communism. Some Jews were very rich, and Hitler needed an excuse for dispossessing them.

In his 1924 polemic *Mein Kampf*, Hitler wrote: 'Therefore, I believe today I am acting in the sense of the Almighty creator: by warding off the Jews I am fighting for the Lord's work.'

The Source of Hitler's Anti-Semitism

Vernon noted that anti-Semitism was part of the social milieu in which Hitler grew up. Vernon himself admitted that he avoided the only Jewish boy in his school.

While in Vienna as an aspiring artist, Hitler came into contact with violent anti-Semitic literature, and it is in this period that Hitler claimed that his deep-rooted hatred for the Jews was born.

Vernon suggested that there were certain psychological and cultural reasons for the strength of this pathological hatred of Jews. Vernon surmised the following list of possibilities: Hitler is a common Jewish name; in Vienna he was teased about his Jewish appearance; there was the mystery of Alois Hitler's true parentage – which Adolf may have known. Furthermore, many of the people who helped Hitler, who gave him food, who bought his paintings, were Jews; and to have to accept kindness from people he 'disliked' would not increase his love of them.

When Hitler came across his first conspicuously Jewish person in Vienna, he recorded: 'I suddenly came across a being clad in a long caftan, with black curls. Is this also a Jew was my first thought.' He then listed what he considered were the repellent traits of the Jew: 'Later the smell of these caftan wearers often made me ill. Added to this was their dirty clothes and their none-too-heroic appearance. Aside from the physical uncleanliness, it was repelling suddenly to discover the moral blemishes of the chosen people.'

Even prior to Hitler joining the Nazi Party, he held extremely nationalist, racist and anti-Semitic views. After he joined the party, he expanded upon and marketed these ideas.

Hitler had a racist world view. He believed that people could be separated into a hierarchy of different races, in which some races were superior and others inferior. Hitler believed the German race – the 'Aryans' – to be the superior race, while he and the Nazis considered Jews to be an inferior race of people who had set out to weaken other races and take over the world. Hitler considered that Jews were particularly destructive to the German Aryans and did not have any place in Nazi Germany.

Hitler also wanted to rid Germany of the disabled, homosexuals, the Romani and Sinti, and any other minorities that did not fit in to his idea of an Aryan race. The Nazis labelled all these groups 'a-social'.

Hitler was an extreme nationalist, believing the German Aryan race should dominate. His expansionist policies sought *Lebensraum* ('living space') for the German people. Hitler also wanted to create a generation of young Aryans who were physically fit and totally obedient through programmes such as the Hitler Youth. He believed that these policies would unite Germany and ensure it was the strongest nation on earth.

Physically, Hitler was not a very imposing figure – certainly not the ideal of a great fighting leader or the deliverer of Germany and creator of a new Reich. In height he was only a little below average. His hips were wide and his shoulders relatively narrow. His muscles were flabby; his legs short, thin and spindly, the latter being hidden in his youth by heavy boots and more recently by long trousers. He had a large torso and was hollow-chested to the point where it is said that he had his uniforms padded. He would thus certainly not pass the physical requirements of his own elite bodyguard.

His dress, in the early days, was no more attractive: he frequently wore the Bavarian mountain costume of leather shorts with white shirt and suspenders. These were not always very clean, and with his mouth full of rotten brown teeth and his long dirty fingernails he presented rather a grotesque picture. At this time, he also had a pointed beard, and his dark brown hair was parted in the middle and pasted down flat against his head with oil. Nor was his gait that of a soldier. He walked daintily, in small, ladylike steps. He nervously cocked his right shoulder as he walked, and his left leg snapped up as he did so.

1945

Thursday, 13 September: Dr Theodor Morell
Dr Morell, Hitler's personal physician, was interrogated at the United States Forces European Theatre (USFET) Interrogation Centre on the subject of his final experiences in Berlin. Morell seemed physically decayed and 'mentally

gaga'; he was unsure of most of the facts he gave and was felt to probably be genuinely so.

Morell said that he was in the bunker of the Chancellery until he left, but took no part in any discussions. He said that he left at about 1.00 am on 22 April from an unknown aerodrome via Gladow to Munich, where he landed between 5.00m and 6.00 am. He thought the plane might have been a Kondor. Other passengers were a male stenographer and a number of women, believed to probably be the wives of drivers and other personnel.

When Morell left, he said there remained in the bunker Hitler, Goebbels and his family, Bormann, Gruppenführer Johann Rattenhuber and an unknown small general with a monocle.

Accoding to a report in the *News Chronicle* on 16 May 1945, Gerhardt Herrgesell, one of Hitler's secretaries, stated that after the conference of 22 April, he left Berlin in a plane with several women and Dr Morell: 'We took off at 1.45 am and landed at Munich at 4.15 am.' This roughly fitted in with Morell's description. Morell was unable to recall the name of Herrgesell, but he was presumably the male stenographer to whom he referred, 'a member of Hitler's staff of confidential typists'. Luftwaffe General Karl Koller, who left Berlin on the night of 22/23 April, stated that upon arrival at Munich aerodrome he found 'fat old Morell' standing there. In reply to a question, Morell had said: 'I have just come from Berlin in one of the Führer's courier "Staffel" aircraft.' Thus it seemed that Morell left Berlin on the night of 22/23 April, not (as he stated) 21/22 April.

Morell was the subject of a large number of intelligence reports, all of which referred to him in a most uncomplimentary manner. Some reports described him as a shrewd money-crazed quack who believed in his own quackery, while others claimed his hygienic habits were those of a pig.

Morell first met the Führer at a dinner party in 1936, with Hitler suffering from severe stomach cramps and colossal flatulence. Morell convinced the hypochondriac Hitler to swallow capsules of Mutaflor, which contained a strain of hydrolyzed E. coli, and Dr Kuster's anti-gas pills, which contained traces of strychnine. Hitler's symptoms immediately improved. Morell soon had him on a daily dose of Vitamultin, a mysterious powder in gold foil packets that made Hitler's energy levels go through the roof.

Morell had succeeded where other doctors had failed. Convinced of Morell's medical miracles, Hitler appointed him as his personal physician in 1937. However, Hitler's inner circle found it difficult to accept Morell, with many regarding him as a charlatan.

Morell was described as rotund, suffering from excessive sweating and halitosis and having a distinct body odour. Hitler's mistress, Eva Braun, who was later also a patient of Morell's, was initially repulsed by him. In response, Hitler told her: 'I don't employ Dr Morell for his fragrance; I employ him to treat me medically.'

Morell soon became Hitler's shadow, following him into bunkers, military meetings, on holidays and even to survey territory conquered during the war. These moments were captured in Morell's exhaustive medical diary, which provided a unique account of the daily health and mindset of Hitler. In his notes, the doctor referred to Hitler as 'Patient A', a precaution to protect both Hitler's privacy and himself should his notes fall into enemy hands in the event of the Nazi leader's death.

Hitler became seriously ill in August 1941. Up until that moment, he had been receiving daily injections of vitamins and glucose, but they were no longer proving effective. Nervously, Morell turned to more medically dubious animal hormones.

Hitler's injections thereafter included metabolic stimulants, sex hormones and extracts made from the seminal vesicles and prostates of young bull and pigs' livers. While Hitler did not eat meat, he was having animal substances injected directly into his bloodstream.

The medical medley increased from there, with Morell promising Hitler 'instant recovery'. However, as Hitler's body got used to the compounds injected into his system he required higher doses and stronger drugs to have an impact.

Hitler was soon on 'uppers' and 'downers' in tandem. If he couldn't sleep, he received a dose of barbiturates and morphine; if he needed to wake, then he was given injections of ever-stronger stimulants. This miscellany of injections earned Morell the nickname of the 'Reichmaster of Injections'.

In 1943, Morell began injecting high doses of opiates into Hitler. The Führer's health was declining, and he often appeared stooped and considerably aged according to those closest to him. Eukodal (oxycodone), the pharmacological cousin to heroin, became Hitler's panacea. It made him euphoric, and with the frequency of high doses injected it seems likely that he became addicted.

But soon even Eukodal was not enough. On July 20 1944, Hitler sustained minor bomb blast injuries from an assassination attempt in the Wolf's Lair. This time, he was treated by Dr Erwin Giesing, who had a favourite remedy of his own: cocaine. From then on, the Führer daily received Eukodal combined with two doses of high-grade cocaine.

When the Allies began bombing pharmaceutical companies such as Merck in Darmstadt December 1944, production of Eukodal suddenly came to a halt. Indeed, in January 1945 Hitler ran out of opioids just before he descended into the Führerbunker. According to author Norman Ohler, Hitler then turned into a physical and mental wreck. He had been held together by his injections, but now the most important substances allowing him to function, the opioids, were gone.

Morell stayed on as Hitler's physician almost to the end. In the last days of the war, Hitler granted him permission to leave the Führerbunker, Morell escaping Berlin on one of the last flights out. Hitler, without his doctor, allegedly flew into a rage, informing those around him that he would commit suicide.

According to Morell's notes, Hitler received a total of 800 injections and varying medications on 1,100 occasions between August 1941 and April 1945.

Morell was never convicted of war crimes; he was never ideological, and his membership of the Nazi Party was seen as strictly for personal gain. He got rich during the war from abattoirs and factories manufacturing his hormone concoctions and Vitamultin. He was also funded by the contracts that supplied the Nazi military machine with his drugs.

October 1946

Another of Hitler's doctors, Major Erwin Giesing – an ear, nose and throat specialist – was in the hands of the US. He was exhaustively interrogated. A claim was made by Giesing – who during May 1945 served in a military hospital in Bavaria – that an X-ray of Hitler's head had shown one displaced bone.

Monday, 15 October

1st Lieutenant Arthur D McKibbin (US Infantry, Editing Section) produced a report after the interrogation of Hitler's doctors who had examined and treated him during the year up to his death. The report was published to provide:

(a) Medical data useful for the identification of Hitler or his remains.
(b) Further material for the debunking of numerous 'Hitler myths'.
(c) The knowledge needed to expose those frauds who in later years may claim to be Hitler, or who may claim to have seen or talked to him.
(d) Research material for the historian, the doctor and the scientist interested in Hitler.

The physicians were questioned separately. Some of the information was produced from memory. The physicians were as follows:

Name: Dr Erwin Giesing, referred to as source (G).
Position: Oberstabsarzt in charge of the ear, nose and throat section of Reserve Lazarett II. He was called in to treat Hitler on 22 July 1944. His treatment lasted about three months.
Interrogated: 30 August 1945.

Giesing was called in by Dr Von Hasselbach, one of Hitler's regular physicians, to treat the Führer and others following the 20 July 1944 assassination attempt. He was the only ENT specialist in the area.

Professor Carl Otto von Eicken, chief of the ENT clinic at the 'Charite' hospital in Berlin and a surgeon who performed two operations on Hitler in 1934 and 1944, thought highly of Giesling's ability. Von Eicken said Giesling appeared to have examined Hitler more thoroughly than his personal physicians. His opinions were regarded as reliable, and his examination of Hitler appeared to have been an exhaustive one.

Name: SS Gruppenführer Dr Karl Brandt, source (B).
Position: Reich Commissioner for Health and Medical Services.
Interrogated: 30 August 1945.

Brandt was a 41-year-old surgeon and was rather young for the positions he held. He accompanied Hitler to Venice in 1934, became Hitler's personal physician and remained on the medical staff until relieved in September 1944 at the instigation of Dr Morell. On 23 May 1945, he was interned at Flensburg. Brandt was considered to be reliable.

Name: Dr Hanskarl von Hasselbach, source (vH).
Position: Oberfeldarzt, Chief Surgeon of Army Field Hospital 2/562.
Interrogated: 10 September 1945.

One of Hitler's accompanying surgeons from 1934 to 9 October 1944, he was the first doctor to treat Hitler after the 20 July bomb plot. He was considered by his peers to be a very critical doctor – possibly one of the few people associated with Hitler not to fall under his spell. Von Hasselbach was also considered reliable. During October 1942, he transferred to Hitler's Headquarters to take over part of Dr Brandt's duties. On 9 October 1944, he was dismissed from his duties at Hitler's Headquarters and transferred to the army.

The physicians gave the following comments about their medical observations of the Führer:

Hitler's State of Health and Medical Characteristics

'G' 'Hitler gave the impression of being about 56 years of age in 1944 [he would have been about 45]. His nutritional state of health was good. Weight was about 72 to 74 kg, height 175 to 177cm. Temperature, pulse and respiration was normal on several occasions.'

'vH' 'Up to 1940 Hitler appeared to be much younger than he actually was. After that date, however, he aged quite rapidly. From 1940 to 1943 he actually looked his age, while after that he gave the appearance of having grown old. His hair turned quite grey during the last months. Hitler's body began to stoop, which may have been due in part to lack of exercise; Hitler didn't like to walk, even short distances. A tremor of his head and hands was quite noticeable, particularly when bringing a cup to the mouth or signing documents. Toward the end, his features still appeared to be smooth and relatively juvenile. Nutritional state of health appeared to be good up to 1944, but declined afterward. Hitler was aware of his predisposition toward adiposity [obesity] and limited his food intake. His appetite was good.'

'B' 'Hitler appeared to be about 55 years of age in 1944. Nutritional state of health was good. Weight was about 80kg, height 175 or 176cm. Temperature, pulse or respiration not taken. "B" stated that Hitler was definitely a psychopathic personality.'

Medical History

'G' 'Hitler suffered from intestinal cramps over a long period, particularly after 1933. These may have been of hysterical origin, or may have arisen from an overdose of drugs. Hitler exhibited a pulmonary apical pathology [a lung condition] in childhood, which disappeared in later years. He was operated on twice, in 1935 and November 1944 – both times for a laryngeal polyp. Both operations were performed by Dr von Eicken in Berlin. Hitler showed signs of jaundice (August–September 1944); bronzing of face and icteric discolouration of sclera. This was probably due to a strychnine intoxication brought about by two years use of "Dr Koester's Anti-Gas pills". In September to October 1944, Dr Von Eicken also carried out a maxillary sinusitis draining and washing.'

'vH' 'Hitler complained of meteorism [swelling of the abdomen caused by gas in the intestines or peritoneal cavity] especially after eating black bread and cabbage and an abnormal feeling in the epigastric region. These symptoms were due to a neurosis, since occasional errors in his diet (such as the intake of lentils and peas) brought only the normal amount of complaining. Furthermore, the prescription of unsuitable and useless drugs brought about improvement for those complaints.'

'B' 'Epigastric cramps and vomiting was noted during 1944–45. These probably were the result of constant strychnine and atropine medication and not of hysteric origin.'

Scars

'G' 'A double-bean sized, non-irritating contracted linear scar was on his left leg. It was possibly caused by shrapnel during the First World War. Shrapnel fragments may well have been found in the soft tissue in that region.

'A scar was located on the right knee. The length of the scar was about 1cm, width 2mm. It resulted from injuries from 20 July 1944 [the bomb plot].

'A thin, superficial skin scar, of rice-corn size, was located in the extensor region of the right hand. Immunisation scars were definitely not recognised.'

'vH' 'No knowledge of scars prior to 20 July 1944. The injuries of that date consisted of tearing of the skin on lower third of both thighs, hematomas on the right elbow and on the dorsum of the left hand. There were also minimal injuries to fingers. These were superficial skin wounds, which would probably have left minimal scars. After the 20 July "Putsch", a bean-sized thickening of the extensor tendon of the third finger of the left hand. The tumour moved when the affected finger was exercised, indicating probable injury to the tendon.

'On other than those places no blush was noted. Hematoma [blood outside of blood vessels] was gradually absorbed, with tenderness continuing no longer than normal. Dr Morell applied a bandage soaked in acid aluminium acetate on the elbow. This resulted in dermatitis with pruritus [itchy skin] which lasted about two weeks.'

'B' 'Hematoma was present on the extensor region of the right forearm close to the elbow joint. This was a result of the 20 July explosion.'

Skin

'G' 'Colour of face and body was white and pale. Texture of skin was fine. Skin tone of face was slightly decreased. A temporary eczema was noted in July 1944 on both lower extremities (shins). Sensitivity of skin was normal. Dermography on skin of chest, back and forearms showed an abnormal response. This was probably due to continued medication (strychnine-atropine pills prescribed by Dr Morell).'

'vH' 'Skin of face was rosy-white and of a healthy colour. The rest of the body was pale-white. (Hitler did not like to expose himself to the sun.) Turgor [skin elasticity] and tonus of the face was good. Hitler was disposed to acquire pustules and small furuncles [individual boils] in the posterior aspect of the neck. However, they never required incisions or patches. Petechiae [a small red or purple spot caused by bleeding into the skin] or cicatrices [the scar of a healed wound] were not observed. Sensitivity of his skin was normal so far as observed. After the 20 July attack, Hitler remarked that for some time he had noticed a disturbance in sensation in his left leg. Normal sensation returned to that leg after the attack.'

'B' '[His] skin was pale and white, sensitive to sunlight and of very fine texture. Hair growth and distribution was moderate. Skin showed no evidence of petechiae. Psoriasis was not present on extensor surface of the leg.'

Face

'G' 'Hitler's face showed distinct nasolabial folds (indentation lines on either side of the mouth that extend from the edge of the nose to the mouth's outer corners). No asymmetry was noted. Turgor of soft tissue over both maxillary sinuses was decreased. Facial expression at the time of examination, July 1944:- fatigued, exhausted, with an appearance of senility.'

'vH' 'Facial expression was impressive, vivacious, but changeable. His large, coarse nose disturbed the fine facial features, but his fascinating eyes compensated. Pictures were unable to produce the suggestive power of his face. It was not conspicuously asymmetrical.'

'B' 'There was a slight asymmetry of the eyes (left slightly lower than the right). A minimal degree of hypertelorism (an abnormally large distance between the eyes) was noted in the region of the maxillary sinuses.'

Scalp

'G' 'Hair was dark brown, almost black; grey in region of the temples. His hair was beginning to thin.'
'vH' 'Hair was thick and showed no sign of thinning.'
'B' 'Hair was dark brown, slightly grey on temples and less so on scalp and moustache. It [the hair] was parted on the right.'

Eyes

'G' 'A slight suggestion of exophthalmus [bulging or protruding eyeballs], and a slight ocular hypertelorism was observed. Movement of lids were normal and showed no lag. Pupils were normal in size, regular. They showed normal consensual reaction to light. Turbidity to corpus vitreum [a transparent jellylike substance filling the interior of the eyeball behind the lens] was noted by an eye doctor in 1936. (Hitler's eye doctor was Dr Loehlein.)

'Turbidity became worse and Hitler complained about it in 1944. Some hyperopia [far-sightedness] of the right eye developed. Conjunctiva, sclera and cornea showed no evidence of pathology. The colour of the eyes were blue but with a slight shading of grey.'
'vH' 'Exophthalmos slight. Ocular movements were normal and coordinated. Lids showed no evidence of pathology. Pupils were not examined. Conjunctiva was normal. Cornea was transparent and no vascularisation was noted.'
'B' 'Eyes blue in colour with a fine shading of grey. Eyes were hyperopic.'

Ears

'G' 'Neither ear showed any deformity. A pea-sized scar was present in the right ear.'
'vH' 'Hearing was good until 20 July 1944, after which it was impaired.'

Nose

'G' 'His nose was straight, somewhat fleshy.'
'B' 'Distal portion of nose broad and fleshy. Nostrils large.'

Mouth

'G' 'No abnormality of pathology of upper or lower lips was observed.
   'The upper, lower right and left second and third molars were missing. The upper right lateral incisor [and] the lower left lateral incisor had a porcelain jacket [crown]. Gold crowns and a fixed bridge were observed.
   'The tongue appeared to be small.
   'The right and left tonsils showed adhesions. The left tonsil was walnut size, the right, one-third larger. A scar was found, possibly as a result of acute tonsillitis.
   'No fetor ex ore [halitosis] was present.'
'B' 'Upper and lower lips were small. Tongue was very often furred.'

Neck

'G' 'The neck showed normal mobility. No enlargement or symptoms referring to thyroid was observed. False vocal cords were present; true vocal cords were of medium size and smooth.'
'vH' 'Thyroid, while not examined, did not appear to be enlarged, and no symptoms of thyrotoxicosis [excess thyroid hormone action] were present.
   'The larynx was not examined. However, frequent clearing of the throat indicated that a mild pharyngitis, laryngitis or pharyngolaryngitis was present.'
'B' 'Neck was normally mobile. The thyroid was normal. Larynx, pharynx and vocal cords were not examined.'

Heart

'G' 'Blood pressure at rest was taken by Dr Morell (25 August 1944) [and] showed systolic pressure of 143mm Hg, diastolic pressure of 87mm Hg. The systolic pressure rose to 175mm Hg when Hitler was mentally excited. No murmurs and thrills were found. Slight respiratory arrhythmia [abnormality of the heart's rhythm] was present. No efficiency tests were made.'
'vH' 'Hitler complained of having a weak heart. He had avoided all forms of exercise since 1938. He avoided going to the "Kehlsteinhaus", or Eagle's Nest (1,800 meters above sea level) because he felt a tightening of his chest when he was there. However, his capacity

for work did not diminish. It was concluded that the symptoms, like epigastric pains [pain or discomfort right below the ribs in the area of the upper abdomen] and cramps, were of hysterical origin. However, no test was made.'

'B' 'No examination.'

Abdomen

'G' 'Contour was normal. There was no evidence of hypertrichosis [excessive hair growth anywhere on a person's body]. No scars were observed. There was no palpable liver or spleen enlargement. No pains over Mac Burney's point [a point over the right side of the abdomen]. Cremaster reflex normal [superficial reflex found in human males that is elicited when the inner part of the thigh is stroked].'

'vH' 'No examination.'

'B' 'Contour was normal. No scars were observed. Examination revealed no rigidity or tenderness. Intestinal activity was abnormal. No masses or tumours were palpated [felt].'

Lymphatic Glands

'G' 'Small lymph nodes were palpated in the inguinal regions [groin], but no tenderness was detected.'

Back

'G' 'A slight kyphoscoliosis of the thoracic spine [causes extra pulmonary restriction of the lungs] was present.'

'vH' 'Acquired kyphosis [curvature of the spine that causes the top of the back to appear more rounded than normal] of the dorsal spine was present.'

'B' 'Slight occupation kyphosis. Mobility of spine normal. No tenderness over spine, kidneys or pelvis noticed.'

Extremities

'G' 'No evidence of varicosities [varicose veins] was noted.'

'vH' 'Slight varicosities on both legs. Hitler did not complain about them.'

'B' 'No varicosities noted.'

Neurological study

(a) Cranial nerves
I. Nervus olfactorius [related to smell]
'G' 'Subjective: No complaints of impairment of smell of olfactory hallucinations.
  'Objective: No test for response to oil of cloves was made.'
'vH' 'No examination was made.'
'B' 'Subjective: No impairment of smell or olfactory hallucinations were complained of.
  'Objective: No examination.'

(b) Nervus Opticus – Optic Nerve
'G' Subjective: Hitler complained of impairment of vision. No evidence of visual hallucination was apparent.'
  'Objective: Acuity, colour blindness and fundoscopic examination were not made.'
'vH' 'No examination.'
'B' 'Subjective: Visual examination absent.
  'Objective: Eye examination(s) made by Dr Loehlein.'

(c) Nervus trigeminus [main sensory nerve of the face and motor nerve for the muscles of mastication]
'G' 'Subjective: Hitler did not complain of neuralgia, numbness, paresthesia [burning or prickling sensation].
  'Objective: No evidence of sensory disturbance nor sensory pathology was present. Corneal and sneeze reflexes were not indicative of pathology. No deviation of the jaw was noted. Mastication was normal.'
'vH' 'No motor deviation of the jaw was noted. Mastication normal.'
'B' 'Neuralgia, numbness, paresthesia absent. Facial sensation was normal. Corneal and sneeze reflexes not tested. No deviation of jaw.'

(d) Nervus Facialis (facial nerve)
'G' 'Subjective: Taste sensation of anterior of two-thirds of the tongue not tested. Facial spasm absent. Lacrimation [tear flow], salivation normal. No facial distortion noted.
  'Objective: No deformity in facial expression. Hitler could wrinkle forehead.'

'vH' 'No evidence of paralysis, transient or permanent, noted. Otherwise no examination.'
'B' 'Facial spasm or facial asymmetry absent. Lacrimation and salivation normal.'

(e) Nervus Auditorius (ear nerve)
'G' 'Nervus Cochlearis [cochlear nerve]: Slight hearing from 20 July explosion. No complaints of ringing or crackling in the ears. The ticking of a watch was heard on both sides. Whispering was heard on both sides at a distance of 6m.

'Rinne Test [used primarily to evaluate loss of hearing in one ear]:(Tuning fork on mastoid, then to ear). Left ear normal. Right ear negative.'
'vH' 'No examination.'
'B' 'No examination.'

(f) Cerebrum
'G' 'Concentration excellent. Euphoria, personality changes, incontinence not observed. Sensation intact, force grasping or clumsiness not observed. Masked facies [the loss of facial expressions most commonly associated with Parkinson's disease] observed during accidental meeting in the Reich Chancellery, 13 February 1945, a distinct tremor of the left hand.'
'vH' 'Ability to concentrate excellent. The persistent hope for victory undoubtedly did not originate in a frontal lobe lesion or other damage; it's believed either a conscious or unconscious stupefaction of judgement was responsible for the delusion. No disintegration of personality occurred up to October 1944 [when 'vH' was dismissed]. However, Hitler's actions did become less intelligible after 20 July 1944. It was assumed that a slight commotio cerebri [an injury to the brain] occurred after the attack, but no signs such as coma, vomiting or pulse disturbances, were evident. Hitler's state of excitement was more of a psychgenic nature.'
'G' 'In agreement with "vH".'

(g) Psychiatric data
'"G", "vH" and "B" agreed that Hitler's was excellent, his memory for events – both near and remote – good, and though he was somewhat relentless, his attention (power of concentration) always met the needs of the moment. Reaction to environment was normal. Flow of

words was coherent and speech relevant. No phobias or obsessions were noted by the three physicians. Hitler was emotionally labile [liable to change, easily altered]. "VH" observed that Hitler could hate deeply in some fields, while almost forgiving anything to those he loved. "G" noted that Hitler believed he was chosen by fate to be the leader of the German people, and that he felt that his ideas must be carried out – even if Germany and her people were destroyed in the process. "G" believed that this may have indicated megalomania.'

'Vh' 'Observed that Hitler's mental endurance was "astonishing", and he loved to be merry and gay [light-hearted and carefree]. Hitler generally appeared to be calm and deliberate – but on occasions he reacted with vehement attack of anger, which subsided and disappeared quite rapidly. Hitler complained of bad sleep, but was inclined to sleep long hours.'

(h) Urological data
'None of the three sources knew of any indication of pathology in this field. "B" attributed pain in the abdomen to meteorism [swelling of the abdomen caused by gas in the intestines or peritoneal cavity] – possibly the result of large doses of strychnine and atropine.'

(i) Sex characteristics
'"VH" observed that he was not in possession of any information which would indicate venereal disease. He said that Hitler's sex instincts were neither increased nor depressed, and was certain that he was neither a pervert nor a homosexual. The total of Hitler's utterances regarding sex lead to the conclusion that his sex instincts were normal, or only slightly repressed.'

(j) X-rays
'X-rays of Hitler's sinuses were taken during September 1944 at the ReserveLazarett, Rastenburg, and were on the files of HQ United States European Theatre Military Intelligence Service centre.

'X-rays of Hitler's teeth were taken by his personal dentist, Hugo Johannes Blaschke (and the chief dentist on the staff of Reichsführer-SS Heinrich Himmler) during the spring of 1942 and again during autumn of 1944.

'Dr Loehlein, who made detailed eye examinations of Hitler, was interrogated at the centre (mentioned above). Steps by that unit were undertaken to obtain X-rays, cardiograms and the results of laboratory test.'

1946

Tuesday, 5 February
Hitler's Teeth/Treatments

Dr Hugo Johannes Blaschke, a Brigadeführer, was Hitler's personal dentist. He had been called in to treat Hitler by Hermann Göring in the early part of 1934, and was Hitler's dentist from that time until Blaschke's departure from the Reich Chancellery and Berlin during the night of 20/21 April 1945. His last treatment of Hitler was sometime in mid-February 1945. Neither he nor anybody else treated the Führer after that time. The information was published in order to provide:

(a) Data useful in the identification of Hitler or his remains.
(b) Knowledge needed to expose any frauds who in later years may claim to be Hitler, or who may claim to have seen him or talked to him.
(c) Research material for the historian, the doctor and the scientist interested in Hitler.

What follows is a translation of notes written for the report by Blaschke, giving Hitler's abridged case history as a dental patient in the years 1934–45:

'In the beginning of the year 1934 I was, at the instance of the then (Prussian) Prime Minister Göring called to the Reich Chancellery. I was told that Adolf Hitler had a toothache. Upon examination I found a swelling of the gingiva [gums] of the left lower jaw, extending from the left central incisor to the left cuspid. The lower left lateral incisor had at its distal end a cavity which extended as far as the pulp cavity. The pulp was dead and the tooth sensitive to pressure. All lower incisors, especially the ones on the left, were very loose.

'The pains could be caused either by an abscess in the area of the root-tips or by an abscess in the gingival pocket of the lower left lateral incisor.

'After opening of the root canal and removal of an abundance of tartar the pains soon decreased in intensity and disappeared completely overnight.

'The X-ray photos showed the following: A lentil-sized light spot around the tip of the root of the lower left lateral incisor. Strong atrophy of the alveoli, most pronounced around the lower right central incisor and the lower left central and lateral incisors …

'During the following days, besides the treatment of the root of the lower left lateral incisor, tartar was thoroughly [*sic*]. The gingivitis healed and the teeth became steadier and again fit for use. The treatment of the root took a normal course. The tooth was filled with iodoform-paste and temporarily closed ...

'In the upper jaw much more extensive work was necessary. There existed on either side bridges which were connected by an arch behind the left incisors. Three-fourths of the upper left lateral incisor was broken off. The arch connecting the two bridges caused annoyance because food particles got caught in it easily. The gingiva had receded considerably from the edges of existing gold crowns, so that the necks of the teeth were exposed. Caries [tooth decay] had started at some of these points.

'The old bridges had to be removed and replaced. As the upper right central incisor was already absent and replaced by part of the bridge and as, in addition, the lateral incisor was ¾ broken off, the gaps would have impeded speech. Hitler refused a temporary replacement through a removable dental plate for the period of manufacture (of the new replacements). It was then possible to remove both bridges in their entirety. They were taken out at each sitting and temporarily fastened again afterward. The root of the upper left lateral incisor, which had to be completely removed for the fitting-on of the new crown, received a new pivot-tooth.'

Blaschke was presented with a problem in the upper jaw after the removal of the old bridges. Two possibilities offered themselves:

'1. A removable, supported prosthesis, restoring the ability to masticate as far as the the bridge in the lower right jaw would allow.
'2. A fixed bridge with a slightly smaller masticating surface. Since in Hitler's case an edge-to-edge bite was present, the ability to masticate would have been sufficient despite the missing molars.'

'Hitler rejected a removable prosthesis. He remarked that for him, as a vegetarian, the fixed bridge would suffice since he had a special kitchen at his disposal at all times.

'Hitler's treatment was finished. The treatment of the root of the lower left lateral incisor was repeated during one of the last sittings (for the fitting of the bridge), after an X-ray had revealed a noticeable reduction of the infection of the root-tip.

'I agreed with Hitler that I would have to examine his teeth in intervals of three or four months at the most, since only constant supervision, especially of the lower incisors, could tend to avoid similar extensive work in the upper jaw.

'I was able to make these check-ups fairly regularly until the outbreak of the war.

'New extensive work was not necessary during those years …

'Treatments were performed at either the Berlin Chancellery or the Berghof on Obersalzberg. Dental stations existed in either place.

'In the years 1938–39, I did not succeed for a long time (I think it was a little more than a year) in treating Hitler. Whenever I called I was told that treatment was not possible at the time, and that I should wait until notified. When I was finally called pain was present …

'In contrast to previous years, treatments from now on were more difficult to carry out, since Hitler had very little time. He was in addition very worried about pains that might be caused by the treatments and demanded the greatest caution to have them avoided. I could never be sure whether a treatment scheduled would come off or it would be postponed indefinitely.

'At the "Wolfsschanze" [Wolf's Lair] headquarters treatments were performed in a truck-mounted dental station provided by the guard battalion of the regiment "Grossdeuschland". Later, on account of the air-raids, a dental station was installed in one of the shelters.

'Towards the end of September (1944) I was called to the headquarters. Hitler complained about slight tenderness of the gingiva of the upper left jaw. He was bed-ridden. He was, as Prof Morell told me, suffering from an inflammation of the Nasopharyngeal area.

'From the middle of January 1945, Hitler was constantly in the Berlin Reich Chancellery. Again and again he postponed the treatment of the upper left incisor. He came once to the dental station for a short while in mid-February for a superficial examination. Besides the removal of tartar … no treatment was performed on that occasion.

'The patients' file cards as well as the X-ray pictures of their teeth were, since the middle of January 1945, constantly kept at the dental station in the Voßstraße shelter of the Reich Chancellery.

'On the night of 20/21 January 1945, I was ordered to be ready for movement, with a minimum of baggage, within an hour. I was helped in packing the little portable dental station which I wanted to take with me by my dental helper … and my assistant Dr Rohkamm. It is possible and even likely that the files were put in the same box as the dental station. My baggage was then supposed to be sent from the Tempelhof airfield to Salzburg in a transport plane carrying baggage exclusively. This plane never arrived at Salzburg, and from the Obersalzberg, it could never be ascertained what had become of it.'

Blaschke also stated that he treated Martin Bormann regularly from 1937–45, for the last time in March of that year. During that period, Bormann was not treated by any other dentist.

Blaschke treated Eva Braun too at irregular intervals from 1935–45, for the last time at the Berlin Reich Chancellery in March 1945. Treatments were performed at the Chancellery and at the Berghof on the Obersalzberg. When in Munich during Hitler's stays at his field headquarters or during his travels, she was treated by a local dentist.

It later transpired that Hitler had a fear of illness. Carl Otto von Eicken was one of Hitler's ear, nose and throat specialists, treating the dictator for voice problems for ten years from 1935. Hitler said to von Eicken: 'If there is something bad, I absolutely have to know.' Hitler attached enormous importance to his voice, which was crucial in his speeches to whip up support for his cause. One operation to remove a polyp was postponed until after a speech because von Eicken advised that he would need to rest his voice after the procedure.

Von Eicken, when questioned about his actions on treating a man whose actions led to the death of millions and asked why he didn't kill Hitler, replied: 'I was his doctor – not his murderer.'

Chapter Six

The New Flensburg Government and the State of Germany

1945

Saturday, 28 April
Admiral Karl Dönitz received a radio telegram from Martin Bormann, Hitler's Party secretary, sent from the Reich Chancellery in Berlin, informing him that Himmler had engaged in secret surrender negotiations with the Western Allies via Sweden and calling it a clear act of treason. The same day, Hitler sent Ritter von Greim, the new chief of the Luftwaffe after Göring's downfall, to Plön to tell Dönitz to arrest Himmler. Greim arrived on the 29th, but Dönitz took no action.

Monday, 30 April
Dönitz decided to travel down to Himmler's headquarters at Lübeck to question him about the surrender negotiations, but the Reichsführer-SS lied to his face, assuring him that allegations of his treason were false.

Dönitz had hardly returned to Plön when he received another telegram from Bormann in Berlin at 6.30 pm:

> 'In place of the former Reichsmarschall Göring the Führer has appointed you, Herr Grossadmiral, as his successor. Written authorization underway. You are to immediately take any measures which the present situation demands. Bormann.'

Dönitz thus became Head of State of the German Reich and Supreme Commander of all armed forces, Hitler having named him his successor in his political testament drawn up the day before, a will that came into force when he committed suicide in his Berlin Führerbunker.

A military man without any political aspirations, Dönitz's appointment as Hitler's successor came as a complete surprise to him. He had assumed that Göring would succeed Hitler; if not him, then Himmler. However, both men had been thrown out by Hitler, but Dönitz was not sure whether Himmler would peaceably accept the new state of affairs. To find out, he phoned Himmler and asked him to come to Plön.

The Reichsführer-SS arrived shortly before midnight, accompanied by six bodyguards, but walked into Dönitz's office alone. Unsure about how Himmler would react, Dönitz had put his pistol under some papers on his desk. He brought out the telegram announcing his appointment as Hitler's successor and asked Himmler to read it. As Himmler did so, his face went pale. After a short silence, he said: 'In that case, please let me become the second man in your state.' Dönitz rejected the offer, saying: 'That is impossible. I have no job for you.' To Dönitz's relief, Himmler accepted the new situation. They talked for an hour before the Reichsführer-SS left.

Tuesday, 1 May
Goebbels became the new Head of Government and Chancellor of Germany (Reichskanzler) in accordance with Hitler's last will and testament. Reichskanzler Goebbels and Bormann sent a radio message to Dönitz at 3.15 am, informing him of Hitler's death, and Dönitz was appointed as the new President of Germany (Reichspräsident) in accordance with Hitler's last wishes.

Albert Speer recalled that after he had reached Dönitz's headquarters at Plön, he was unpacking his bags and found a framed photo of Hitler that his secretary had included. Speer said: 'When I stood the photograph up, a fit of weeping overcame me. That was the end of my relationship to Hitler. Only now was the spell broken, the magic extinguished. What remained were images of graveyards, of shattered cities, of millions of mourners, of concentration camps.'

Himmler's Capitulation Explanation
The new government was called to Plön. Feldmarschall Ritter von Greim, the new head of the Luftwaffe, and his partner the test pilot Hanna Reitsch were to receive orders from Dönitz as to the immediate Luftwaffe activities. They would also be able to meet Himmler and confront him over the betrayal story.

Himmler arrived late, so all the others were in the conference room, leaving Reitsch alone when he walked in. 'One moment Herr Reichsführer, a matter of the highest importance, if you can spare the time?' Reitsch asked.

Himmler seemed almost jovial as he said: 'Of course.'

'Is it true, Herr Reichsführer, that you contacted the Allies with proposals of peace without orders to do so from Hitler?'

'But, of course.'

'You betrayed your Führer and your people in their very darkest hour. Such a thing is high treason, Herr Reichsführer. You did that when your place was actually in the bunker with Hitler.'

'High treason? No! You'll see, history will weigh it differently. Hitler wanted to continue the fight. He was mad with his pride and his honour. He wanted to shed more German blood when there was none left to flow. Hitler was insane. It should have been stopped long ago.'

'Insane? I came from him less than 36 hours ago. He died for the cause he believed in. He died bravely and filled with the honour you speak of, while you and Göring and the rest must now live as branded traitors and cowards.'

'I did it to save German blood, to rescue what was left of our country.'

'You speak of German blood, Herr Reichsführer? You speak of it now? You should have thought of it years ago, before you became identified with the useless shedding of so much of it.'

At that moment, a sudden strafing attack by an Allied aircraft terminated their conversation.

The Last Orders to Hold the Russians

Greim later indicated that little had been decided at the first Dönitz war council. However, everyone was in accord that, at best, resistance would only be possible for a few days longer. In the meantime, commanders against the Russians were to hold to the last man to enable as many civilians as possible to flee from the Red Army's advance. Reitsch claimed that Greim, whose injured leg was becoming increasingly worse, insisted upon flying immediately to Feldmarschall Ferdinand Schörner, in command of troops in Silesia and Czechoslovakia, to instruct him that he should resist even after the capitulation order was released, to give the civilians time to flee to the American zone.

On the flight to Schörner, Greim's foot became so bad that he had momentary lapses of consciousness. Upon arrival, Schörner indicated that he had already decided to hold on as long as possible and had issued orders to that effect even before their arrival.

It was decided to fly to Generalfeldmarschall Albert Kesselring with the same instructions, but Greim's leg was by now so critical that further movement was impossible. From 3–7 May, he had to remain at Schörner's headquarters in Königgrätz, where Reitsch nursed Greim until he could move about again.

At 10.53 am on 1 May, Dönitz received a second telegram from Bormann: 'Testament in force. I will come to you as quickly as possible. Until then, in my view, hold publication. Bormann.'

Another signal arrived at 3.18 pm, this time jointly signed by Bormann and Propaganda Minister Joseph Goebbels:

'Grossadmiral Dönitz. Führer died yesterday 1530. Testament of April 29 transfers to you the office of Reich President, Dr Goebbels the office of Reich Chancellor, Reichsleiter Bormann the office of Party Minister, Reich minister Seyss-Inquart the office of Foreign Minister. By order of the Führer the testament has been sent out of Berlin to you, to Generalfeldmarschall Schörner and to assure its preservation for publication. Reichsleiter Bormann will try to reach you today to clarify the situation. Form and time of announcement to the troops and public is left to you. Confirm receipt. Goebbels, Bormann.'

Subsequently, in a short message broadcast by the Hamburg radio station at 10.26 pm, Dönitz announced Hitler's death to the German public and that he had been appointed his successor. In his order of the day to the armed forces, he said: 'Against the English and Americans I must continue the fight for as far and as long as they hinder me in the execution of battle against the Bolsheviks ... The oath of loyalty which you gave to the Führer is now due from each one of you to me as the Führer's appointed successor.'

Wednesday, 2 May
The Allies broke out of their Elbe bridgehead at Lauenburg, east of Hamburg, and slashed through to Lübeck and Wismar on the Baltic coast, thereby closing the 'last gate' to the West for withdrawing troops and refugees. Upon hearing the news, Dönitz made two decisions. Firstly, as it was now pointless to continue the fight, he realized the time had come to bring an end to hostilities as quickly as possible to prevent further bloodshed. Thus, he instructed Admiral von Friedeburg to take up contact with Field Marshal Bernard Montgomery, the commander of the British 21st Army Group, and begin surrender negotiations. Secondly, since the British at Lübeck were now only an hour's drive from Plön, he ordered his HQ to move north another 65 miles, to the naval port of Flensburg on the Danish border. The transfer took place during the night of 2/3 May.

The so-called 'Flensburg government' was headed up by Grand Admiral Dönitz. There were ministers, but they didn't have a ministry. There was a Minister for Finance without any money, and there was a Minister for Foreign Affairs but there were no people working for him.

On the way to Flensburg, Dönitz rendezvoused with Admiral Hans-Georg von Friedeburg – his successor as commander-in-chief of the Kriegsmarine – at 9.00 pm on the highway bridge over the Kaiser Wilhelm Canal at Levensau near Kiel, and briefed him on his assignment. Von Friedeburg was to offer to Montgomery the surrender of all German forces in north-western Germany, but also to try to negotiate for the remains of Heeresgruppe Weichsel to be allowed to retreat to the west and surrender to the British. Von Friedeburg was to be accompanied on his mission by General der Infanterie Eberhard Kinzel, Chief of Staff of the OKW-Führungsstab Nord, Konteradmiral Gerhard Wagner, military representative on Dönitz's staff, and an OKW staff officer, Major Hans Jochen Friedel. After wishing von Friedeburg good luck, Dönitz motored on northwards.

Thursday, 3 May
Arriving at Flensburg in the early hours, Dönitz set up his headquarters in the Marine-Schule Mürwik, the naval cadet school on the bluff overlooking the Flensburg Fjord in Mürwik, an eastern suburb of the town. Moored along the quay within the school complex was the *Patria*, an 8,000-ton Hamburg–America Line passenger ship, which was where the admiral set up his initial quarters. The following morning, he was joined there by Keitel and Jodl and their small OKW staff, as well as by Speer, who had returned from Hamburg. Looking for a place to house his headquarters and the OKW staff, Dönitz turned to the commander of the naval school, Kapitän Wolfgang Lüth, who immediately offered him the use of the complex's Sportschule (sports school building). A large red-brick building of several wings, it included a gymnasium, classrooms, offices and dormitories. Lüth also offered Dönitz the use of two rooms in his Commander's Villa as personal quarters for the Grand Admiral and his adjutant, Korvettenkapitän Walter Lüdde-Neurath. The Marine-Wach-Bataillon 'Dönitz', a unit comprised of former U-boat crews and commanded by Korvettenkapitän Peter Erich Cremer, formed a perimeter guard around the Marine-Schule, with armed sentries at all entry roads.

As Flensburg seemed about to be occupied by British forces, several people started pressing Dönitz to move his government to either Denmark or Prague. Himmler in particular felt drawn to Prague. Dönitz refused to do so, considering such a move pointless and dishonourable. Others were making plans for escape. Gauleiters Erich Koch of East Prussia and Hinrich Lohse of Schleswig-Holstein each demanded a submarine so that they could escape to South America, but Dönitz flatly refused both requests.

Friday, 4 May
Dönitz gave von Friedeburg full authority to accept Montgomery's conditions. Also, as soon as the surrender to Montgomery had been completed, he was to fly on to SHAEF headquarters at Rheims in north-east France to negotiate a separate surrender in the West. Dönitz's two emissaries returned to Lüneburg

Heath, taking with them another OKW staff officer, Oberst Fritz Poleck, and shortly after 6.00 pm von Friedeburg, Kinzel, Wagner, Poleck and Friedel signed the capitulation of all German forces in northern Germany, the Netherlands and Denmark, to come into effect at 8.00 am the following day.

Saturday, 5 May
Dönitz ordered Heeresgruppen Mitte, Süd and Südost (Centre, South and South-East) to fight on to prevent as many Germans as possible from falling into 'Bolshevization and slavery', calling for absolute obedience and iron discipline. On the other hand, he ordered an immediate halt of all U-boat warfare. The structure of Dönitz's new government was slowly emerging. On 2 May, while en route to Flensburg, Dönitz had asked Schwerin von Krosigk, his Finance Minister and newly appointed Foreign Minister, to form a new cabinet. Schwerin von Krosigk agreed, but to underline the temporary character of the new administration he insisted that it be called an 'acting Reich Government' and that he himself be titled Principal Minister instead of Reich Chancellor.

Schwerin von Krosigk presented his 'acting government'. It was designed as a 'non-political' cabinet made up of specialist ministers. Schwerin von Krosigk himself became Principal Minister, as well as Minister of Finance and Minister of Foreign Affairs. Albert Speer was Minister for Industry and Production; Dr Wilhelm Stuckart, who had been a State Secretary in the Ministry of Interior, was Minister of the Interior (in place of Himmler) and Minister of Culture; Dr Julius Dorpmüller, until then Minister of Traffic, became Minister of Post and Traffic; Dr Franz Seldte, Hitler's Minister of Labour, became Minister of Labour and Social Affairs; and Dr Herbert Backe remained Minister for Food, Agriculture and Forests. Three ministries – the Propaganda Ministry, the Air Ministry and the Ministry for the Eastern Territories – were abolished.

Late in the afternoon, Admiral von Friedeburg and his party were negotiating at SHAEF headquarters at Rheims over a separate surrender in the West. The Supreme Allied Commander, General Dwight D. Eisenhower, was uncompromising and insisted on an immediate and unconditional surrender on all fronts, including the Russian.

Sunday, 6 May
During the morning, General Kinzel returned to Flensburg to report to Dönitz. The Grand Admiral felt he could not accept Eisenhower's position and decided to send Jodl to Rheims to try to get agreement to a surrender in two stages; first in the West, then at least four days later in the East, thus enabling more troops to get away from the Soviets.

Monday, 7 May

At 2.41 am, Jodl – seconded by Admiral von Friedeburg and Jodl's aide, Major Friedrich Wilhelm Oxenius – signed the unconditional surrender of all German forces, effective from 0.01 am on 9 May. Still, Dönitz's evacuation efforts and delaying tactics at the negotiations had enabled some two million Germans to escape the Soviets.

At 12.45 pm, Schwerin von Krosigk broadcast to the German nation, announcing the unconditional surrender, and was followed next day by Dönitz, who pointed out that the Nazi Party had stepped aside and that political power now rested with the occupying powers, who would decide whether or not he would remain in office.

Tuesday, 8 May

In an effort to assuage the Soviets, a repeat surrender ceremony was staged at Berlin-Karlshorst. Generalfeldmarschall Keitel was the main German signatory, with Generaloberst Hans-Jürgen Stumpf, the Chief of Luftflotte Reich, signing for the Luftwaffe and Admiral von Friedeburg for the Kriegsmarine. The Germans signed at 10.16 pm, and the ceremony was completed at 10.43 pm. The war in Europe was over.

Back at Flensburg, the new German government was doing its best to at least keep up the appearance of administrative activity. The cabinet ministers and their assistants spent their days writing reports and memoranda on the present state of affairs and on how Germany could be set on its feet again. Every morning at 10.00 am, Schwerin von Krosigk chaired a cabinet meeting in the so-called Cabinet Room, a former classroom in the Sportschule building, engaging in serious discussions on matters such as the food situation, traffic, finances and foreign policy. Many of those involved recognized the farcical aspect of it all. Speer in particular thought that the tragedy was turning into a tragi-comedy; he was of the opinion that they were making themselves ridiculous by carrying on with this charade. He also noted that SS and other Nazi uniforms had vanished overnight, their wearers (such as Dr Stuckart and Dr Backe) suddenly appearing in civilian clothes.

With Germany having capitulated, Speer and several others opined that the Dönitz government had done its job and should wind up its activities. However, Schwerin von Krosigk and Stuckart took a different view, arguing that Dönitz must stay on to preserve the continuity of the German Reich and not imperil the legitimacy of a future German government. Dönitz agreed with them. He was still besotted with the idea that his government had to preserve 'the most beautiful and best that National Socialism has given us – the unity of our racial community'. The very idea that prominent democrats and trade unionist should be invited to take part in government was totally unacceptable to him and his entourage, feeling that their experience of the Weimar Republic had shown democracy to be unworkable. Speer alone argued that it was essential to form a government acceptable to the Allies, but none of the others could believe that they had done anything wrong under Hitler or that the Allies could possibly object to them. When confronted with the horrors of the concentration camps, they merely replied that the German people knew nothing of these crimes. There was no hint of shame, horror or repentance at these monstrous crimes against humanity. Dönitz considered that where camp inmates had been treated inhumanely, the perpetrators should be dealt with by German courts, but said that in any case most of these people were 'hardened criminals', 'morally degenerate' or 'anti-social elements' that deserved to be incarcerated in such camps.

Thursday, 10 May
Three days after the surrender at Rheims, the British 11th Armoured Division arrived in the Flensburg area, having been tasked with the occupation of the northernmost districts of Schleswig-Holstein. Responsible for the sector around Flensburg was the division's 159 Infantry Brigade. Driving into town that morning, the brigade commander, Brigadier Jack Churcher, was faced with a bizarre situation: the streets were crowded with German staff cars filled with German officers, German army buses lurched through the town and the docks were patrolled by fully armed German naval and military police. The Luftwaffe was also still in charge of the airfield. The area was crawling with thousands of German troops, who occupied every barracks and building they could get into.

Churcher found the Dönitz government still in being, set up within its own enclave, protected by armed German guards of the Marine-Wach-Bataillon. The German enclave, about 4 miles long and a mile wide, extended along the Baltic shore from just east of Flensburg town to and inclusive of Glücksburg. It was only a small area, but it included three large military facilities: from west to east, the Marine-Torpedo- und Nachrichten-Schule (Naval Torpedo and Signal School), the Marine-Schule Mürwik (Naval Cadet School) and the MarineKaserne Glücksburg-Meierwik barracks. Also included, at the eastern end of the enclave, was the massive Schloss Glücksburg castle.

As Dönitz's government and the OKW and OKM were apparently operating with Allied approval, and lacking orders from SHAEF to the contrary, Churcher decided that for the moment he would have to respect the enclave. He issued orders that his troops should in no way interfere with the functioning of the government and the military commands, and should not enter the German area. As the Germans had all the best barracks, Churcher set up his command post in the town's main police station at No. 1 Norderhofenden.

Friday, 11 May
Generalfeldmarschall Busch broadcast a message from the Flensburg enclave. Describing himself as OB Nordwest, he declared: 'By order of Grossadmiral Dönitz and with the agreement of the British occupation authorities I have taken command of Schleswig-Holstein and the areas occupied by the troops of Field-Marshal Montgomery. All German military and civilian authorities there are subordinated to me.'

Busch was referring to an agreement made on 5 May by which 21st Army Group established a German chain of command through which it could direct the initial disbandment of the enemy forces. However, his broadcast brought heated protests from all over the Allied world. It gave offence because it conveyed the message that the Dönitz government took priority over the Allies, and furthermore it was sent from a transmitter in the Flensburg enclave, which British troops were not able to enter. In London, angry questions were asked in the House of Commons. General Eisenhower promptly ordered firm control over the Flensburg radio and censorship of all future transmissions. Brigadier Churcher sent a commando party of technicians to the transmitting station to remove the vital parts and ordered the station closed. The incident gave Churcher an opportunity to enter the enclave and visit Dönitz's headquarters in the Marine-Schule. One of the first people he saw upon entering, although he darted into a passage to escape recognition, was Himmler. Churcher demanded to see the senior German officer, whereupon he was shown into the office of Generaloberst Jodl. When he asked about Himmler, Jodl denied that the former Reichsführer-SS was there. Churcher proceeded to give Jodl instructions concerning the evacuation of German troops from the Flensburg area and the construction of PoW camps. He stipulated the exact limits of the German enclave and limited the number of guards that Jodl was allowed to employ to 300.

Saturday, 12 May
Major General Lowell W. Rooks, Deputy Chief of G-3 Division at SHAEF, and his deputy, British Brigadier E.J. Foord, the Chief of Operational Intelligence of SHAEF's G-2 Division, arrived in Flensburg with a staff of thirteen Americans and ten British, and set up headquarters on the *Patria*.

Albert Speer was working in his office in Schloss Glücksburg when he was approached by two Americans, Lieutenant George Sklarz and Technical

Sergeant Harald Fassberg. They introduced themselves as members of the US Strategic Bombing Survey (USSBS) group, which was compiling data on the effects of the Allied bombing campaign, and asked him whether he would be willing to cooperate. Speer agreed, and for the next week sat in the castle with various members of the USSBS discussing the effects, mistakes and peculiarities of the bombings on both sides, and providing the USSBS with important wartime reports. Major General Frederick L. Anderson, Deputy Commander of Operations at Headquarters, US Strategic Air Forces in Europe, travelled to Glücksburg to personally thank Speer for his co-operation and compliment him on his wartime achievements as Minister for Armaments and War Production.

Despite such examples of co-operation, there were several incidents which led to demands in the United States and Britain for the termination of the Dönitz government and the elimination of the enclave. Busch's controversial broadcast of 11 May had been the first incident. There was growing alarm over the fact that the Allies had no precise knowledge of the situation inside the German enclave. It was suspected that it contained a number of high-ranking officers and Reich ministers who were listed as war criminals and eagerly sought after by British Intelligence.

Sunday, 13 May
Major General Rooks, in his first interview with Dönitz, ordered the arrest of Generalfeldmarschall Keitel (who was wanted for war crimes) and his replacement by Generaloberst Jodl. He explained that all subsequent instructions to the German forces would be in the name of the Supreme Allied Commander and that his control party were to have complete access to the offices and files of the OKW.

Later that day, Rooks interviewed Jodl, who with Keitel arrested and taken away was now the chief OKW officer. Jodl assured Rooks that he would undertake to carry out SHAEF directives in the interest of maintaining order and saving the German people from catastrophe.

Monday, 14 May
Political Intelligence Report – Germany, by the Joint Intelligence Sub-Committee
The purpose of this report, sections of which are quoted below, was to stress those factors which might have an effect on the security of the Allied armed forces or cause the Allied High Command embarrassment.

The policy of Germany's new leaders
'The German armed forces died hard. But the events of the past week prove that Germany still does not regard the struggle as over. The Nazi Party may have collapsed, its leaders for the most part either dead or in our hands and her armies herded into prisoner of war camps; but this extraordinary country is still fighting with weapons which she forged and used with success during the years 1919–1939 – the weapons of political intrigue. The great German military critic, Clausewitz, said that a country went to war only when it had failed to achieve its object by diplomacy. The converse is also true. When a country cannot wage war any longer, it will give up the military struggle and once more patiently wage political warfare. This is what Dönitz and the other German leaders will try to do – they are standing Clausewitz's old dictum on its head and are carrying on the battle by other means.

'What is the battle and what is the policy of these men? The battle is a clear cut issue. However bitterly the Germans have fought against the Allies, Soviet Russia has always been the enemy they detested and feared most desperately. They fear that the bestialities which the Germans visited on Russia will now return a hundred fold on them. During the last days of the war, German units on the Western Front were ordered to turn their backs on the Allies and march to join battle on the Eastern Front. Fighting still continues in Czechoslovakia, where Schörner's army fought a rear-guard action to cover the retreat of German soldiers and civilians to Allied-occupied Germany. Hitler and Goebbels chose to die (if reports of their deaths are true) in Berlin and on the Russian Front. Jodl, though he tried to dicker and procrastinate, signed the armistice at Reims with a dignified and correct bearing: Keitel signed at Berlin with every mark of arrogance and contempt for the foe which occupied the German capital.

'Their policy is also quite simple; embroil the Allies at all costs with the Russians. Every independent act of the Dönitz government has been directed to this end. The Flensburg radio under Dönitz stated that the armistice with the Allies made possible the transfer of German forces to fight the Russians in the East (this was of course a lie). Up to the last Jodl tried to lengthen the surrender negotiations to gain time for Schörner. Whole German armies on the Eastern Front have tried to surrender to the Allies instead of to the Russians as they were bound by the terms of surrender. Germans on Bornholm [a Danish island in the Baltic Sea] resisted the Russians landing and asked the Allies to land and receive their surrender. Meanwhile a whispering campaign had begun that at an appropriate moment the Allies will attack the Russians. Prominent personalities in our hands do not scruple to try to make trouble by hinting that we are afraid to do so.

'The lines on which Germany's official leaders will conduct the campaign is becoming clear. They will take every opportunity of licking the Allies' boots in order to make us grudgingly acknowledge that they are "correct". At the same time they will do everything they can to cheat the Russians, thus engendering in the Soviet mind, quick to be suspicious, that the Allies are behind this German trickery. They will appeal to the Allies whenever the Russians do not stick by the letter of the surrender agreement. They will give the impression, whenever possible, that the Allies are protecting Germans, a Western race, from the barbarians from the East. Since Russian negotiations are often marked by obduracy and seldom by speed, they will try to come to quick agreements with the Allies and thus face the Russians with a fait accompli.

'This is a cold and perfectly calculated campaign. It springs moreover from a determination to prove that Hitler's conception of history was true. The German argument is now as follows. "The Nazi Party (which was responsible for losing the war) was a wicked institution since it forced the Anglo-Americans to destroy Germany; it has now been swept away and its place in the struggle against Bolshevism is now taken by the Allies. Germany must therefore help the Allies and oppose the Russians. By fooling the Allies into rebuilding Germany as a bulwark against the Russians, Germany will regain its place as a Great Power." To bolster up this argument the Germans can draw support from certain organs of the press of many countries, particularly from Spanish newspapers under the control of the repulsive ragamadolio General Franco.

'Present German policy is therefore one step in the great campaign for the renaissance of Germany. The men, who signed the acknowledgement of Germany's complete defeat, were junior commanders or staff officers in 1918. To them 7th May 1945 is just another episode in Germany's eternal struggle for domination. They saw their country destroyed and rebuilt and they believe in their hearts that it can be done again. To parody General De Gaulle's famous aphorism, Germany has lost another war, but it has not lost the chance of making another. Just as some of the German generals expect that the Allies will in the end use them in local government to prevent Communist uprisings, Germany's present leaders are already at work to gain for Germany the status of co-belligerent against Russia. They are working in reality to defeat the Allies in the hour of their victory.'

General conditions in Germany
'The general orderliness and apathy of the population continues. Requisitions, except in obvious cases of looting, are accepted as the price of defeat, the main complaint being that the Nazis and the rich are not stripped first. A popular method of attempting to gain personal advantage and of currying favour with the Allies is to inform on the Nazis, and gifts are sometimes pressed on Allied officials with a characteristic Teutonic tactlessness. Non-fraternisation is regarded with some dismay both as an obstacle to easing restrictions and as a humiliation to "good" Germans. The Allied billeting policy has, however, come as something of a shock especially in view of the housing shortage.

'Though there is now widespread feeling against the Nazis, the army has escaped the odium of defeat. Deserters are exposed by German civilians, but numerous attempts were made by soldiers to change their uniform for the safety of civilian clothes. In a group of 83 civilians, 32 were found to be soldiers. While all the stories which circulated in 1940 of German parachutists descended to earth disguised as nuns may not be true, one German NCO was recently apprehended in the cassock of a Franciscan monk complete with a six days' growth of beard and a genuine monk to substantiate his story.'

Security
'Wire-cutting has been reported from some areas and a fire destroyed the town hall at Freudenstadt which the French state is alleged to have been caused by a phosphorous bomb which had been left as a booby trap. Two other fires broke out and destroyed several other buildings in the same city. Buried explosives and demolition equipment were also found by the French in the Black Forest region. The French have begun to collect Germans [aged] between 18 and 45 and put them at the disposal of combat units for road clearance.'

Thursday, 17 May
Major General Rooks and American diplomat Robert Murphy were received by Dönitz at his office in the Sportschule. When asked about his status as head of state, he showed them copies of the first two telegrams from Bormann that appointed him as Hitler's successor and informed him of the Führer's death. He implored them that he was merely trying to do his duty and carry out orders from the authority which he considered legitimate.

As it happened, a Russian delegation, a fifteen-man party led by General Truskov, arrived in Flensburg and joined the SHAEF Control Party on the *Patria*. This made the required co-ordination with the Soviets much easier.

Friday, 18 May
A British search party entered the enclave, cordoned off the hospital and, despite German protests, went in looking for Alfred Rosenberg, the Nazi ideologue and head of the NSDAP Office of Foreign Affairs. He was found in bed in a state of drowsiness; it was feared he had taken poison but it turned out he was just drunk. Rosenberg was tried for war crimes at Nuremberg in October 1946, found guilty and executed.

Saturday, 19 May
Eisenhower directed the 21st Army Group to consult with the SHAEF Control Party and then arrest the members of the Dönitz government and the OKW. Their archives were also to be seized and secured. Members of the Kriegsmarine HQ were for the moment to be exempted from the order. Members of the US Strategic Bombing Survey group requested to keep the decision secret for a day or two as they had not yet finished their very useful discussions with Speer and his staff on the results of Allied bombing.

Tuesday, 22 May
Major General Rooks issued his summons to Dönitz, Jodl and Admiral von Friedeburg to present themselves aboard the *Patria* at 9.45 am the following day. The Grand Admiral had been expecting to be arrested for some time, so when his adjutant, Korvettenkapitän Lüdde-Neurath, informed him about the summons he had no illusions about what it meant. 'Pack your bags!' he remarked.

Wednesday, 23 May
British soldiers respected the Flensburg enclave for the government and did not hinder people from going in and out.

In a ruined country, Britain believed Dönitz's government could help provide stability. The theory was that Germans were more likely to listen to other Germans. Furthermore, the enclave attracted Nazis on the run. 'All the rats from the Nazi regime went to Flensburg, a lot of SS people also got new papers from this last government, so they changed identities, then they were able to escape from the Allied troops,' said Kriegsmarine captain Joerg Hillmann.

Yet British patience with the Flensburg government finally wore off, and its members were taken into custody. The institution had been exposed as a fantasy – seemingly in denial about the defeat of Nazi Germany. Dönitz was eventually jailed for ten years at the Nuremberg trials, having maintained his belief that he was Germany's true leader.

During the morning of 23 May, Dönitz, Jodl and von Friedeburg left their respective billets, each in their own car, and drove the short distance to the *Patria*, arriving there punctually at 9.45 am as requested. As Dönitz's car reached the quayside, Lüdde-Neurath got out first and held the door open for Dönitz, who was carrying his field marshal's baton. Stepping on to the gangway, the Germans noted that things were very different from what they had been on previous visits. The British lieutenant-colonel who was usually there to welcome them was absent, and there was no presenting of arms by any of the guards. On the other hand, there was a host of press photographers standing around. On board ship, they were shown into the spacious lounge bar. Before them was a long table, covered by a white tablecloth. Dönitz, Jodl and von Friedeburg sat down. Dönitz remarked: 'It's easy to guess why we've been asked here today.'

They sat alone in silence for six minutes, while their ADCs and other accompanying officers paced the linoleum floor. The Germans were kept waiting for several minutes to ensure they were still aboard at 10.00 am when 159 Brigade moved into the enclave. When the Allied Control Party entered, Dönitz and his commanders rose to their feet. There was no formal salute. Major General Rooks sat opposite the Germans with Brigadier Foord and General Truskov on his right and left and an interpreter, Herbert Cohn, to one side.

Rooks immediately came down to business:

'Gentlemen, I am in receipt of instructions from the Supreme Headquarters, European Theatre of Operations, from the Supreme Commander, General Eisenhower, to call you before me this morning and tell you that he has decided, in concert with the Soviet High Command, that today the acting German government and the German High Command, with the several of its members, shall be taken into custody as prisoners of war. Thereby the acting German government is dissolved. This is now going on. Troops of the 21st Army Group are taking the several members, civilian and military, and certain records into custody. In conformity with instructions, each of you is to consider yourself a prisoner of war from this moment. When you leave this room an Allied officer will attach himself to you and escort you to your quarters where you will pack, have your lunch and complete your affairs, after which they will escort you to the airfield at 1330 [hours] for emplaning. You may take the baggage you require. That's all I have to say.'

When he had finished, Rooks asked Dönitz if he wished to say anything. The Grand Admiral, who had listened with a tight face but was otherwise calm, merely retorted: 'Comment is superfluous.' Jodl, his face red and blotchy, let a sheaf of papers slip through his fingers on to the floor. Von Friedeburg, for whom this was his fourth capitulation in three weeks, just sat apathetically, tears in his eyes.

The main operation to seize the enclave and arrest the other members of the Dönitz government and the OKW had started at 9.30 am. The assigned units had moved into position, stopping short and keeping out of sight of the German sentry posts. At 10.00 am, Brigadier Churcher gave the signal for the troops to go in. The Cromwell tanks of the 15th/19th Hussars rolled forward and took up position at the enclave exits. The two infantry battalions and the Royal Marines party entered the German area and quickly closed in on their objectives. The whole enclave surrendered quickly. Not a single shot was fired.

Arrest of Grand Admiral Karl Dönitz
Admiral Sir Andrew Browne Cunningham, Britain's First Sea Lord and Chief of the Naval Staff, referred to General Eisenhower's intention to arrest Grand Admiral Dönitz and other German leaders. Cunningham thought that the War Cabinet Chiefs of Staff Committee should consider whether the arrest of these German leaders was desirable, and if they were arrested, who was to be put in their place. He said some German commanders would be required as a medium for the control of the German armed forces and thought that the arrests might cause trouble at Bergen in Norway, where there were several thousand Germans and some forty U-boats. He had already received indications of possible trouble in that city. He drew attention to the fact that all signals from U-boats at sea had ceased as from 5.00 am that morning.

Dönitz, Jodl, Speer and the other high-ranking Nazi prisoners were taken to the 159 Brigade headquarters at the police station on Norderhofenden in the centre of Flensburg. There they were sat in a room, surrounded by their suitcases. One by one, they were summoned to an adjoining room to be registered as prisoners, and were then taken behind a screened area in the corner where they were subjected to a full body search. No crevice was left unexamined. Meanwhile, their baggage was being searched and all documents and valuables taken out. Examining Dönitz's suitcase, a Field Security officer found the Grand Admiral's field marshal's baton and his so-called interim baton. Emerging from behind the screen, he showed the field marshal's baton to a Captain Hugh Williams. Both men would have liked it as a souvenir, but they decided it must be handed over to the brigade commander, so the baton was taken to Brigadier Churcher's office and placed in his safe. Two days later, Dönitz wrote a formal protest, asking for the return of his two batons, but without effect.

The humiliating body search and the rifling of their luggage severely upset the Germans. Depending on their dispositions, they emerged from the room angry, insulted and depressed. Shortly after, the three main prisoners – Dönitz, Jodl and Speer – were paraded to the rear courtyard of the police station, where Brigadier Churcher allowed members of the Allied press to film, photograph and question them. The three Germans took it calmly and stoically. Speer made an effort to give the impression that the spectacle did not concern him. One reporter tried asking Jodl a question, but the general icily replied: 'I am a prisoner of war and not required to say anything but my name and rank.' The reporter grinned and said: 'OK, give me those.' Jodl shot back: 'Generaloberst Jodl, chief of the Oberkommando der Wehrmacht.'

All the prisoners were loaded onto trucks and taken to Flensburg airfield where they were put on board two C-47s and flown to the Allied Internment Centre at Bad Mondorf, Luxembourg. Dönitz's government had lasted just twenty-three days.

Two of the escorting officers, Captains Hugh Williams and Derek Knee, flew in the same aircraft with the Germans. Williams recalled:

'We had a little trouble with the American crew who wanted to get autographs. We took off. After a while the little man seated opposite me rose, raised his Homburg hat and said: "Where are we going?" Not to be outdone, I got up, bowed and said: "I'm afraid I can't tell you." "Ah," he said, "it's a secret." "Yes," I said. As far as I was concerned it was a secret as no one had told us where we were going. The 159th Brigade Quartermaster had pushed two wooden crates aboard, one containing tins of corned beef and the other tins of biscuits. A little later my little friend rose again and we went through the bowing and hat raising. He said: "Is this for us?" "Yes," I replied. Now one of the failings of the German government was that they never taught their politicians and senior Wehrmacht officers how to open tins of bully beef. So, standing in the middle of the plane at 200 knots, I demonstrated how to open a tin of corned beef. Dönitz said his wife had put some sausage in his briefcase, so could he have a knife. I gave him mine.'

Future of Mission No. 30: Exchange of Information with the Soviet Union
The purpose of Britain's Military Mission No. 30 in Moscow was to liaise with Soviet military personnel and share information useful to the common purpose of defeating Nazi Germany. Also included were military situation reports on the Eastern Front, including summaries of battles and operations, reports on the Soviet Army, assessments of German strength and strategy on the Eastern Front and discussions of Germany's need to secure a supply of oil.

The Chiefs of Staff Committee was informed that the Foreign Secretary had some doubts as to the value of the continuation of Military Mission No. 30 and considered whether it would not be better to revert to the normal system of dealing with the Soviet High Command through military attachés on the staff of the Ambassador. An alternative proposal was that advantage should be taken of the appointment of Lieutenant General Gammell as head of the military mission to make a firm approach to the Russians pointing out that the mission had been of little value to the British and that, if it were to be kept in being, the British should expect to be afforded treatment comparable to that given to the Soviet Mission in England. It was proposed to hold an informal meeting between representatives of the Foreign Office, the Ambassador in Moscow and General Gammell to discuss the matter.

Tuesday, 13 November
General Karl Kolle's Memoirs
The memoirs of General Karl Koller, Chief of the General Staff of the Luftwaffe, included the following:

> 'I went to the briefing [on 27 April, 1945] which was held by the OKW in the Forester's house in woods near Furstenberg. Großadmiral Dönitz and the Reichsführer were expected, they came late.
>
> 'The Reichsführer greeted me before the briefing. When I spoke to him about the Reichsmarschall he remarked: "The Reichsmarschall matter is an unfortunate business" (which did not make it clear whether he meant that the Reichsmarscall's sections or the measures taken by Führer-Bormann were unfortunate). I remarked that when the Reichsmarschall heard of the Führer's decisions he could not have acted in any other way, in order to draw the Reichsführer into a lengthy discussion, but this was unsuccessful because [Field Marshal Wilhelm] Keitel interrupted and the conversation was ended. The Reichsführer remarked that he wanted to talk to me later. But he did not have any time for me after the briefing either and said he had other conferences. Then he left suddenly when a tank alert was given.

'The Grossadmiral greeted me as always, [and] did not mention the Reichsmarschall matter. I did not have time to mention it to the Grossadmiral until after the briefing.

'The briefing, which did not take long, was attended by the Grossadmiral and by the Reichsführer. It was held by Jodl. Nothing special [was mentioned], the successes of the attack of the 12th Army were being awaited. I was able to correct some errors concerning the situation in the southern zone.

'After the briefing I spoke to the Grossadmiral concerning the arrest of the Reichsmarschall, which I did not consider to be justified. The Grossadmiral said that he was convinced that the Reichsmarschall was impelled by the best interests, but he ended the conversation by saying he must go to lunch. He wanted to speak to me later, but he left very suddenly.

'I then spoke to Keitel again to find out at least what he thought of the overall situation and the plans for the immediate future. The conversation was immediately guided into trivial channels. (I had expected that the seriousness of the overall situation and the Reichsmarschall matter, along with the appointment of Greim to the rank of Feldmarschall and to be supreme commander of the Air Force, which had just been announced, would be the main topic in all personal conversations. These matters were very urgent. But I was given the impression that nobody wanted to talk about the Feldmarschall or about the seriousness of the general situation. It has always seemed to me that these people were living on a different planet and that they were afraid to open their mouths.)

'Jodl smiles in passing and remarks "Don't fly to Berlin under any circumstances."

'I make use of the quiet which settles over the hut during the meal in order to call up the Führerbunker in Berlin. Reception bad at times.

(a) I asked for the Führer in order to report my presence. The exchange in the Bunker answers, "The Führer has retired and cannot be disturbed."

(b) Then I ask for the Feld[marschall] von Greim and am immediately connected. Report to Greim that I have arrived at Rechlin, that I am now at the OKW and that I have orders, forwarded by Bormann's office, to come to Berlin and report to the Führer. At the same time I congratulated him on his promotion but could only offer my condolences on his new appointment in view of the situation. I also asked him whether he intended to appoint someone else [as] the Chief of the General Staff or whether I am to remain at my post. Furthermore, I asked about his wound and about his health. Feld[marschall] von Greim described how he had been wounded and said it was not serious, but he must remain in bed at present. The Führer repeatedly sat at his bed for long periods and discussed the matter with him.'

Kohler wrote that the following conversation then took place between him and Greim:

[Kohler:] 'I know nothing about your leaving to report to the Führer. I gave your written report to the Führer. He read the report but did not make any comment. Do not fly to Berlin under any circumstances; in the first place this is entirely unnecessary and in the second place you will never get through, and if you did get through, then it is questionable whether you will be able to get out again. I do not believe that it will be possible for me to get out any more and then we would be sitting here in the Bunker. That would be an impossible situation.' I told Greim as much of the air situation as I knew and that we would attempt to land aircraft on the Axis [in Berlin] during the evening or the night in order to get him out.

[Greim:] 'Good, try that, but do not stay too long and leave that to [General Eckhard] Christian. You must fly out tomorrow night; otherwise, there will be confusion in the command down there. You know how it is.' (Greim is still thinking as AOC of the Luftlotte 6 [one of the primary divisions of the Luftwaffe.])

'You will naturally remain at you post as Chief of the General Staff; I would not be able to carry on without you. I also told that to the Führer and I am convinced that we will be able to work very well together.'

[Kohler:] 'Now I know what I must do, but we will not be able to work together very long. We can't make very much out of the Air Force any more, Herr Feldmarschall, the end is approaching.'

[Greim:] 'Just you wait and don't lose hope, everything will still end up well, the presence of the Führer and his strength have braced me up considerably, this is as good as a fountain of youth for me here. Everything is like in a lunatic asylum. I simply do not understand it and I often ask myself if I am so stupid that I cannot follow the spiritual soarings of these men and that I cannot recognize the path to salvation. Or they must have a sixth sense that enables them to see things to which we ordinary mortals are blind. But there is no such thing and one begins to doubt one's sane thinking. There are so many things about us that a normal person cannot grasp.'

Their conversation then turned to cover the following matters:

'(a) The Me.262 units. According to the Führer's orders they are to remain in the Prague area and the units not already there are to be sent there.

'(b) Operations in the area south of Berlin: point of main effort for all aircraft whose range permits them to reach Berlin: support of the relief of Berlin. (I told Greim that in my assessment of the situation the relief of Berlin cannot succeed. There is no chance of success when one considers the strength of the opposing forces, the condition of the equipment of our troops and our supply situation. Greim emphasizes that the relief must succeed and will succeed.)

'(c) KG.51 [Luftwaffe bomber wing] is also to transfer to the Prague area.

'(d) Jagdverband 44 [a special fighter unit of top German fighter ace pilots], distribution of the Me.262 aircraft. Greim agrees with me that the special Plenipotentiaries must finally be done away with. He wants to get the Führer to order this and empowers me to ignore them for the time being.

'(e) Chain of command in the South German area:
  'OKL in command of–
  'Luftflotte 6, in command of Lw.Kdo. West.
  'Luftwaffenkdo. 4.
  'Luftwaffenkdo. 8.
  'Kdr General der Lw. Italian (AOC in Italy).
'Greim approves the proposal to place the Lw. Kdo. 4 and the Kdr Gen Der Deutschen Luftwaffe in Italy under the command of the Luftflottenkdo. 6 at the proper moment.

'(f) Greim orders (after a discussion with Gen Oberst Stumpf before taking off for Berlin on the 26th April) that Genltn Schmidt Ob.Lw.Kdo. West is to be relieved of his post immediately and is to be replaced by General Harlinghausen. My question whether Gen Schmidt is to be given a reason, is answered by Greim in the negative, he says it is not necessary for him to give a reason. (The reasons were evident.)
  'Other changes in personnel:
  'Gen Oberst Dessloch as Deputy AOC Luftfl. 6.

The New Flensburg Government and the State of Germany 165

> 'Gen Deichmann as Deputy AOC Luftwaffenkdo. 4.
>
> '(g) Greim informs me of the Führer's order dated 25th April which I had already received from Winter and which is recorded here under the 26th April.
>
> 'Slogans (given by Greim): Assumption of command of the Air Force; promotion to Feldmarschall; first task relief of Berlin; faithfulness to the Führer; expects the Air Force to follow a straight and honourable path.
>
> '(h) Greim also asks me to inform his wife and give her his regards.'

The conversation then ended.

During and after the conversation with von Greim, Kohler said the following took place:

> '(a) A tank alert had been given at the OKW because Russian tanks had broken through at Prenzlau and were advancing towards Lychen and Wolbeck. Everybody must be ready to leave within two hours.
>
> '(b) I went to Jodl and informed him of my conversation with Greim.
>
> '(c) A tank alert call came for me from the Bunker. Greim was calling, repeated parts of the first conversation and ended by saying that he was handing the line to the Flugkapitaen. Hanna Reitsch came to the telephone. She asked me to inform her mother and her sister in Salzburg and to explain to them that she could not refuse Greim's call. Then she gave a detailed description of her flight, often repeating herself. As it was impossible to stop her, I put down the receiver after 20 minutes and stopped the conversation. That was the only line to the Bunker and was required for more urgent business.
>
> '(d) If I wanted to organize anything to bring Feldm Greim out of Berlin, it would be necessary for me to return to Rechlin. Of course, Christian and his men had made all the necessary preparations, but I wanted to convince myself personally. I said goodbye to Jodl and Buechs and drove away. The treks along the roads had increased since this morning, traffic was blocked in some places.'

After Kohler's arrival at Rechlin, he recorded that events occurred in the following manner:

> '(1) Six Fieseler Storch with 30 escort fighters had been assembled in Rechlin. The Storches were supposed to fly under fighter cover to the Axis in Berlin sometime in the evening. Twelve Ju.52s were in

readiness for the night. They were also supposed to bring SS men back to Berlin. The Storches mission failed, [as] the formation was scattered in a strong shower. The single Storch that managed to break through was unable to find the Axis in the smoke-haze and in the rain, some met heavy AA fire, [and] were damaged, others had to make emergency landings, [and] two were missing at first. None of the Storches landed on the Axis.

'(2) Oberst Rudel decided against making any further attempts himself and intended flying back that night. I approved this decision. I did not see Rudel any more after that. I do not know whether he flew away or not.

'(3) Rudel had a discussion with General Christian concerning organization, the units, the operational strength, the ammunition supply, the fuel supply, [and] questions of command. In detail: with Oberstetten. Panitzki operational questions, command, organizational for the flying units; with Major Dickel the same question with regard to the AA; with Major Falk supply; with Major Repenning communications. The conditions in this liaison staff are not fortunate. Christian seems to be at odds with his men. Confidential relations troubled. Ironed out as much as possible. An exchange of personnel would be senseless now.

'(4) Christian complains about Gen Oberst Stumpf; Christian and Stumpf seem to have fallen out completely. This is confirmed by a telephone call to Stumpf and a long conversation with Christian. (Each placed the blame on the other.) Stumpf does not want to take orders from Christian and does not want to realize that Christian is only carrying out orders from the OKL or OKW. Christian was supposed to have an arrogant tone and interfere with details. On the other hand, Stumpf makes Christian's work very much more difficult by his well-known prima donna temperament, [and] Stumpf thinks everything would be alright if I were to replace Christian personally or [if he was replaced] by Schultz. I gave Christian appropriate instructions and asked Stumpf to show some understanding and not make working together unnecessarily difficult. I held it to be unwise in these times to exchange Christian for Schultz, each of whom was acquainted with conditions in his own area. It is terrible how small-minded these people are, they are even governed by personal vanity in these hard times.

'(5) The first Ju.52 returns from night operations to Berlin without success[;] the crew searched for the approach to the Axis for an hour without finding it. The second plane returned badly damaged, the third was missing, the fourth returned and reported that the D/F station on the Axis had refused to accept any more aircraft. This led to the assumption that the third plane had probably crashed on the Axis and Greim confirmed this assumption later. There would probably be no more operations to Berlin that night. I set my take-off for Rechlin for 3 o'clock.'

1946

Tuesday, 12 March
The following details were learned following an interrogation of Julius Weitmann, Press Referent to Admiral Dönitz from 30 January 1943 to 20 May 1945:

'Admiral Dönitz moved his headquarters to the Tiergarten Bunker during the night of 20/21 April, [19]45, and owing to Russian fire the headquarters was again moved to Plön [at] 0400 hrs on 22 April, [19]45. During these twenty-four hours Admiral Voss, personal representative of Dönitz at Hitler's headquarters, was interviewed together with Keitel by Dönitz in the Tiergarten Bunker. Voss then returned to Hitler's headquarters, and Weitmann has not seen him since that date, nor has he heard any mention of Voss since 30 April, [19]45.

'On 30 April, [19]45, Dönitz received a telegram ... the contents were in special code and a special machine was used for de-coding. Dönitz had been in a nervous state for the ten to twelve days prior to receiving that message and his condition is said to have worsened on the receipt of the telegram. The following day at 1400 hours a second telegram was received, again in special code and dated 30.4.45 ... Dönitz was apparently not surprized, his nervousness increased and he immediately ordered Weitmann to make preparations for him to broadcast at 1800 hours that evening. Measures were taken immediately but it was 2145 hrs before Dönitz eventually broadcast.'

Weitmann further stated that he was informed by a Dr Schweisser of the Propaganda Ministry, whom he met after the capitulation, that State Secretary Werner Naumann entered the Ministry at 6.00 pm on 30 April 1945, informed the staff of Hitler's death and then left.

Chapter Seven

Political Statements and Hitler's Will

1945

Sunday, 29 April, Early Morning
In his underground bunker, Adolf Hitler readied himself for death. Instead of surrendering to the Allies, the Führer had decided to end his own life. Having already written his last will, Hitler then concentrated on his political statement.

Hitler's Will
Hitler's will was a short document which stated that they had chosen death over capitulation, and that he and his wife, Eva Braun, were to be cremated. It named Martin Bormann as executor.

As the bunker shook and shuddered under ceaseless barrages, a pale and visibly trembling Hitler sat down with Traudl Junge to compose his political statement.

Political Statement
Frau Junge had overslept. Hurriedly, she rushed to Hitler's study and breathlessly apologized for being late. Hitler understood and gestured her to sit down. She started to take the cover off of the typewriter, but Hitler told her to leave it; he wanted her to take down what he had to say in shorthand before she typed it.

The political statement was a lengthy document made up of two sections. In the first, Hitler laid all the blame for the war and Germany's defeat on 'International Jewry' and urged all Germans to continue fighting. In the second section, Hitler expelled Hermann Göring and Heinrich Himmler and appointed their successors. He appointed Grand Admiral Karl Dönitz as the new president of the Third Reich. He then vowed that he would never leave Berlin, preferring to remain to direct the defence of the city, even if it cost him his life.

He said to Junge:

'Since there are not enough forces to withstand the enemy attack at this point and our resistance is slowly being weakened by blinded and spineless characters, I wish to join my fate to that which millions of others have taken upon themselves and remain in this city. In addition, I do not wish to fall into the hands of an enemy who, for the amusement of its incited masses, needs a new spectacle directed by the Jews.'

Hitler had drafted the text for his final documents on the evening of his marriage ceremony and dictated them to Frau Junge while the party continued next door. Nobody else could have drafted them, according to the Führer's secretary, Frau Gerda Christian, because Hitler had called in Goebbels and Bormann only for short consultations from time to time. The dictation, including the consultation with Goebbels and Bormann, took about two hours. Frau Christian did not know how many pages were typed, but she knew that the special typewriter with large type was used. She also did not know how many copies were typed, but assumed that one original and three or four copies were made, as was customary for Hitler's speeches. Everybody at the party knew that Hitler was dictating his last will, and no pledge to secrecy was required; Christian believed, however, that as a matter of discretion the people present would not have spread their knowledge among other occupants of the bunker. Frau Junge did not mention anything to her about the contents of the testament; nobody else discussed its contents. The composition of a new Reichsregierung had previously been discussed and Frau Christian knew about it, but she was not aware of the fact that this matter had been included in the testament. Christian did not know whether anybody was sent out with copies of the testament; she knew that Dönitz was informed, but did not know through whom. She was unaware of any letter of transmittal written by Goebbels, Bormann or anyone else, and also claimed ignorance of the prospective recipients of the copies. Confronted with a large list of names and asked to select likely messengers who might have carried copies, she named the following:

(a) Wilhelm Zander. She found out from the newspapers that Zander had been in possession of a copy. She was unaware of this before and would not have thought him a probable choice.
(b) Nikolaus von Below. She said he would be the most logical person for a mission of this kind, but Christian thought that he had left the bunker before the testament had been written. She appeared genuinely surprised when informed of the fact that von Below's signature as a witness appeared on the document.

(c) Martin Bormann. Christian believed it very probable that he had a copy. She believed that this may have been one reason for Bormann's anxious desire to leave Berlin.
(d) Heinz Lorenz. She remembered distinctly that he left after the completion of the testament. She was not aware of any assignment for Lorenz, but considered him a good choice on account of his intelligence.
(e) She commented on the fact that a considerable number of other military personnel were coming and going at various time, but was unable to indicate any likely names.

Hitler's Personal Will:

'Although during the years of struggle I believed that I could not undertake the responsibility of marriage, now, before the end of my life, I have decided to take as my wife the woman who, after many years of true friendship, came to this town, already almost besieged, of her own free will, in order to share my fate. She will go to her death with me at her own wish, as my wife. This will compensate us for what we have both lost through my work in the service of my people.

'My possessions, in so far as they are worth anything, belong to the Party, or if this no longer exists, to the State. If the State too is destroyed, there is no need for any further instructions on my part.

'The paintings in the collection bought by me during the course of the years were never assembled for private purposes, but solely for the future establishment of a picture gallery in Linz on the Danube.

'It is my most heartfelt wish that this will be duly executed.

'As Executor, I appoint my most faithful Party comrade, Martin Bormann. He is given full legal authority to make all decisions. He is permitted to hand over to my relatives everything which is of worth as a personal memento, or is necessary for maintaining their present standard of living, especially to my wife's mother and my fellow-workers of both sexes who were well known to him. The chief of these are my former secretaries, Frau Winter, etc, who helped me for many years by their work.

'My wife and I chose to die in order to escape the shame of overthrow or capitulation. It is our wish for our bodies to be burnt immediately on the place where I have performed the greater part of my daily work during the course of my 12 years service to my people.

'Berlin, 29 April 4.00 hours.
'A. Hitler
'Witnesses: Martin Bormann
Dr Goebbels
Nicolaus von Below'

Goebbels's Appendix to Hitler's Personal Statement:

'The Führer has ordered me to leave Berlin if the defence of the Reich capital collapses and to take part as a leading member in a government appointed by him.

'For the first time in my life I must categorically refuse to obey an order of the Führer. My wife and children join me in this refusal. Otherwise, apart from the fact that on grounds of fellow feeling and personal loyalty we could never bring ourselves to leave the Führer alone in his hour of greatest need, I would appear for the rest of my life as a dishonourable traitor and common scoundrel, who would lose his own self-respect as well as the respect of his fellow-citizens, a respect I should need in any further service in the future shaping of the German nation and German State.

'In the delirium of treason which surrounds the Führer in these most critical days of the war, there must be at least some people to stay with him unconditionally until death, even if this contradicts the formal, and from a material point of view, entirely justifiable order which he gives in his political statement.

'I believe that I am thereby doing the best service to the future of the German people. In the hard times to come, examples will be more important than men. Men will always be found to show the nation the way out of it tribulations, but a reconstruction of our national life would be impossible if it were not developed on the basis of of clear and understandable examples.

'For this reason, together with my wife, and on behalf of my children, who are too young to be able to speak for themselves, but who, if they were sufficiently old, would agree with this decision without reservation, I express my unalterable decision not to leave the Reich capital even if it falls and, at the side of the Führer to end a life which for me personally will have no further value if I cannot spend it in the service of the Führer and by his side.

'Berlin 29 Apr. 45 ... 5.30 hours
'Sgnd. Dr Goebbels.'

Other Documents

Christian claimed that she and Frau Junge did not type any other documents at all between 20 and 30 April. Their last work assignment was typing two press reports for Goebbels on 10 April. She explained that this situation was quite natural, since Hitler dictated very little to his secretaries in normal times, with the exception of speeches, personal letters to foreign statesmen such as Mussolini or Ion Antonescu in Romania and certain special projects. Christian claimed that during the days in the bunker, all military matters were entirely handled by military personnel. On the other hand, Frl Krueger, Bormann's secretary, was very busy during this time, as Bormann dictated and composed quite a number of documents during the last few days and appeared very active. Christian had no idea of the subject of Bormann's work, but was fairly sure that Frl Krueger would know. Christian again mentioned a vague recollection concerning some contact between Bormann and the Gauleiter at Munich.

Friday, 23 November
Jacob Otto Dietrich

Dietrich was a German SS functionary during the Nazi era, who served as the Press Chief of the Reich and State Secretary to the Propaganda Ministry and was also a confidant of Adolf Hitler. After the war, he was interrogated by the Combined Services Detailed Interrogation Centre, or CSDIC (WEA).

Dietrich was shown the signature on Hitler's political and personal testaments in the presence of two officers. Regarding Hitler's own signature, Dietrich stated that the 'A' and 'H' were correct, but the 't' 'appeared to be lacking'. The signature was considerably less clear than the originals he had seen up to about a year previously, but might be Hitler's genuine signature written under mental stress or excitement.

Dietrich recognized the signatures of both Goebbels and Bormann without hesitation, but he was not prepared to state on oath that they were genuine. However, he admitted that had he himself received a document bearing those signatures, he would have accepted them without question as coming from Goebbels and Bormann.

Dietrich did not recognize the remaining three signatures on the documents. He stated that he had not to his knowledge seen them before, with the possible exception of the signature of von Below.

Saturday, 24 November
Heinz Lorenz
The wills of both Hitler and Goebbels were given to Heinz Lorenz, Hitler's shorthand typist and DNB journalist, on 29 April 1945 by State Secretary Naumann. Lorenz was responsible for picking up broadcast news and bringing it to the bunker. He was told to leave Berlin on 29 April and to try to preserve the will for posterity. Other copies were given to various people with similar missions.

Hitler's and Goebbels's Wills
Britain's Secret Intelligence Service felt that the documents were genuine. The evidence supplied by them was consistent in all particulars with that derived from other sources concerning the last days in the Führerbunker.

The existence of these documents was implied in the telegram sent by Goebbels to Dönitz on 1 May, after Hitler's death. That telegram stated:

> 'Führer died at 1530 yesterday. Will dated 29.4. confers office of President on you; office/Chancellor on Reichminster Dr Goebbels; office of Party Minister on Reichsleiter Bormann; office of Foreign Minister on Reich minster Seyss-Inquart. By the Führer's order, the Will is to be brought out of Berlin to you and Fm Schörner for security and publication. Reichsleiter Bormann is trying to come to you.'

The telegram also referred to the document entitled 'Second Part of the Political Statement'.

The existence and some of the terms of Hitler's will were also implied in the 29 April telegram sent by Bormann to Dönitz, in which Bormann stated: 'In place of the former Generalfeldmarschall Göring the Führer has appointed you, Herr Großadmiral, as his successor. The written authority is on its way to you.'

The expulsion of Göring and Himmler was entirely consistent with the attitude of Hitler at that time as known from previous evidence, as was the silent omission of Albert Speer, with his replacement as Minister of Armaments by his assistant Karl Saur.

Lorenz himself was known to have been in the bunker with Goebbels and Werner Naumann, and his functions were known to have been as stated by him.

The witnesses who signed the documents were also known to have been present in the bunker on 29 April.

The documents also explained satisfactorily why Goebbels – whose decision to commit suicide was known to Hitler – nevertheless reported to Dönitz that he had been appointed by Hitler as Reichskanzler.

If the original document was in typescript, it would presumably have been typed by either Frau Christian or Frau Junge. The typist would be able to find evidence of its authenticity, which was an additional reason to trace Frau Christian.

Tuesday, 4 December
Heinz Lorenz, DNB Journalist
Heinz Lorenz was interrogated in connection with Hitler's will. His version of events tallied in all but a few minor points with the British statement on the circumstances of Hitler's death issued on 1 November 1945, and the Commandant of CSDIC (WEA), who had interrogated Lorenz personally, was convinced that he had told the truth.

The main points were that he received the will and personal statement personally from Bormann and Goebbels with instructions to get them through, if possible, to Dönitz or the nearest German high command, and failing this, to preserve them as historical documents. Lorenz admitted that he had two companions: Major Johannmeyer, Hitler's military adjutant, and Standartenführer Zander, one of Bormann's adjutants who had received similar missions. Zander was also given a copy of the Hitler/Braun marriage certificate. Lorenz provided descriptions and details of these two men, which were circulated to all Corps Districts and to USFET.

Lorenz stated that after the capitulation, all three of them decided that it would not be possible to contact Dönitz or any of the German military HQs, and they were only interested in their own personal fates. There were telegrams from Bormann and Goebbels to Dönitz which referred to the will of 29 April 1945, of which copies were sent to him. It was known that the copy sent to Dönitz failed to arrive. Frl Krueger, secretary to Bormann, was asked about the typing of the documents.

The signatures on the will were seen by Captain Jim Skardon, a handwriting expert from the MI5 Liaison Section, who had pronounced them genuine. They were also shown to Otto Dietrich, a confidant of Hitler, who immediately recognized them but said that as he was not a handwriting expert he could not swear an oath that they were genuine.

The question of the publication of the will then arose and whether it should be delayed until Zander and Johannmeyer had been apprehended. On the other hand, it was felt that publication of the will would not have made it more difficult to trace the pair, and it would be advisable to release the information

Political Statements and Hitler's Will 175

in order to forestall any possible leakage. The following brief was released for the press (*italics* as annotated in the original):

'Hitler's Will has been discovered. It was found on Heinz Lorenz, [a] DNB journalist who had been attached to Hitler's staff since 1936.

'Before the war Lorenz attended a number of important Conferences between Hitler and foreign statesmen and recorded the proceedings in shorthand. During the war he was attached to the Führer's Headquarters and took down news received from foreign broadcasts and passed it direct to the Führer's staff. In this capacity he was working at the Bunker in the Reich Chancellery from 18th April onwards, his receiving set acting as the only link between the outside world and the Führer's Bunker (he was unable to transmit messages).

'It was he who broke to Hitler the news of Mussolini's death and also of Himmler's negotiations with Count Bernadotte.

'He [Lorenz] was arrested in the British Zone, where he was living under an alias, taken to an internment camp and there searched. Sewn into the shoulder padding of his coat were found the following:

'1. Hitler's personal will.
'2. Hitler's political statement.
'3. An appendix by Goebbels to Hitler's political testament.

'He has been interrogated in detail on how he came into possession of these documents and he has given a story of the last days in Hitler's Bunker which agrees practically in every detail with that already given to the Press on 1st November. As he was so frequently in the Bunker he was in contact with Hitler's adjutants and member of his staff and was able to obtain a very good idea of what was going on. At 0400 hrs on 29th April Hitler made his Wills, which were witnessed by Bormann, Goebbels, General Krebbs, General Burgdorf (Chief military ADC to Hitler) and Colonel von Below (Luftwaffe Adjutant at Führer HQ).

'Between 0900 and 1000 hrs. on the same morning, Lorenz was summoned by Bormann who gave him Hitler's personal and political wills. He was then given Goebbels's declaration by Goebbels himself. He was instructed to leave Berlin at once in civilian clothes and convey the Wills to Dönitz if possible, or failing him, the nearest German High Command. He was told by Goebbels that if all else failed; he was to publish the wills for historical purposes.

'Bormann told Lorenz that he had been given this mission because as a young man with plenty of initiative, it was considered that he had a good chance of getting through.

'Lorenz left Berlin on 29th April at midday and was subsequently not present at the time of Hitler's suicide. As he found it impossible to reach Dönitz he decided to live under a cover name and to await events.

'Lorenz's story has been checked against all available evidence and appears to be entirely reliable. The signatures on the documents have been compared with other signatures of Hitler, Bormann, and Goebbels and pronounced by an expert to be genuine. They have also been shown to Otto Dietrich, Hitler's Press Chief, and were immediately recognised by him. The wills bear out the evidence we have from other sources that Hitler intended to commit suicide and have his body burnt together with that of Eva Braun. He definitely states this in his personal will in which, *after announcing his decision to marry Eva Braun*, he leaves all his possessions to the Party (or the State if the Party no longer exists), except for his paintings which are to be used for a picture gallery at Linz, and any personal mementos which his family or his former secretaries might wish to keep.

'His political testament is divided into two parts, the first being a tirade disclaiming all responsibility for the war and blaming it on *the ruling political clique in England, who were in turn the tool of "international Jewry"*. In this he again states that he had no intention of falling into enemy hands, but he will instead stay in Berlin and choose death voluntarily at the moment when he feels his position can no longer be maintained. The rest of the German people *however must* continue fighting with all possible means. *He shows his distrust of the Army whose will to resist he compares to that of the Navy.*

'In the second part of his political testament he dismisses Göring and Himmler from all their offices because of their so-called treachery to himself and appoints a new Government headed by Dönitz as President, with Goebbels as Chancellor, Bormann as Party Ministry and [Arthur] Seyss-Inquart [an Austrian Nazi politician] as Foreign Minister.

'*An interesting feature is the replacement of* [Albert] *Speer as Armaments Minister by his deputy* [Karl] *Saur. Speer was in disfavour on account of his opposition to the "Scorched Earth" policy.* In an appendix to Hitler's will, timed 0530 hrs Goebbels states that *for the first time he must categorically* refuse to obey the Führer's order to leave Berlin and take part in the new Government. *In contrast to general "delusion" of treachery around him he declares that he* intends to stay together with his wife and family and die at the Führer's side. *His children, if they were old enough, would agree with the decision which has been taken for them.*'

Thursday, 6 December

It was reported to the CIB that on 20 April 1945, the following people were given copies of Hitler's will with the mission to get them to Admiral Dönitz or General Ferdinand Schörner.

SS-Standartenführer Zander

Adjutant to Martin Bormann, Zander was described as aged about 37, of slim build, height about 1.75m, weight about 135lb, with brown hair which was very thin at the front, dark eyes and a rather dark complexion. He was normally clean-shaven, but he had recently grown a small moustache. He had slim, delicate hands, and his general appearance was slim. He had a deep voice. He was last seen wearing a dark civilian suit at noon on 11 May 1945, in his parents-in-laws' house in Hannover. His wife lived in Bad Wiessee or Tegernsee (Bavaria). Zander's parents-in-law were called Ahlring or Eilring and had a tobacconists shop in Hannover; this was bombed out and they moved to another flat.

Zander was carrying a copy of Hitler's personal and political wills and also the Hitler–Braun marriage certificate. It was possible that he may have left this at his father-in-law's house.

Major Willy Johannmeyer

The last Heeresadjutant to Hitler, Johannmeyer was aged 30, of slim build, height about 1.78m, weight about 150lb, with fair hair, light eyes (no glasses) and a fair complexion. His nose and chin were described as normal, his teeth white and good, and he was generally clean-shaven (however, on the night of 9–10 May, he had not shaved for several days). His general appearance was said to be of the typical blond German officer type. He had the Oak Leaves to the Ritterkreuz. His nationality was German and he spoke only German, his harsh voice having a Westphalian accent. He was last seen wearing a dark civilian suit with a grey-green shooting jacket on the night of 9/10 May in a train at Wunstorf station near Hannover. He had intended to go to Iserlohn, where his parents lived; his wife lived in Säckingen.

Friday, 14 December
Frau Zander

Frau Zander was arrested and transferred to PoW Camp 031 in order to discover the whereabouts of her husband, SS-Standartenführer Wilhelm Zander. It appeared that Frau Zander had told a number of lies in her original statement when she said that she had not seen her husband since April. According to the CIB, it transpired that after visiting his parents-in-law at Hannover, Standartenführer Zander had walked from the British Zone to Tegernsee, Bavaria, and was in hospital there during May and June with an injured foot. Zander had taken out false papers and was apparently now travelling under a false identity.

Frau Zander stated that the American Counter Intelligence Corps occupied her house in Munich, but that was not true: all that happened was that she was interrogated by some American officers.

It was felt that Frau Zander was more likely to tell the truth if she was told that other people knew about her husband's presence in Bavaria, had been arrested and were talking; the name Greiter should be mentioned to her as one of those arrested.

Frau Zander was in Munich during May and June, and it was thought most unlikely that she did not know that her husband was in Tegernsee at that time.

The Allies wanted to know whether Zander had mentioned to his wife his possession of Hitler's will and the Hitler–Braun marriage certificate.

Major Johannmeyer
The General Staff (GS) felt that:

> 'Johannmeyer should be thoroughly searched. His clothing needed to be examined carefully as it was possible that he may have concealed Hitler's Political Testament and possibly Hitler's personal Will in his clothing.
> 'His house and personal effects [needed] to be searched.
> 'He should be interrogated on the subject of the disposal of the Will.'

It was suggested that Johannmeyer may be able to provide some information about the location of SS-Standartenführer Zander, who was also believed to have a copy of the Führer's will.

The GS suggested that as Johannmeyer was ill, it was not feasible to move him to CSDIC (WEA) as there were no facilities there for invalids. They also suggested that if it were at all possible, Johannmeyer should be interrogated with particular reference to what he experienced at the time of Hitler's 'assumed' death.

1946

Thursday, 3 January
A number of questions were raised regarding the discovery of Hitler's will, as noted by Charles Wighton, a British United Press (BUP) correspondent:

(1) A letter to *The Daily Telegraph*, 1 January 1946, alleged that Hitler's marriage certificate may have been a German plan to trick the Allies. It was pointed out that it did not appear to have been typed on a machine of German manufacture, that no dieresis (marks placed over vowels to show they are pronounced separately) were shown, that one word was misspelt and that the dateline was not in German style.
(2) Where was the policeman Karnau (who told his story in June 1945)? Where was Kempka?
(3) Why had all the witnesses of Hitler's fate never been brought together and confronted with one another in a bid to find discrepancies?
(4) Why didn't the Intelligence Service dig up the cremation trench outside the Chancellery?
(5) Why had no mention been made of the allegation that two Storches that landed at Charlottenburger chausse on 30 April 1945?
(6) What information was there on the three men who escaped after the three messengers?
(7) Was it not agreed that all evidence regarding the alleged burying of Hitler's body was hearsay – sometimes second or third party – and would not hold water in a court of law?
(8) Why had the testimony of material witnesses in Soviet hands been ignored?
(9) Why was the documentary evidence to justify the claim that Hitler was dead not produced (interrogation reports etc)? Instead, the position was left merely to the Intelligence Branch claim without proof. And why were sections of the private report to the Cabinet kept secret?

Thursday, 10 January
The Discovery of Hitler's Last Will: HQ XXX Corps District
It had been known for some time that Hitler had made a will before his suicide. The evidence of this was in the captured telegrams sent on 1 May 1945 to Admiral Dönitz. The first of these was sent by Bormann and merely stated that Hitler's will was in force, i.e. that Hitler was dead. The second, sent by Goebbels, said that Hitler died at 3.30 pm on the previous day, 30 April, and that his testament of 29 April appointed Dönitz as President of the new government.

Next came the discovery of copies of Hitler's personal and political wills and an appendix by Goebbels. These were found sewn into the shoulder padding of Heinz Lorenz, Hitler's Deputy Chief Press Secretary, who had already been arrested as a case of doubtful identity. Lorenz was sent to an Interrogation

Centre and questioned closely on how he had obtained the documents. Meanwhile, the authenticity of the documents had been established by a handwriting expert and the contents compared with facts already known. Lorenz had at first stated that he did not know how many copies of the will had been made or to whom they had been given, but he eventually admitted that two other emissaries had been sent with him from Hitler's bunker on 29 April to take the wills to various destinations. SS-Staf Wilhelm Zander, assistant to Bormann, was given Hitler's personal and political wills and the Hitler–Braun marriage certificate, with the task of delivering them to Admiral Dönitz. Major Willy Johannmeyer, adjutant to Hitler, had Hitler's political testament for delivery to General Schörner, German C-in-C in the south. Lorenz himself was instructed to take the will to Dönitz or otherwise to Munich for eventual publication. It was known that Johannmeyer was in the bunker during the last week in April, but very little was known of Zander. Those people needed to be pursued to find the copies of the documents.

Johannmeyer was found living at Iserlohn in his parents' house. He maintained that he had merely acted as an escort for Zander and Lorenz and had not carried any documents himself. It was impossible to shake him from that assertion. To resolve the deadlock, Zander's case was then taken up. Zander's parents-in-law lived in Hannover and Zander's wife, who had previously been living in Munich, arrived there at about the same time. Zander had spent a fortnight at Hannover around 10 May and then departed to the south to try to find his wife, but nothing further was heard from him. Frau Zander appeared to be very anxious to help find him, producing photographs, addresses of his brothers and other evidence, but it was not possible to make any further progress until a British officer visited Munich and began work in conjunction with the American CIC. He learned that Zander was alive and living under an assumed name in the area. It was also discovered that he was known as Paustin and that he had been to hospital under that name, and had worked for a market garden in Tegernsee. Zander was subsequently tracked down without much difficulty. He saw that the game was up and was prepared to speak freely. His version of events agreed with that of Lorenz and revealed the location of the documents. It was, however, unnecessary to collect them, as the woman with whom Zander's documents had been deposited became frightened as a result of the local enquiry and handed them over voluntarily. The documents consisted of Hitler's two wills, the marriage certificate and a covering letter from Bormann to Dönitz.

Johannmeyer was now confronted with the facts, and although for a long time he persisted in his story, he eventually realized that as his two comrades, who were older and highly protected Nazi Party men, could so easily betray a trust which was laid on them chiefly by the Party, he as a purely military man with no Party connections had no reason to continue in this attitude. He therefore led his interrogator to a corner of his garden in Iserlohn and dug up a glass jar containing Hitler's political testament and a covering note from General Burgdorf.

Wednesday, 16 January
Heinz Lorenz
An anonymous letter had been received by Oberpräsident Kopf of Hannover. The letter was type-headed Otterndorf, near Cuxhaven, and posted at Cuxhaven on 22 December 1945, addressed to Herren Oberpräsident Kopf, Persönlich-Hannover, and OberPräsidium. The letter read as follows (text in italics annotated by the author):

'Herr Oberpräsident,
'The reason I am writing this to to you is that you may see what the people are thinking, and what their opinion is of you. I am writing you [sic] for the simple reason that we knew you when you were Landrat [district administrator]; at that time we had an opportunity to admire your ability. At present you are the highest official in the Province. What has, however, given us the courage to write to you, and indeed to renew our activity, is the fact that some weeks ago Reichsleiter Bormann brought us the Political Testament of our beloved Führer. Now at least we know where we stand, and the reasons for the collapse – treachery and sabotage even in the highest places. Now we know that the Anglo-American thieves stole from us the Atom bomb with which Adolf Hitler would, in June, have blown the British Isles to smithereens within 48 hours. However, our Führer's testament indicates what lines of action we are to follow in order to establish – even *if only* after decades – the National Socialist great German Reich. We shall not rest until the last enemy is driven from German soil, and until German traitors – you included – are hanging from the lampposts! Are you ashamed, Herr Oberpräsident, to act as toady to foreign rulers? We here in Land Hadeln [a town in northern Germany] always knew that your ability was not very great, but not that you were without Honour. Until now, you and all the other "personalities" of the new system have lost no opportunity to scoff at the shortage of the Third Reich; better would it be that you give proof by your deeds, your aper [sic] of the Nazis ... In all your speeches you forgot one thing, which is that the ruins surrounding us were caused not by Adolf Hitler, but by the Anglo-American terror bombers; that the

misery of the refugees is not of Hitler's doing, but that of the Bolshwilks [*sic*]! But you cannot bow and scrape sufficiently under the Oppressors! You pitiable wretch!

'We National-Socialists can neither be converted nor deprived of our faith by such as you! The Führer in his testament has shown what our goal is. Only one reproach have we to make against our unforgettable Reichsführer-SS Heinrich Himmler, and that is he was too gentle. Much too gentle! If only he had hanged the whole bunch of Jews and people of your sort, they would not be able to gabble today! Or do you really think that we believe in the Nurnberg [*sic*] *circus*, the sentence of which has already been decided on by 3 arch-swinderlers in Potsdam.

'And now just one thing more. Are you really so naive or foolish to believe that the Bolsheviks – whose goal is world revolution – intend to stop at the frontiers of Hannover Province? Are you really so stupid as not to perceive that [when] the Anglo-American gangsters refer to National Socialist or the Third Reich they really mean German or Germany? Now enough of words –– action calls us.

'*It is a question of avenging the dead Führer, making you and all your kind innocuous and one day establishing the* ... Nationalistische Grossdeutsch Reich.'

The letter, a personal attack on Oberpräsident Kopf, contained the usual type of Nazi propaganda. Frau Zander was interrogated on the subject, but it seemed unlikely that she wrote it or posted it herself. It was believed possible that Lorenz mentioned the existence of the will to a fellow internee at Westertimke, and it was therefore requested by the Intelligence Bureau that Lorenz be asked if he did mention or show the will to any other person, and if so, to whom. It was felt that would assist in tracing the author of the letter.

On the back of the envelope was printed Gemeinde Otterndorf (a town on the North Sea coast). Frau Zander's movements since 17 December when she left Munich were checked, and it was hard to see how she could have posted the letter in person; that would have been putting a too complicated construction on the whole affair. It thus seemed more probable that the leakage of information about Hitler's political testament took place at Westertimke, where Lorenz was interned from June to November, when he was transferred to Fallingbostel.

Friday 25, January
It was Artur Axmann's strong assertion that Bormann had personally carried copies of Hitler's political and personal testament, but when the question was

put to Axmann of how many copies of the testaments existed, he professed not to know. He was then asked who, in his opinion, had been entrusted with copies. His initial answer was: 'Bormann and the three military aides of Hitler.' Upon further questioning, he eliminated Voss, the naval aide, from the list, leaving his final choice of the three most likely names as Bormann, von Below and Johannmeyer. From a series of names which were put to him without any special emphasis, he dismissed several for various reasons, including Lorenz, who in his opinion was not close enough to Hitler to be considered and whom he had not seen in the Reichskanzlei after 28 April. When asked for the destination of the various copies, Axmann stated that all the copies were sent to Dönitz, dismissing the suggestion that Schöoerner or anyone else was to receive a copy.

Monday, 4 March
Answers to Queries re von Below by Press Correspondents Chamberlain and Wighton
Von Below was satisfied that the personal will he signed was identical to the one published in the papers. He had been shown a photostat of it and identified it as genuine. He said he never saw the political testament in the bunker, but thought the will was typed by one of Hitler's secretaries.

The machine on which they were typed contained umlauts, as was clear on the photostat issued to the press on 30 December. There was nothing un-German in the style of the date-line.

The marriage certificate, of which only photostats were held, appeared to have been blotted because it was folded over in a hurry. The date was, however, perfectly clear – Berlin, morning, 29 April 1945. The photograph that was published in the press on 30 December appeared to have suffered in transmission.

Tuesday, 19 March
According to HQ, US Forces European Theatre, Bormann had been spreading rumours of an atom bomb. Hitler's political statement, however, made no reference to an atom bomb, nor to treachery and collapse as a cause of ruin, and neither did it indicate any line of future action for the establishment of the Nazi Reich. Therefore, it was clear that the writer of the letter to the Oberpresident of Hannover had not seen the document, but had merely heard of its existence and invented its contents in order to apparently add authority to a threatening letter. It was therefore reasonable to assume that the writer had not seen Bormann, who would have known the true contents of the testament.

It had not been possible to discover who actually wrote the letter, but investigations suggested two possibilities:

(a) It was possible, though not probable, that Frau Zander herself wrote the letter; she was questioned as to her movements after she left Munich on 17 December 1945.
(b) It was possible that information leaked out through Lorenz at Fallingbostel. Lorenz had been interrogated and stated that the only person to whom he mentioned the matter was Erich Beck, editor of the *Breman Nachrichten*, to whom he spoke on 15 November, the day after the papers had been taken from him. Beck had also been interrogated and stated that that he told no one until 15 December, when he informed Koltermann, who circulated the story around the camp. On 20 December, four men from that camp were released who had homes in the Land Hadeln district, which included Otterndorf and Cuxhaven, but it seemed unlikely that they would have written such a letter on the very date after their return home.

Thursday, 20 June
Interrogation of Günther August Wilhelm Schwägermann
According to HQ, Military Intelligence Service Centre, US Forces European Theatre, Schwägermann said that he only heard from Frau Junge and Frau Goebbels that Hitler had dictated his last will, and he knew that Dönitz was to be the Führer's successor, with Goebbels as Reichskanzler. The number of copies and recipients were unknown to him, he claimed.

Schwägermann vowed that he did not know whether Goebbels left a last will or whether he wrote an appendix to Hitler's testament. He was under the impression that Goebbels wrote nothing during the last few days in the bunker. He said that if Goebbels wrote a last will and testament before living in the Führerbunker, his long-time confidential secretary would know. However, the secretary was not in the Führerbunker at the time. The secretary had custody of all personal documents and manuscripts of Goebbels, and since Schwägermann was not aware of any destruction of Goebbels's personal papers, he said the secretary would be the logical man to know about their location. The secretary had kept notes of Goebbels and possibly a diary; these had been kept in a special safe in the cellar of the house in Hermann-Göring-Straße 20. Schwägermann said he did not know what happened to those documents.

Chapter Eight

Did Hitler Die?

It must be noted that a lot of German men at the time copied the 'Hitler look', either out of respect or adoration for their leader. Newsreels of German soldiers and civilians had shown plenty of men with toothbrush moustaches and slip-down forelocks. It was therefore entirely feasible that men who looked like Hitler could be mistaken for him.

In June 1945, Hitler was allegedly spotted in Ireland, dressed as a woman. In August that year, according to one 21st Army Group report, the Führer had visited Tokyo, while by October he had supposedly travelled to Egypt and converted to Islam. However, the British Foreign Office believed such rumours to be 'sheer poppycock', their belief being based on the accumulated evidence.

From May 1945, British officials had been collecting information concerning Hitler's last days. Signals intelligence and interrogation reports all suggested that the Führer had killed himself.

For example, in June 1945, the British interrogated Hermann Karnau. As a guard on duty outside the Führerbunker, Karnau was witness to the bodies of Hitler and his new wife, Eva Braun, on fire 'two metres' from the bunker's emergency exit. He even drew a map showing where their bodies were buried.

During the summer of 1945, reports of Hitler's survival were inspiring Nazi resistance movements, which hindered British and American efforts to de-Nazify and democratize Germany. Such was the scale of such reports that three years later, in 1948, the British and American Intelligence Divisions had to disprove a rumour which claimed that Otto Skorzeny's paratroopers (famous for rescuing Mussolini) had rescued Hitler and other leading Nazis from Berlin, taken them to a secret airfield in Hohenlychen and helped them escape.

When even the Soviets claimed that Hitler was hiding in British-controlled Hamburg, enough was enough, and the highly regarded British intelligence officer, Major Hugh Trevor-Roper, was assigned the task in November 1945 of finding out what had really happened to Hitler.

By this time, rumours of Hitler's survival had merged with those concerning the alleged escape of his private secretary, Martin Bormann, who, according to a Miss Gunn of MI5, was seen 'sitting in state on a high mountain beside his pallid Fuehrer' or even 'riding the Loch Ness Monster'.

The only conclusive evidence that Hitler was dead would have been the discovery and certain identification of his body. In the absence of this, the sole positive evidence consisted of circumstantial accounts of certain witnesses who were either familiar with the Führer's intentions or eyewitnesses to his fate.

Clearly, the best of such witnesses would be those people who were intimate with Hitler in the last days of his life, who lived with him in the bunker and who took charge of the execution of his decisions, including those in respect of the disposal of his body. These people were Dr Goebbels, Martin Bormann and Hitler's surgeon Dr Ludwig Stumpfegger. Of those three, Goebbels was dead (suicide on 1 May 1945, along with his wife and their six children), while Bormann was stated by two reliable and independent eyewitnesses to have been killed in Friedrichstaße on 2 May. Stumpfegger was last seen either dead (according to one witness) or seriously wounded, if not dead (according to another witness) after the same incident involving Bormann.

Both Bormann (in general terms) and Goebbels (explicitly) informed Admiral Dönitz on 1 May that Hitler was dead. It was presumed at that stage (November 1945) that on 1 May either Bormann or Goebbels officially informed General Weidling (the last commander of the Berlin Defence Area during the Battle of Berlin) that Hitler had taken his own life, as in consequence Weidling released his soldiers from their oaths of loyalty to the Führer.

For a definitive answer to Hitler's fate, witnesses would need to be interrogated. These fell into various categories:

(a) Certain politicians, generals and confidants who were with Hitler between 22 and 30 April and were familiar with his plans and intentions. There was a considerable body of evidence from people such as Albert Speer (in the bunker 23/24 April), Field Marshal Ritter von Greim (there 26–29 April) and others. However, none of those witnesses were present at the death, burning or burial of Hitler. They could add only second-hand details.

(b) The personal secretaries of Hitler and Bormann, who were in the bunker on the last day and were familiar with the details of the events, would be more pertinent witnesses. Hitler's two personal secretaries at the time were Frau Junge and Frau Christian, while Bormann's secretary was Frl Else Krüger (allegedly his mistress). Of these, Frau Junge had been last seen on 3 May at a village near Havelberg, where she was left as she was not equipped to travel further, and Frau

Christian was reliably reported in the British Zone and was being traced. Frl Krüger had been examined and was one of the witnesses whose evidence would be used.

(c) More significant witnesses still would have been the personal adjutants or servants of Hitler who were present at the end. Of these, the most important were: SS-Sturmbannführer Günsche, Hitler's personal adjutant; SS-Sturmbannführer Linge, his personal assistant; and SS-Sturmbannführer Erich Kempka, the officer in charge of his transport. All these actually took part in the burning of the bodies of Hitler and Eva Braun. Of these, Günsche was missing, Linge was suspected to be a Russian PoW (a witness thought she saw him in a line of German prisoners in Müllerstraße in Berlin) and Kempka was in American hands and had been interrogated.

(d) Members of the SS-Begleitkommando on guard duty in Hitler's bunker on the last day could also be very useful. They were: SS-Sturmbannführer Franz Schedle (missing), SS-Hauptsturmführer Otto Hansen (missing), SS-Hauptsturmführer Helmut Beerman (possible US PoW), SS-Obersturmführer Hans Reisser (missing), SS-Obersturmführer Pat Lindlof (missing), SS-Hauptsturmführer Hermann Dirr (missing), SS-Obersturmführer Helmuth Frick (missing) and SS-Hauptsturmführer Griesenboeck (missing). The SS-Begleitkommando had been under the command of Schedle, and it was felt that its members were probably detailed to perform various duties in connection with the disposal of Hitler's body. Schedle was known to have given a message for transmission to his wife that he would not fall alive into Russian hands. Of the other officers of the SS-Begleitkommando, Beerman was recorded as having been captured by the US 9th Army.

(e) Members of the RSD, which was responsible for the personal safety of Hitler, might also potentially help clarify matters. A detachment of the Dienststelle was on duty at the bunker at the end. The head of the RSD, SS-Brigadeführer Johann Rattenhuber, was in the bunker and would be a valuable witness if alive, as it was believed that he had given orders in connection with the burial of the remains of the bodies. According to a Russian communiqué on 7 May, he was captured by the Russians. His deputy, SS-Obersturmbannführer Peter Högl, head of Dienststelle 1, was thought probably dead. Of the other members of the RSD guard known to have remained in Berlin, the following were on duty at the relevant period: Harry Mengershausen, Hilco Poppen, Hermann Karnau, Hans Bergmüller, Max Koelz, Erich

Mansfeld and Hans Hofbeck. Of these, Mengershausen was sought in Bremen, while Karnau and Mansfeld were in British and US hands respectively and had been interrogated as accidental witnesses of the burning of the bodies. Koelz was believed to know about the burial of the remains, but was missing, as was Hofbeck, who was said to have witnessed the burning. Poppen was in British hands and had been interrogated.

Evidence from Available Sources
Apart from the above well-defined categories of witnesses, there were certain casual witnesses who could possibly add details. One of those was a woman, who was given accommodation in one of the bunkers through her personal connection with an officer in the Begleitkommando and went to Hitler's bunker for meals, and had given useful evidence. There were other potential witnesses of that kind, but it was thought unlikely that they would be able to add significant details to that part of the story that remained obscure.

Knowledge of Hitler's intentions was confined to highly placed officials and intimate friends, and could not have influenced the evidence given by the RSD guards on duty outside the bunker who were merely accidental eyewitnesses of the fulfilment of the plans.

Hitler's original intention had been to fly to Berchtesgaden on 20 April. When the day came, he delayed his departure, and on 22 April, vacillating as he received conflicting advice, he suffered from an attack of nervous prostration, announcing for the first time that he despaired of victory. The Führer then decided to stay in Berlin and to take his own life there. Goebbels took the same decision. Thereupon, Hitler dismissed many of his advisors; others left of their own accord. Hitler remained surrounded by his 'family circle' and those officers connected with the defence of Berlin. By 23 April, he had reportedly recovered his composure, and for the rest of his time he appeared in a state of mental serenity. The decision to leave was never reconsidered, with attempts by others to alter it forbidden.

From 22–30 April, Hitler waited for the outcome of the Battle of Berlin in some kind of peace of mind. The problem was simple: if Berlin could be saved, Hitler would live; if it fell, Hitler would commit suicide. In the latter case, he told Albert Speer (on the night of 23/24 April) and von Greim (between 26 and 28 April) that plans had been made for the destruction of his body so that it would not fall into enemy hands.

By 29 April, the question as to whether Berlin would stand or fall – and therefore whether Hitler would live or die – was no longer in doubt. As Soviet troops closed in on his bunker, Hitler accepted the inevitability of his defeat. He set into action his plan to take his own life.

Late into the night of the 29th, the inhabitants of the other bunkers were told not to go to bed as the Führer wished to say goodbye to the ladies. At 2.30 am on 30 April, they were summoned. They included officers of the SS-Begleitkommando and about ten women, who collected in the dining corridor of the bunker as Hitler entered. He then shook hands with all of the women and spoke to most of them, before leaving and returning to his own room.

1945

Von Below stated that Hitler had first voiced his and Eva Braun's suicide intentions after making his decision to remain in Berlin on 22 April. Eva Braun also declared that she was willing to follow the Führer in suicide. Generals Burgdorf and Krebs told von Below on or about 28 April that Hitler and Braun intended to take their own lives. None of the others in the bunker, except Goebbels, intimated any suicide intentions to von Below.

Von Below declared that the following were given poison phials by Hitler: Eva Braun, the Goebbels family and von Below himself. Below knew of no orders given to Günsche, Kempka or Rattenhuber regarding the burning of the bodies. At the time von Below left the Bunker (midnight 29/30 April), he said no date had been fixed for the suicide and no definite plans had been made in that connection.

Von Below stated that Greim and Reitsch were given no instructions to return to Berlin. They took off early in the morning of the 29th, von Below himself accompanying them to the exit of the Chancellery.

He added that the pilots Baur and Beetz were given no orders to fly out Hitler, either dead or alive.

As von Below left the Bunker on 30 April, he said he did not know anything about the alleged landing of two Storch aeroplanes on the Charlottenburger Chausse. He considered it impossible for any aircraft to have taken off or landed in Berlin after he had left.

Von Below said there was no question of trying to rescue Hitler at the last moment: 'It would have been an impossible task and against Hitler's wishes.' He knew of no scheme by which the Führer was to be drugged and removed at the last moment. While some people had tried to persuade Hitler to leave Berlin, he consistently refused to do so.

Von Below said he was told by General Burgdorf of an SS plot to murder Hitler and hand over his body to the Western powers. He claimed that

Fegelein was interrogated, probably by Rattenhuber and Hoegel, after the news of Himmler's treachery reached the bunker, and may have revealed the existence of the plot. He added that he knew further about the subject.

According to von Below, Hitler had finally given up all hope of the relief of Berlin by General Wenck's aby the time von Below left the bunker. There was no question of procrastination; Hitler was determined to commit suicide.

There were various reasons why von Below believed that Hitler was dead:

(a) His personal wish to end his life was frequently and openly expressed.
(b) The impossibility for Hitler to escape from Berlin or live incognito.
(c) He did not consider that Hitler had the physical or moral strength to go on living.

Von Below said he reached the River Elbe on 8 May but was unable to find any means of crossing it until 22 June. Assuming an alias, he spent this time doing odd jobs for a hotel proprietor in return for his keep.

On 6 May, he had met a soldier who had left the Chancellery on 1 May. This person told him: 'Hitler and Eva Braun committed suicide on the afternoon of 30 April. Hitler shot himself and Eva Braun took poison. Afterwards the bodyguards burnt the bodies.' Apart from that witness, who was not now available to interrogate, he had not met anyone who had been in the bunker when he left.

The BAOR (British Army of the Rhine, formed in August 1945 to control the British Zone in Allied-occupied Germany), during an exhaustive enquiry into Hitler's death in order to establish definitively whether or not Hitler actually died, and under what circumstances his death occurred, published the following:

(1) An exhaustive list of names of people who had not reported to HQ BAOR as being under arrest and who could supply information regarding Hitler's death.
(2) Entourage of Hitler and Himmler:

Hitler
(a) Immediate party and government associates
SS-Obergruppenführer Martin Bormann.
Age 46. May 1941 was appointed Chancellor and also became Hitler's Secretary. Although the office of Deputy to the Führer was abolished after [Rudolf] Hess's flight in 1941, the duties previously attached to that office had devolved to Bormann. Bormann lived in Munich and

was married with children. He was said to be extremely energetic and hardworking and according to British press reports, had made violent attacks on the Christian faith which he considered incompatible with the National Socialist Point of view.

SS-Obergruppenführer Philip Bouhler.
Age 46. Head of the Führer's Chancellery. A member of the Reich Culture Senate and had made contributions to National Socialist literature.

SS-Obergruppenführer Franz Xaver Schwarz.
Age 70. Head of the Party Treasury. He was a Reichsleiter (second-highest political rank of the Nazi Party) and an expert on questions of administration and finance.

SS-Obergruppenführer Dr Hans Heinrich Lammers.
Age 67. Head of the Reich Chancellery. He was a member of the Secret War Cabinet and of the Council of Defence of the Reich. Married with four daughters.

SS-Gruppenführer Hermann Fegelein.
Age 39. Liaison Officer of the Reichsführer-SS [Himmler] at Hitler's HQ. Described as flamboyant, brave, energetic and ambitious but lacking organisation. Said to be very popular with Himmler. Fegelein was believed to be a ruthless and dangerous individual. He was one of the youngest senior officers.

(b) <u>Personal Adjutants</u>
SS-Obergruppenführer Julius Schaub.
Age 48. Chief aide and adjutant to Hitler. Schaub took care of Hitler's personal belongings, papers and travel journeys, making him a notable figure in Hitler's inner circle.

NSKK Gruppenführer Albert Bormann.
Age 44. Hitler was fond of Bormann and found him to be trustworthy. In 1938, Bormann was assigned to a small group of adjutants who were not subordinate to Martin Bormann. The relationship between Martin and Albert became so caustic that Martin referred to him not even by name but as 'the man who holds the Führer's coat'.

NSKK Brigadeführer Alwin Albrecht.
Age 43. [On] 1 July 1939, Hitler appointed Albrecht an NSKK Oberführer and made him one of his adjutants. Hitler went on to meet Albrecht's wife and liked her. Under Reichsleiter Philipp Bouhler, Albrecht remained on Hitler's staff and worked in the Reich Chancellery in Berlin.

SS-Obergruppenführer Fritz Darges.
Age 33. Hitler's last adjutant.

SS-Hauptsturmführer Richard Schulze.
Age 31. From October 1941 and at intervals thereafter, he was an SS ordinance officer and SS adjutant for Hitler. He was placed in charge of administration, guidelines for training, discipline, deployment and transfer of members of the unit.

(c) <u>Other appointments</u>
SS-Gruppenführer Dr Karl Brandt.
Age 42. Hitler's personal physician.

SS-Brigadeführer Hans Baur.
Age 48. Hitler's personal pilot.

SS-Brigadeführer Hans Rattenhuber.
Age 49. Head of Hitler's personal Reichssicherheitsdienst, bodyguard from 1933–45. Basically, commander of the Führer's Escort.

SS-Hauptsturmführer Otto Günsche.
Age 29. Orderly Officer to Hitler.

<u>Himmler</u>
SS-Brigadeführer Rode.
Age 57. Chief of Himmler's Field HQ.

Obersturmbannführer Werner Grothmann.
Age 31. Aide-de-camp to Himmler from 1940 until Himmler's death in 1945.

SS-Obersturmführer Graf Dohna.
[Age unknown.] Adjutant.

SS-Obersturmführer Wittig.
Age 36. Possibly Martin Wittig. Adjutant.

SS-Hauptsturmführer Franz Conrad.
Age 40. Adjutant.

Monday, 10 September
There was a considerable amount of comment in the press on the subject of whether Hitler was still living or not. The German Burgermeister of Berlin added to the confusion when he stated that he believed the Führer to be still alive. The Russians had told him that they had no satisfactory evidence that he was dead and were anxious to review the evidence on the subject with the other occupational powers. The CIB agreed on behalf of the British Zone to pool its evidence.

Most of the evidence appeared in the CSDIC reports and the man who kept the closest tabs on the matter was Major Hugh Trevor-Roper. The CIB were anxious that Trevor-Roper prepare a brief for a quadripartite discussion.

The CIB enlisted the help of the War Room in London, specifically MI5's intelligence officer, Lieutenant Colonel T.A. 'Tar' Robertson. Robertson was in the War Room when he received a letter from the CIB, BAOR, saying that he may have noticed that there was much being written in the press about whether or not Hitler had actually died. What the CIB wanted was that the principal witnesses were in fact 'War Room characters', such as Berger, Kohle, Dolmann and Ernst Kaltenbrunner. The CIB reported that outside that field of witnesses, a great deal was available in CSDIC reports.

The CIB felt that such a task, unless it was carried out immediately, would never get done, and unless it was done by a 'first-rate chap, would not be worth having. As well as being useful for the quadripartite powers – Britain, the US, Russia and France – it would be a work of considerable historic interest. If it was not completed by 10 October, after which it was feared that Trevor-Roper could be demobilized, it was hoped that the military necessity clause could be operated – with Trevor-Roper's agreement – to retain his services for another month or so. Trevor-Roper was quite prepared to accept such an arrangement.

Wednesday, 12 September
Frau Grape-Anderson
A Frau Gertrude Grape-Anderson told Air Staff Intelligence that she felt the rumours about Hitler's survival could finally be verified one way or the other by Dr Karl Gebhardt, as he was in charge of the Hohenlychen Sanatorium

right up to the end of the war. She felt it her duty to report the matter before Gebhardt was executed (he was sentenced to death at Nuremberg).

Grape-Anderson visited Hohenlychen to collect personal belongings and to find out whether she could establish further details of the alleged visits there by Hitler during the last few days before his reported death. In particular, she mentioned that there used to be a Frau Ritche, wife of the director of the Adolf Hitler Schule, who claimed to know that Hitler used to visit Hohenlychen.

Frau Grape-Anderson was a rather fragile old lady of apparent complete integrity. She was advised in her own interests not to indulge too actively in the role of private detective while in the Russian Zone, but was told that if she should come across anyone who claimed personally to have seen the Führer at Hohenlychen at the end of April 1945, then details upon her return to the British Zone should be reported to BAFO (the British Air Forces of Occupation).

It was the opinion of BAFO's Chief Intelligence Officer that Frau Grape-Anderson was quite honest in her account and intentions, though they naturally assumed that the stories she had heard probably amounted only to rumour and gossip.

Harold Kingston Graham-Hodgson

Radiologist Harold Kingston Graham-Hodgson, of the Middlesex Hospital, wrote to the Minister of Health, Aneurin Bevan, saying that he had read in the press, on more than one occasion, that it was uncertain as to whether Hitler was alive or dead, and whether he was an 'inmate' of the grave at the Chancellery in Berlin. Graham-Hodgson believed that Hitler's skull was X-rayed in 1944 after the July bomb plot incident at the Wolf's Lair near Rastenburg. He said that a radiogram was as accurate a method of identification as fingerprints, since no two people had the same shaped sinuses, mastoid processes etc. Provided that the X-rays of Hitler's skull taken in 1944 were obtainable, he believed it would be an easy matter to tell, without a doubt, whether the skull in Berlin, purported to be Hitler's, was actually his or not. Furthermore, any person in the future who was suspected of being Hitler could have his head X-rayed and be immediately identified. Graham-Hodgson added, as a postscript, that as he was in charge of the X-ray department of the British Red Cross and they had several mobile X-ray vans on the Continent, he could easily go and carry out the necessary X-rays.

Wednesday, 19 September

The following list of names of people wanted in connection with determining the truth surrounding Hitler's death was distributed in a 'SECRET' note by the commander of VIII Corps District:

Frau Marzialis, secretary in the Reichskanzlei.
Freytag von Loringhoven, staff officer responsible for the preparation of reports for Hitler, Lieutenant-Colonel Rudolf Weiß and Rittmeister Gerhard Boldt, all probably on the staff of General Hans Krebs.
Major Johannmeyer, personal assistant to Hitler.
Werner Naumann, State Secretary in Joseph Goebbels's Ministry of Public Enlightenment and Propaganda.
Walther Hewel, Botschafter (Ambassador), representative of von Ribbentrop at Führer HQ.

In order to obtain further evidence about Hitler's alleged death, statements were taken from three further relevant people:

Fräulein Else Krüger, secretary to Martin Bormann.
Professor Fritz Fischer, surgeon at Hohenlychen hospital.
Professor Karl Gerhardt, Chief Surgeon at Hohenlychen hospital.

Friday, 21 September
Nazi Underground Installation, Berlin
The manager of a Siegen factory, Fritz Muesse, said the owner of the business, Karl Klingspor, was imprisoned by the Gestapo in the middle of 1943 for defeatism and only saved from death because he was working on a special textile invention. He added that Klingspor was transferred to Brandenburg, Berlin, and unless he had met his death just before the capitulation he would still be there.

Muesse produced this information as part of a written application for permission to reopen the Klingspor factory and to travel to Berlin to find the owner. He had been there many times in the course of the last two years in connection with the Klingspor case. He continued with a frankly incredible story:

> 'Thus I had dealings with the SS HQ in Berlin, especially with Dr Saltpeter, head of Himmler's legal dept, and got to know by sight several SS leaders. At one particular conference held in September 1944 in connection with the Klingspor affair, at the main office of the Berlin SS at Lichterfelde, I overheard a discussion through the open door from which I gathered that in the Ketshendorf/Fürstenwalde/Spree region there was an underground structure called "Foxhole" [Fuchsbau]. From about that time, Hitler was kept there in custody, and was guarded day and night by armed Sturm Führers. Since then everything done in Hitler's name

was in fact done by Himmler. In this Foxhole (28m underground, 25m sand and 3m concrete) there was a whole collection of secret documents.

'This was confirmed to me in December 1944 by an SS man in charge of the office of the Foxhole – viz, that since September 1944 Hitler had been interned there and that Himmler issued thence the OKW communiqués.

'I still think there's a great deal of secret stuff hidden there, if it's not been already unearthed. It's more likely though, that it has been blown up, and Hitler's corpse will almost surely in that case be found down there.

'An acquaintance of mine, Friedrich Schmidt, manager of a big farm at Spreenhagen (13km from Fürstenwalde) can probably give information as he knew certain of the SS officers connected with the Foxhole.'

Monday, 8 October
Hanna Reitsch

The possibility that Hitler might have escaped from the bunker was dismissed as absurd by Reitsch when interrogated by Robert Work of the Air Corps. She was convinced that the Hitler when she left the shelter was physically unable to have gotten away. 'Had a path been cleared for him from the bunker to freedom he would not have had the strength to use it,' she said.

Reitsch also believed that at the very end he had no intention to live, and that only the hope of relief by Wenck's troops stayed his hand from putting the mass suicide plan into operation. News that Wenck could not get through, she felt, was the catalyst that set off the well-rehearsed plans of destruction.

When Reitsch was confronted with the rumour that Hitler might still be alive in the Tyrol and that her own flight to that area, after she left the bunker, might be more than coincidental, she appeared deeply upset that such an accusation could entertained. 'Hitler is dead!' she cried. 'The man I saw in the shelter could not have lived. He had no reason to live and the tragedy was that he knew it well, knew it perhaps better than anyone else did.'

Wednesday, 10 October

Kingston Graham-Hodgon's letter (12 September) to the Minister of Health caused a lot of interest. An official from the Foreign Office contacted Lieutenant Colonel Green at the War Office and enclosed a copy of the letter.

The official feared that it was only too likely that an occasional imposter here and there would, in the future, claim to be Hitler. Consequently, there would be some advantage in having an infallible method of demonstrating that he was not the Führer.

Saturday, 13 October
In connection with Hitler's death, an officer of the General Staff said there were three individuals still required for investigation who were thought to be in the British Zone. Two of them were members of the SS-Begleitkommando who were on duty in the Chancellery on the day of Hitler's death: Otto Hansen, Hauptsturmführer; and Hermann (surname illegible), Hauptsturmführer. It was believed possible that they had escaped from Berlin and returned to their homes.

The third individual wanted for interrogation was Frau Gerda Christian (née Daranowski), whose description was given as follows:

Age: about 35.
Height: 1.70m.
Build: medium.
Eyes: blue.
Hair: blonde.
Complexion: a bit yellow.

Frau Christian had been in the bunker of the Chancellery at the time of Hitler's death. She had been traced to the French Zone, where her mother-in-law has been interviewed and had stated that Frau Christian had left her home at the end of September in order to find work in the British Zone, probably as a secretary to a commercial firm, possibly in Hamburg or Hannover. If located, it was suggested that Frau Christian was not to be arrested but informed that she was required for interrogation regarding Hitler's death.

The General Staff of the CIB also felt that it was necessary to interrogate an officer of Hitler's bodyguard, Harry Mengershausen, a member of the Reichssicherheitsdienst who had protected the Führer during the last days of the war in Berlin. Mengershausen was believed to have lived at Theodore/Körnerstraße, Bremen. It was requested that arrangements for his location be sent to the General Staff in order that a specialist officer could undertake his interrogation.

Monday 5 November.
A 'SECRET' memorandum was sent from the BAOR to (GSI), HQ, XXX Corps District on the subject of Hermann Karnau, who had been a guard outside the Führerbunker:

'1. The recent detailed investigation into the last days of Hitler renders it desirable that Karnau be further interrogated on one particular matter.

'2. Evidence from other sources shows fairly conclusively that the body was carried out of the Bunker in a blanket, and that Hitler had previously shot himself. Karnau does not mention a blanket, but gives details by which he recognised the body as that of Hitler.

'3. May he be closely questioned on the following points:

    (a) Was the body, when he first saw it, covered in a blanket?
    (b) If there was a blanket on the body, did it burn quickly, otherwise how could Karnau give details of the face etc?
    (c) Were there any signs of violence on the body, if so what?
    (d) In the earlier Canadian report, Karnau said that the head was split, but in the later Canadian report that there were no signs of violence on the body. When Karnau was under interrogation at this HQ in June, he stated that he could not say that Hitler's head was split open.
    (e) What clothes was the body wearing? Give detailed description.

'4. In view of the importance which this subject has assumed, it would be appreciated if the interrogation could be dealt with as a matter of urgency.'

Tuesday, 13 November
Josef Wehrberger
Weheberger was an Allgemeine SS-Obersturmführer who was interned at PoW Hospital Centre number 4, Bad Mergentheim, and claimed to be an intimate personal friend of Hitler. A Weekly Counter Intelligence Report from the hospital centre for the week 28 October to 3 November 1945 included the following:

'Subject [Wehrberger] claims that he talked with Hitler for the last time in the spring of 1944. He states that he heard from a very reliable friend that Hitler was seen in Munich on 21 April 1945. Subject claims that he is very familiar with Hitler's personal habits, ideas and intentions, having been associated with him for a long time, especially in the early stage of Hitler's fight for power in Bavaria.'

1946

Monday, 7 January
Alleged Discovery of Hitler's Body; Memo from G.H Leggett
An article in *Nachtexpress* of 2 January 1946 had read:

> 'According to an Associated Press report, the correspondent of *France Soir* reported on Tuesday that the body of Adolf Hitler had been found on December 19th by the Russian High Command and had been identified.'

The *Daily Telegraph* of 2 January quoted Reuters as the authority for the report, but a Reuters correspondent in Berlin stated that the source was from *France Soir*.

Major G.H. Leggett from the CIB rang the offices of the French press camp but was informed that there was no correspondent in Berlin representing *France Soir*, and indeed all the regular correspondents were away temporarily.

Leggett then rang a Colonel Volkov's office and drew the attention of the Russians to the press reports, asking a Lieutenant Perminov to obtain an explanation or comment. Perminov was rung again on 4 January but could only say that he had no official information on the subject. The urgency of the matter was stressed, and Perminov promised to continue investigations into the matter, but in spite of several further telephone calls, neither Perminov nor Volkov or any other officer could be contacted.

Major Leggett annotated his memo on the subject:

> 'It was was also intended to ask the Russians about Gen Krebbs, Himmler's deputy in Bohemia ... and a signatory of Hitler's Will who, according to the *Daily Telegraph* of Jan 2, was about to be handed over by the Allies to the Czechs. This ... if in fact he is still alive, [would] be a valuable witness in the investigations of Hitler's death.'

Thursday, 10 January
Opinion Regarding Hitler's Death
A Hans Merten received a Confidential Censorship Civil Communications communiqué from a G. Gleichmann of Torgau/Elbe which ran as follows:

> 'Do you believe that Hitler is dead? The Russians swear by all that is Holy that he is still alive. Many say that he will come back as a Social Democrat. There is much in favour of this theory. The husband of an acquaintance of mother's, who worked on an airfield, says that he saw

Hitler and Bormann get away in an aeroplane. Who knows? Besides, it is a fact that Göring was here at the bridge-head (Brückenkopf) during the last days!! ... Of course, much to do everywhere. Why were we betrayed so terribly! It is certain now that the troops will leave in February, but whether we will be governed by the British or will remain Russian, nobody can tell.'

Monday, 9 September
Dr Ramon von Ondarza

Dr von Ondarza told the Hamburg Regional Intelligence Office he had been called up as Truppenärzte to the Military Staff of Hermann Göring, remaining in that post until he was taken prisoner by the Americans in May 1945. He was released by the Americans five months later. During January 1946, he went to Hamburg and was employed there as a doctor in a refugee camp for Ostflüchtlinge in Reinbeck.

As Truppenärzte to Göring, von Ondarza had travelled with him wherever he went in Europe. Taking care of Göring's health, he naturally became very friendly with the Feldmarschall. On 23 April 1945, he was arrested with Göring and the rest of his staff in Berchtesgaden by the SS on the orders of Himmler from Berlin, and was informed that the whole staff, together with Göring, had been sentenced to death on account of Göring's attempt in April to arrange an armistice with General Eisenhower. The officer in charge at Berchtesgaden was, however, dubious about the whole affair, and they were eventually captured by the Americans in May 1945.

Saturday, 28 September

The British Intelligence Division in occupied Germany launched an investigation named Operation *Conan Doyle* in September 1946 following 'spiritualist revelations' that a woman named Eva Hücker was in fact Eva Braun.

A letter from Brigadier C.E.I. Hirsch to Major General J.S. Lethbridge, of BAOR Intelligence, stated that a Mr L.A. Hall (formerly Private No. 6104231, 84 Coy, Hanover) and his wife had tried to see the Chief of the Imperial General Staff (CIGS, Field Marshal Alan Brooke) on the afternoon of 27 September. They were eventually interviewed by MI4 of Military Intelligence.

It transpired that Mrs Hall's father was a spiritualist, who had died in July that year. Hall and his wife claimed they had begun to receive messages from the deceased father a week ago, telling them to go and see the CIGS and tell him the story of the late Private Stanley Knight and his association with a German woman called Eva Hücker.

Private Knight was a former member of 69 Coy, Pioneer Corps, attached to 185 HQ Hanover, who shot himself on 14 December 1945 due to having contracted VD from Eva Hücker. Before killing himself, Knight wrote to his wife in England and supposedly enclosed proof that Eva Hücker was in fact Eva Braun, and that a 'friend' of hers called Heinrich was actually Hitler. The evidence enclosed in the letters was reputed to include a letter from Eva Hücker's father and Eva herself admitting she was Eva Braun.

The message from Mr Hall's father were alleged to have included a description of Heinrich; he was said to be smallish, wearing a blond wig and a coat with padded shoulders, and having an artificial birth mark on the right cheek from just under the jawbone It was said that he had a facial operation carried out by a certain von Fedawich.

The message from Mrs Hall's father went on to say that Eva Braun was posing as her own twin sister, now married and with one blonde daughter aged about 4. Heinrich and Hücker were reported to live at 189 Podbielskistraße, just outside Hanover. The message claimed there were two small huts in a garden set back from the road with trees on both sides and a wood behind, and there was a well in the centre of the front garden.

The Hall family told MI4 that they were going to an address in Torquay (given to them by the spiritualist messages), where they expected to find Stanley Knight's widow and obtain further evidence.

As a result of Operation *Conan Doyle*, British Intelligence officers did indeed manage to trace Hücker but discovered that she was a prostitute who bore no resemblance to Braun.

1947

Friday, 12 September
Hitler's Last Days, According to Frau Gertrude Grape-Anderson
Gertrude Grape-Anderson had a daughter who worked as a receptionist at the Air Headquarters' Officers' Mess, and through this daughter she was put in touch with an RAF Intelligence Officer. She did not, however, tell her daughter the reason for the introduction.

Frau Grape-Anderson lived in Berlin before and during the war, and shortly before the city's fall she moved to Hohenlychen, in the neighbourhood of Fürstenberg.

A few days previously, Grape-Anderson said she had been back to Berlin with the intention of retrieving some personal belongings, obtaining an official permit for that purpose. While in Berlin, she claimed she repeatedly heard the rumour that 'someone called Galland' (presumed to be former Luftwaffe ace Generalleutnant Adolf Galland) had recently broadcast from Spain a message of good hope to all loyal Nazis. He was alleged to have implied in the broadcast that he had the support of a still-alive Hitler.

Grape-Anderson was unable to trace the rumour down to anyone who actually claimed to have heard the broadcast, but she was disturbed by the fact that many people seemed convinced that Hitler was still alive. This reminded her that in Hohenlychen immediately after the end of the war, no one had believed that the Führer was dead and was said by several people to have been in Hohenlychen as late as 24 April, long after the time when the official version had it that he had begun his final stand in Berlin.

Frau Grape-Anderson herself never actually saw Hitler in Hohenlychen, but it was widely believed that he used to visit the SS Sanatorium there, which was under the direction of Dr Karl Gebhardt. It was a fact that a Fieschler Storch light aircraft used to land frequently on a grassy slope in the area, and people had said that it been bringing Hitler.

Thursday, 2 October
The German daily national newspaper, *Die Welt*, published the following letter from Hanna Reitsch denouncing a book on Hitler published by Hugh Trevor-Roper :

> 'I hear that a reference has been made in your newspaper to the book published inEngland – *The Last Days of Hitler* – by Trevor-Roper. It might be of interest to you to know that the "eyewitness report of Hanna Reitsch" on which the whole book is based and of which extracts have been published in German and other foreign newspapers, does not emanate from me. I have never written it or seen it. The author, who draws far-reaching conclusions throughout the whole book, has never spoken to me, and I believe has never seen me.'

Saturday, 11 October
Dr Karl Gebhardt
A report reached HQ of the Intelligence Division, BAOR, from Air Staff Intelligence, in which it was stated that there were claims that Hitler was seen in Hohenlychen (in the Russian Zone) as late as 24 April 1945, i.e. long after the time when the official version stated that he had taken his final stand in Berlin. According to the report, it had been Hitler's custom to visit the SS Sanatorium there.

The Sanatorium had then been run by Karl Gebhardt, a Gruppenführer in the SS and Generalleutnant in the Waffen SS. Gebhardt was now in Landsberg Prison under sentence of death from the court at Nuremberg, although it was understood that the sentence was not likely to be carried out for some months.

Wednesday, 10 December
Rumours Regarding Hitler's Last Days
As well as running the Hohenlychen Sanatorium, Gebhardt was the personal physician to Reichsführer-SS Himmler and Chief Surgeon of the Staff of the Reich Physician SS and Police (Oberst Kliniker, Reichsarzt SS und Polizei). He was also President of the German Red Cross.

An informant of Air Staff Intelligence, Frau Grape-Anderson – who had been described as a rather fragile old lady but of apparently complete integrity – had made the following statements about Hitler being at Hohenlychen towards the end of the war, repeated from 12 September that year:

> 'According to local gossip in Hohenlychen, Hitler used to visit the SS Sanatorium there which was under the direct control of Karl Gebhardt.
> 'It was stated locally that a Fieseler Storch used to land frequently on a grass slope in the area and that it brought Hitler to the place.
> 'Local people said that Hitler was definitely seen to take a lake-side walk in the same area on 24 April, 1945, i.e. long after the time when the official version had it that he had taken his final stand in Berlin.
> 'People in that area believed Hitler to be alive.'

Grape-Anderson was considered to be honest in her intentions, but it was conceded that the stories she had heard were probably a result of local rumour and gossip.

A story on somewhat parallel lines had been told by Carmen Mory – a Swiss-Nazi German spy and a kapo (inmate or stand-in guard) in the Ravensbrück concentration camp – in the autumn of 1945. According to Mory, a Wehrmacht private was alleged to have stated that he was in the vicinity of Hohenlychen during the closing stages of the Battle of Berlin. He had said there was an airfield concealed in the woods nearby, which in late April 1945 was manned by a detachment of SS-Obersturmbannführer Skorzeny's paratroopers, one of whom had told him they were the detachment who had rescued Mussolini, that they had already removed some high-ranking Nazis to safety and that on 26 April they had taken Hitler away from the airfield, mentioning the Austrian Alps as a destination.

Little credence was attached to Carmen Mory, who had made a number of statements at the time which were glaringly inaccurate. However, there was the coincidence regarding the place and period, which corresponded to that mentioned by the Air Staff Intelligence informant.

HQ BAOR 15 was thus interested in what Gebhardt had to say regarding events in Hohenlychen during the last days of the war, as it was understood that he had been communicative in many other respects. There was also the possibility that other leading Nazi representatives may have visited the Sanatorium.

Friday, 12 December
Hitler's Last Pilot, Peter Baumgart, and the Alleged Flight to Denmark
An article from a correspondent in Warsaw appeared in *The Times*:

> 'Acting on the instructions of the Ministry of Justice here, Polish psychiatrists have examined Peter Baumgart, a German airman who claims to have been Hitler's last pilot, and, in a report published today, state him to be balanced completely mentally.
>
> 'Baumgart, who is now awaiting trial for alleged crimes committed in Poland during the war, has been making fantastic claims that on April 28, 1945, he flew Hitler and Eva Braun, her sister [Gretl], and General Rommer, to Denmark. Because of Allied bombing, the aircraft, a Me108, landed for the night at Magdeburg, leaving the next day for Denmark.
>
> 'Baumgart says that two other German aircraft accompanied them all the time, and gives the names of their pilots as Günter and Urban.'

Thursday, 18 December
The following article appeared in Polish newspaper *Express Wieczorny*:

> 'SS-Officer from Oswiecimor a rebellious pilot?
>
> 'The puzzle of Hitler's pilot before the court.
>
> 'Does the brother of a British soldier and an African by origin tell the truth or does he tell lies?
>
> 'The trial of Captain [Peter] Baumgart of the Luftwaffe, claiming to be Hitler's personal pilot, has been watched yesterday with great interest. The case caused also great curiosity among the foreign correspondents, who have delegated an American of the name Larry Allen to the court at Lezno-Street.
>
> 'Capt Baumgart, wearing a field-dress used by parachutists and shoes with wooden soles is a young man of considerable eloquence. He

answers all the questions willingly and at once. The first sensation came while his identify [*sic*] has been checked by the judge Mr Starzyński, when Baumgart declared that he is a descendant of a Boer from Africa, that he was a British subject before and that he has accepted German citizenship in 1935 after his arrival at Europe [*sic*]. He learnt to fly and after his studies and [upon] completion in the army he was engaged in the air-line Berlin-Africa. He came to Poland in 1943 as an instructor of the Air-Force and in 1944 he was arrested, alleged to be a member of the conspiracy "Freies Deutschland" [Free Germany]. He was advised to join the organisation by a German major who used to deliver letters send [*sic*] by German officers who were taken prisoner by the Soviets. Baumgart was an active member of this movement and he said that he cooperated with emissaries of General Seydlitz who was fighting on the Soviet side.

'After [his] arrest, Baumgart was detained at Klodzko, and when the Soviet attacks on the Nyss-Line increased, Baumgart was released. He was in charge of a regiment he had formed and which was comprised of ex-prisoners.

'Hitler's escape
'The most interesting statement related to Hitler. Baumgart arrived in Berlin on 28 March 1945, where he was told to report. Discipline of the troops stationed in Berlin was getting worse while they were waiting for General Blaskowitz's help. The accused had been transferred to the Headquarters where his duty was to guard Hitler. There were very few planes available. At first Baumgart was in charge of a squadron, later a division. In April he was ordered to convey to Denmark a very high official and there was reason to believe that the person in question must have been Hitler himself. This could be judged from the appearance which was much like Hitler's and from the precautions which were carried out. He had started from the Hohenzollern beach with the Messerschmitt-Typhoon carrying on board also a lady (whom he believed to be Eva Braun in previous interrogations) and General Roemer.

'[Baumgart stated:] "How [did] Hitler behave after landing in Denmark? He was very kind to me however he did not talk during the flight, [but] he shook hands with me after landing and gave me a cheque for 20.000 RM. The cheque, issued for the Reichsbank, was signed by Gen Roemer. I did not try to get cash for the cheque."

'Judge: "How do you explain the fact that as a Boer by origin and as a person involved in a conspiracy you have to be trusted so much and given the mission to convey Hitler?"

'[Baumgart:] "Because there were no experienced pilots and I had to swear for the second time to be faithful."

'[Judge:] "Have you been Himmler's adjutant?"

'[Baumgart:] "No, never. I used to meet him and twice or three times [*sic*] I have been invited by him for supper. Twelve days before Berlin was captured he was already away. I have never been an SS-man. I have been mixed [up] with another Baumgart, an SS officer from Oswiecim, for whom a warrant of arrest has been issued. I have been ill-treated by a British sergeant who interrogated me; he was beating me and used to lock me up in the bunker. In order to get rid of him I have admitted to be a wanted person. I reckoned that when I am in Poland it would be evident before the court that I have never had anything to do with Oswiecim."

'[Judge:] "Well, what finally happened to Hitler?"

'[Baumgart:] "I returned from Denmark alone. I have never seen Hitler again. Later I talked about it with Axmann, leader of the German Youth. He assured me that he was present when [the] corpses of Hitler and Eva Braun were burnt."

Without tattoo

'Baumgart was asked several questions by his defence attorney Krasnodębski. It came to light that Baumgart had a brother in the British Army and who was killed in Norway during the British invasion. Baumgart was suspected [*sic*] by the British whether he was a member of [the] SS and his body was inspected in order to find out if he had the tattoo mark worn by SS-men, the so called "proving of blood". The inspection did not find any tattoo mark on Baumgart. But this had not yet convinced the jury. It has been decided to request the "Najwyższy Trybunał Narodowy" [a war-crime tribunal active in Communist-era Poland from 1946–48] for information if Baumgart or Baumgarten was on the list of war criminals wanted for their beastly activity in the concentration camp Oświęcim [Auschwitz]. The sentence of the court depends very much on the above information.'

1948

Friday, 16 January: Hitler Survival Rumours
An article appeared in the *Lüneburger Landeszeitung* newspaper:

> 'According to the Polish newspaper Express Wieczorny, Peter Baumgart, former captain of the German Air Force, who asserted that just before the fall of Berlin, he had conveyed Hitler and Eva Braun to Denmark, is to be handed over to the British Occupation Authorities.'

Captain Hodges, HQ Intelligence Division, BAOR 15, wanted to know from the Polish Liaison Officer whether Baumgart did in fact make the alleged statements and whether his extradition from Poland had been requested, and if so by whom.

Karl Heinz Küpker
A certain Karl Heinz Küpker of Bohmte had been questioned. He stated that he was a Fähnrich (officer cadet) in NJG 5, flying Ju 88/G6 aircraft, in April 1945. Between 20 and 25 April, he said he flew from Redlin near Parchim to Berlin-Gatow in company with another Ju 88/G6. The latter was piloted by a captain from Lübeck and carried a major or a colonel, wearing a pink or red 'Spiegel' on his collar, as a passenger. The planes returned to Redlin the following morning without the passenger. While at Gatow, Küpker met a pilot who claimed that he had landed Albert Speer.

While at Redlin, and later Husum, Küpker came into contact with a unit that was flying Storch machines to and from Berlin. Among the pilots was one Werner Crewe, who lived in Osnabrück and was subsequently interrogated on his knowledge of the movements of Nazi VIPs in April 1945.

Tuesday, 2 March
Rumours Concerning Whereabouts of Hitler and Other High-Ranking Nazi Personalities
The following statement was made by an informant:

> 'At the end of April 1945, the IV Gruppe des Nachtjagdgeschwader 3/ Stabskompanie was stationed on the airfield at Hadersleben, Denmark. The unit had very few planes left and no flying was done. One afternoon, between 26th and 28th April, a plane landed on the field unexpectedly. It was at first taken for a British Lancaster but turned out to be a French machine, with 4 engines and twin rudder, which the Germans used as

transport. Only the higher ranking officers were allowed to approach the plane and the purpose of the flight did not become generally known. Rumours among the personnel, however, were to the effect that important persons had arrived with the plane from Berlin.'

According to newspaper reports, an ex-captain of the Luftwaffe – Peter Baumgart – was held by the Poles as a war criminal and had claimed that Hitler and Braun flew from Berlin to Denmark on 26 April 1945.

However, from the evidence available at HQ Division, BAOR 15, it was considered practically certain that Hitler and Eva Braun committed suicide on 30 April 1945. Nevertheless, it was thought possible that other high-ranking personalities may have escaped Germany by that method.

It was understood from another source that the commander of IV Gruppe des Nachtjagdgeschwaders was a Major Husemann.

Tuesday, 25 May
Statement that Hitler Lived in a Bunker in Warnemünde in 1947 and was in Upper Bavaria
The following confidential civil communication ('not to be shown to German staff') from a Fr Hilgendorff, Warnemünde, Friedrich-Engels-Straße. 25, was sent to Frau Krüger:

> 'Yesterday I visited a onetime "Bunker", the Stoltera, now blown-up in which Hitler and two women lived in 1947. Adolf Hitler and the women are said to have gone to Upper Bavaria because he was hunted by the Russians.'

Wednesday, 16 June
Werner Grewe
Former Luftwaffe Sergeant Pilot Werner Grewe was interrogated with a view to obtaining particulars of his movements during April 1945 and the possibility of his having any knowledge of an escape plan carried out by Hitler and Eva Braun.

Grewe stated that on 29 April, he was instructed to fly a Storch from Husum to Berlin, but to land at Schwerin before proceeding to Berlin. After waiting in vain all night at Schwerin for further orders, he flew back to Husum on 30 April. On 1 May, Husun aerodrome was captured by the British.

Grewe thought that his flight to Schwerin was connected with some evacuation plan by higher Nazi officials from Berlin to Schleswig-Holstein or Denmark. He did not see any evacuated persons on the aerodrome and knew of no other pilot of NJG 1 who was instrumental in any evacuation from the capital.

Grewe's opinion was that Hitler and Eva Braun were unable to leave Berlin and both had perished there.

Thursday, 17 June
Under interview by three Polish judges, Captain Peter Baumgart claimed that he flew Hitler and Eva Braun to Denmark shortly before the fall of Berlin. Hitler, Eva Braun and a German general with others boarded his plane in Berlin, and it took off for Denmark. The plane made a forced landing in Magdeburg, but, upon Hitler's insistence, he flew the following day through an artillery barrage to the Danish shore.

Baumgart said they landed about 44 miles from the Eiter River in a field. Hitler then shook hands with him, gave him a cheque for 20,000 marks and ordered him to return to Berlin immediately. Baumgart believed that Hitler had subsequently boarded a submarine.

Chapter Nine

The Indomitable Hanna Reitsch and her Opinion of Hitler

Hanna Reitsch's story was remarkable, in that while she played only a small part in the events at the war's conclusion, she had personal contact with the top-bracket Nazis as the end descended upon them. It was also of interest as it was likely that Reitsch was one of the last people, if not the very last person, who got out of the shelter alive. Her information was evaluated by the Allied authorities as reliable, and it was thought that her story may have thrown some light or perhaps have served as an aid to fuller knowledge as to what happened during the last days of Berlin and the war.

It became apparent that Hanna Reitsch once held the Führer in high esteem. However, she was emphatic when she described the apparent mismanagement she observed and learned of in the Führerbunker. For instance, she recalled that Berlin had been depleted of arms to hold the River Oder, and when that line fell it appeared that no coherent defence plan of Berlin had been prepared; certainly, no adequate arrangements had been made to direct the defence from the bunker. It appeared that only at the last moment had Hitler decided to direct the battle from the shelter. However, he did not have the tools with which to operate: no maps, no battle plans and no radio connection with the outside world. That the destruction of Wenck's army had been unbeknown to Hitler for several days was just one example of these inadequacies. In consequence, the Führer was left sitting helplessly in his cellar, impotently playing his table-top wargames.

Reitsch claimed that Hitler the idealist had died, and his country with him, because of his incompetence as a soldier and as a statesman. She concluded that no one who knew him could deny that he was simply incompetent to rule the country, one of his greatest faults being an inability to properly judge the character of those around him, which led to the selection of people equally incompetent to fill important positions. One such example was obviously Hermann Göring and his catastrophic handling of the Luftwaffe.

She repeatedly remarked that never again should such a person be allowed to gain control over Germany or any other country. Strangely, she appeared not to hold him personally responsible for many of the wrongs and evils that she recognized and was quick to point out. Rather, she said: 'A great part of the fault lies with those who lured him, criminally misdirected him, and informed him falsely. But that he himself selected the men who misled him cannot be forgiven.'

When she realized that all was lost, Reitsch said she suggested to Hitler that a squad of suicide pilots should be put together. Hitler, not totally convinced, agreed, but the project never materialized.

'A criminal against the world'
Reitsch claimed that 'Hitler ended his life as a criminal against the world', but she was quick to add:

> 'He did not begin it that way. At first his thoughts were only how to make Germany healthy again, how to give his people a life free from economic insufficiencies and social maladjustments. To do this he gambled much, with a stake that no man has the right to jeopardise – the lives of his people. This was the first great wrong, his first great failure. But once the first few risks had been successful, he fell into the faults of every gambler; he risked more and more, and each time that he won he was more easily led to the next gamble.'

According to Reitsch, it all began with the occupation of the Ruhr, which she said was the first and most difficult gamble of all. When the world did not answer his Ruhr bluff with war, she claimed every succeeding risk became progressively easier:

> 'Each success made the enthusiasm of the people greater and this gave Hitler the necessary support to take the next step. The end result was that Hitler himself underwent a character change that transformed him from an idealistically motivated benefactor to a grasping, scheming despot, a victim of his own delusions and grandeur. Never again in the history of the world must such power be allowed to rest with one man.'

An Evaluation of Reitsch
It was considered that the information given by Reitsch was sincere and that she was conscientious in her effort to be truthful and exact. That her family were dead, her friend von Greim had committed suicide, Germany had been physically ruined and she had endured very trying events during the closing stages of the war had combined to seriously tempt her to take her own life. She

claimed that she only remained alive for the sake of the truth: to tell the truth about Göring, 'the shallow showman'; to tell the truth about Hitler, 'the criminal incompetent'; and to tell the German people the truth about the dangers of the form of government that the Third Reich gave them. She believed that she was fulfilling much of that mission when she spoke to her interrogator. It was therefore felt that her remarks may be considered as her deepest efforts at sincerity and honesty. Captain Robert Work, Chief Interrogator of the Air Corps, reported that she was undergoing a severe mental struggle in her effort to reconcile her conception of honour with her denunciations of Göring, Himmler and Hitler himself. That difficulty appeared not so great when she was speaking to the interrogator than it was when she spoke to civilians; but from civilians who had led her conversation and then, unknown to her, reported the results to the interrogator, it appeared that she was striving to exert a progressively more democratic influence over her fellow countrymen. It was felt that her idealism and exact knowledge regarding many of the faults of the Nazi system, if put to proper use, might eventually be of value in the re-education of the German people.

Conclusion

As the war was reaching its conclusion, Hitler was at breaking point. At one moment he would firmly believe that the war could still go in Germany's favour. But then another less confident belief would envelop him, and he equally firmly believed the war was lost. Like all dictators, he would ignore advice from his generals if it did not fit his narrative and would carry on regardless. For whatever reason, his cogent thought process had deserted him.

Propaganda would declare that Hitler would stay in Berlin fighting to the bitter end; but history reveals a different story.

Some inhabitants of the bunker remained defiantly faithful to the end; people like Joseph Goebbels and his wife, who made the ultimate sacrifice any parent could make.

Hitler, however, began to lose some of disciples; Hanna Reitsch for example. She was no ordinary woman, an extraordinary pilot. Initially, she was very loyal to the Führer. She was adored by Frau Goebbels and admired by Hitler. However, even she eventually saw the dictator as a lost cause and railed against him.

Many of his generals also realized the futility of continuing, but Hitler was defiant until the bitter end, when even he saw that the end was nigh and consequently committed suicide with his wife, Eva Braun.

Bibliography

The National Archives
CAB 79/33/20
WO 280/3781
WO-208-3787
WO 208/3788
WO 208/3789
WO 208/3790
WO 208/3791

Books
Beevor, Antony, *Berlin: The Downfall 1945* (London/New York: Viking-Penguin Books, 2002).
Brendon, P., *Edward VIII (Penguin Monarchs): The Uncrowned King* (London: Penguin, 2016).
Cadbury, D., *Princes at War: The British Royal Family's Private Battle in the Second World War* (London: Bloomsbury, 2015).
Dollinger, Hans, *The Decline and Fall of Nazi Germany and Imperial Japan* (New York: Crown, 1967).
Dorr, Robert, *Fighting Hitler's Jets: The Extraordinary Story of the American Airmen Who Beat the Luftwaffe and Defeated Nazi Germany* (Minneapolis: Zenith Press, 2013, p.210).
Fischer, Thomas, *Soldiers of the Leibstandarte* (Winnipeg: J.J. Fedorowicz Publishing, Inc., 2008).
Hamilton, Charles, *Leaders & Personalities of the Third Reich, Vol. 1* (San Jose, CA: R. James Bender Publishing, 1984).
Hoffmann, Peter, *Hitler's Personal Security: Protecting the Führer 1921–1945* (New York: Da Capo Press, 1979/2000), p.55.
Joachimsthaler, Anton, *The Last Days of Hitler: The Legends, the Evidence, the Truth*, trans. Helmut Bögler (London: Brockhampton Press, 1999).
Kershaw, Ian, *Hitler: A Biography* (New York: W.W. Norton & Company, 2008).
Linge, Heinz, *With Hitler to the End: The Memoirs of Adolf Hitler's Valet* (New York: Skyhorse Publishing, 2009).
McGee, Mark, *Berlin: A Visual and Historical Documentation from 1925 to the Present* (New York: Overlook Books, 2002).
Moorehead, C., *A Train in Winter* (London: Chatto & Windus, 2011).
O'Donnell, James, *The Bunker: The History of the Reich Chancellery Group* (Boston, Ma: Da Capo Press, 2001).
Payne, Robert, The Life and Death of Adolf Hitler (New York: Praeger Publishers, 1973).
Speer, Albert, *Inside the Third Reich* (London: Weidenfeld & Nicolson, 1995).
von Lang, Jochen, *The Secretary: Martin Bormann, the Man Who Manipulated Hitler* (New York: Random House, 1979).

Williams, Max, *Reinhard Heydrich: The Biography, Vol. 2, Enigma* (Church Stretton: Ulric Publishing, 2003).
Ziemke, Earl F., *Battle For Berlin: End of the Third Reich* (New York: Ballantine Books; London: Macdonald & Co, 1969).

Websites
39-45.org/files3945c/8843_Flensburg2.pdf
alexautographs.com/auction-lot/the-interrogation-of-erna-flegel-nurse-to-hitler-_F3C4A6FA29
allthatsinteresting.com/theodor-morell
bbc.co.uk/teach/adolf-hitler-man-and-monster/zbrx8xs
biography.yourdictionary.com/articles/adolf-hitlers-childhood.html
britannica.com/list/9-things-you-might-not-know-about-adolf-hitler
cia.gov/library/readingroom/docs/CIA-RDP78-02646R000100030002-2.pdf
en.wikipedia.org/wiki/Battle_in_Berlin
en.wikipedia.org/wiki/G%C3%BCnther_Schw%C3%A4germann
en.wikipedia.org/wiki/Karl-Jesko_von_Puttkamer#CITEREFJoachimsthaler1999
en.wikipedia.org/wiki/List_of_Adolf_Hitler%27s_personal_staff6 December 1945.
en.wikipedia.org/wiki/Robert_Ley
en.wikipedia.org/wiki/Vorbunker
esquire.com/news-politics/news/a36351/nazi-telegram-hitler-suicide-sale/
forces.net/news/wwii/remnants-nazi-power-75-years-flensburg-government
historyhit.com/british-intelligence-and-rumours-of-adolf-hitlers-post-war-survival/
hydraprod.library.cornell.edu/fedora/objects/nur:01134/datastreams/pdf/content
independent.co.uk/news/world/europe/adolf-hitler-last-bodyguard-rochus-misch-nazi-leader-s-final-minutes-berlin-bunker-eva-braun-a7642871.html
jewishvirtuallibrary.org/a-psychological-analysis-of-adolph-hitler-his-life-and-legend-hitler-as-he-believes-himself-to-be-2
mi5.gov.uk/hitlers-last-days
motherjones.com/politics/2015/02/cia-psychological-profiles-hitler-castro-putin-saddam/
nationalinterest.org/blog/buzz/berlin-falls-inside-inglorious-end-nazi-empire-looked-128637
time.com/3660353/hitler-bunker
psycnet.apa.org/buy/1943-00211-001
smh.com.au/world/papers-reveal-how-goebbels-children-were-killed-20091009-gqv1.html
spiegel.de/international/germany/murder-in-hitler-s-bunker-who-really-poisoned-the-goebbels-children-a-653981.html
time.com/5360342/hitler-valet-excerpt/
trove.nla.gov.au/newspaper/article/69327754
warfarehistorynetwork.com/2020/03/24/hitlers-death-in-the-fuhrerbunker
wikipedia.org/wiki/Hans_Krebs
Articles
Youtube
Felton, Mark, 'Hitler's ashes may still exist'.
Felton, Mark, 'The Fegelein Wedding – Nazi Fairytale or Nightmare'.

Additional sources
Downfall, a Bernd Eichger and Oliver Hirschbiegel film (Constantin Film Produktion GmbH, 2004).